## RESIDUALS: NO

by Daniel Holloway / © Back Stage Magazine / March 30, 2010. Reprinted by permission.
http://blogstage.backstage.com/2010/03/residuals-now-in-color.html

Like most actors, you no doubt often find yourself wondering, "Why doesn't somebody make a color-coded, exhaustively researched chart that explains my residuals and looks kind of like a periodic table of elements on mushrooms?"

Well, wonder no more, left-brain impaired performers. Jonathan Handel – attorney, law professor, and Hollywood union oracle – has just unveiled a labor of love (and insanity): a one-page document that summarizes how all residuals for members of AFTRA, SAG, the WGA, the DGA, and IATSE are calculated.

"I always thought of residuals as a grid," Handel said. "There are roughly [9] media you can make something for and roughly 10 media you can re-release it in. [Nine] times 10 is [90]. That's a grid."

Navigating Handel's grid – and its page of footnotes – can be tricky. Some cells, such as the one that covers theatrical releases rebroadcast on domestic basic cable, contain a single, simple formula. Others, such as pay-TV to pay-TV, are packed to the margins, using a font small enough to make a credit-card billing statement look like easy reading. To make the prospect of deciphering so much info in so small a space less intimidating, Handel whipped out his color wheel.

"I thought very early on that color would make all the difference," he said. "If you imagine it as text against a white background, it would be completely forbidding."

But the decision to get colorful had more to do with function than form. Blue is used for gross-based formulas, shades of pink and violet for formulas based on percentages of minimums, gold and tan for formulas Handel characterizes as "sui generis" (though they could be less charitably called "labyrinthine" or "nuts"), and gray for areas where there are no residuals. The acid-test color scheme has led Handel's friends to describe his work as art.

And like most artists, Handel wouldn't mind getting paid. Though the chart can be downloaded for free at jhandel.com, its creator has set up a site at CafePress – cafepress.com/residuals – where T-shirts, mugs, and even trucker hats emblazoned with the grid can be bought.

"Everybody's been calling this chart pretty," Handel said. "Well, I thought, it's too pretty not to wear."

## NOW – EVEN MORE COLOR

It's fair to say, as Dan Holloway does above, that I "whipped out (my) color wheel" when I created the residuals chart. As you can see, this book takes color to another level – I spun that color wheel like a centrifuge. Preparing the book has been quite a ride – albeit an often bumpy one as I fought frequent software glitches.

Although it may look like my centrifuge flew apart and smashed to bits, I think you'll enjoy the energy and find that the color coding (explained on p. iv) makes the formulas easier to understand.

As Chapter 1 describes, residuals are extremely important. However, they're usually also dry as dirt. I hope adding some color puts a different spin on the subject.

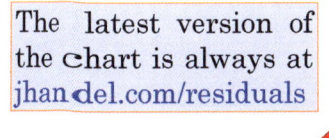

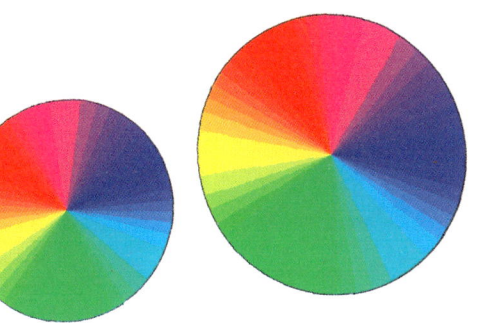

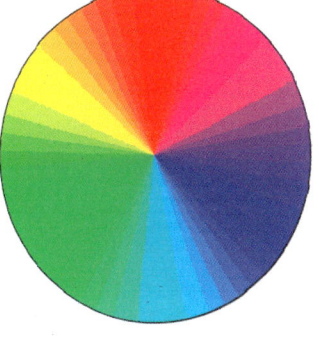

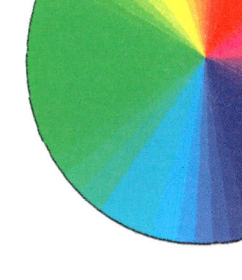

The latest version of the chart is always at jhandel.com/residuals

## PRAISE FROM READERS OF PREVIOUS WORKS

*Jonathan Handel [is] an avid chronicler of Hollywood labor news.*
— *New York Times*

*Handel's work is always incredibly authoritative and a pleasure to read.*
— Patrick Goldstein,
former "Big Picture" columnist, *Los Angeles Times**

Hollywood's most sensible legal eagle. *Jonathan Handel* was one of the most reliable, fair-minded and quotable sources during the Writers Guild of America strike.
— *Kansas City Star*

*I'm going to read this book* [Hollywood on Strike!] *cover to cover.*
— Ken Howard, then-president, Screen Actors Guild (now president, SAG-AFTRA)*

*Jonathan brings the insights of an insider – and the instincts of a reporter – to the complex world of Hollywood labor.*
— Rebecca Keegan, film writer, *Los Angeles Times**

Labor relations in the entertainment industry are complex and incredibly nuanced. Handel's appreciation of the dynamics and his understanding of the issues are commendable.
— Roberta Reardon, then-president, American Federation of Television and Radio Artists (later co-President, SAG-AFTRA)*

[In *Hollywood on Strike!,*] *Handel* chronicles the WGA strike and SAG negotiations with an attorney's eye for detail and a blogger's distinctive point of view.
— Carol Lombardini,
President, Alliance of Motion Picture and Television Producers*

*Handel covers the entertainment labor world as obsessively as any human possibly can.*
— *The Hollywood Reporter*[†]

*Handel's latest article has the kind of detail we love. A major wow with interesting analysis. His work is invariably thought provoking.*
— SAGWatch.net

---

[*] Affiliation for identification only.
[†] This quote predates the author's appointment as Contributing Editor.

# ENTERTAINMENT RESIDUALS

Order copies of this book at
createspace.com/3368594

Download the chart at
jhandel.com/residuals

Sign up for book updates/errata at
jhandel.com/contact

## ALSO BY JONATHAN HANDEL

*How to Write LOIs and Term Sheets:
An Executive's Guide to Drafting Clear Legal Documents
Before Bringing in the Lawyers*

*Hollywood on Strike!: An Industry at War in the Internet Age*

*The New Zealand Hobbit Crisis:
How Warner Bros. Bent a Government to Its Will and Crushed an Attempt to Unionize The Hobbit*

*Entertainment Labor: An Interdisciplinary Bibliography*

## FORMULA COLOR CODES AND TYPICAL USES

**Gray:** No residuals. For theatrical to theatrical, some new media, older product and many IATSE and AFM reuse patterns.

**Light Turquoise:** Percentage residuals. For reuse of theatrical product and reuse in supplemental markets, basic cable and consumer paid new media.

**Pink:** Fixed residuals @ 100%. The residual for each rerun is 100% of something that is roughly related to the union wage scale for the work that the union member performed on the project. For reuse of TV, home video and derivative and original new media product on network primetime.

**Rose:** Fixed residuals – declining percentages run by run. For reuse of TV, home video and derivative and original new media product in other than network primetime, and for basic cable to basic cable.

**Rose (shaded):** Fixed residuals – declining percentages year by year. For high budget SVOD programs.

**Tan:** Hybrid fixed/percentage residuals. Used in foreign reuse of TV and home video product. Very different hybrid formulas are used for reuse of TV, home video and derivative new media product on ad-supported new media platforms.

**Gold:** Various formulas. For pay TV / home video to pay TV / home video.

**Lavender:** Unusual formulas, mostly 100% or more of theatrical and/or TV minimums. For theatrical use of non-theatrical product.

For more information, see pp. 7, 20 and 191.

## TOO PRETTY NOT TO WEAR?

Caveat emptor! In the unlikely event that you'd like to get up close and personal with the residuals chart, you can join the handful of people who have already flocked to www.cafepress.com/residuals and www.zazzle.com/jhandel* (don't forget the trailing asterisk) for t-shirts, hats, coffee mugs and posters. Here's a sampling of what's on offer – and, yes, that last one is a men's tie, 4" wide and 100% polyester.

# ENTERTAINMENT RESIDUALS

## A Full Color Guide

## 2015 Preliminary Edition

**JONATHAN HANDEL**
Entertainment/Technology Attorney

## Jonathan Handel

### Hollywood Analytics • Los Angeles

# COPYRIGHT INFORMATION

## Entertainment Residuals: A Full Color Guide

Copyright © 2015 Jonathan Handel. All rights reserved. No part of this publication may be reproduced, distributed or transmitted in any form or by any means, or stored in a database or retrieval system, without the prior written permission of the author.

**Disclaimer:** This book provides general information and is not intended as legal advice. It does not represent the official position of any guild/union, management organization or company. The laws, rules and contracts discussed in this book are complex and subject to varying interpretations. The union agreements are the definitive reference. Consult a qualified lawyer for specific advice.

Ed2015P C4 B29 Ch2015-2

ISBN: 978-1441439352

Published by
Hollywood Analytics, Los Angeles, California.

Library of Congress Control Number: 2011963518

Cover and book design: Jonathan Handel.

Contact the author at:
- jh@jhandel.com
- http://www.jhandel.com   Twitter: @jhandel
- Facebook: jhandel   LinkedIn: jonathanhandel
- 8033 W. Sunset Blvd. #234, Los Angeles, CA 90046

# ACKNOWLEDGEMENTS

For generously reviewing the residuals chart that inspired this book, I'd like to thank Phillip Ayling (American Federation of Musicians and Recording Musicians Association), David Besbris (then at AFTRA, now SAG-AFTRA), James Cope (Film Musicians Secondary Markets Fund), Dennis Dreith (then at FMSMF), Christopher DeHaan (then at AFTRA, now 42West), Ray Hair (AFM), Kim Roberts (then at AFTRA, now FMSMF) and Joan Halpern Weise (SAG-AFTRA).

I also appreciate the valuable feedback on the chart from students in my UCLA School of Law Entertainment Unions and Guilds course and on the chart and book from students in my similar Southwestern Law School courses.

For kindly permitting me to reprint their materials (see pp. 3, 153, 166 and 169), I thank Daniel Holloway (then with Backstage), writer John August, and Schuyler Moore (Stroock & Stroock & Lavan).

Thanks also to Christopher Barrett (Metropolitan Talent Agency) for helpful discussion in connection with the essay on p. 174 and Tom Markley (also of MTA) for useful conversations on television programming generally.

Many other people helped but preferred not to see their names in print, in light of the confidential nature of relationships in entertainment labor and sensitivity of the issues surrounding residuals.

All titles are for identification only and do not imply endorsement by the respective organizations. Indeed, various aspects of residuals formulas are subject to disagreement, so no book by a third party could do justice to an organization's position. This book does not represent the position of any union, employer, or other organization (including those with which I'm affiliated, TroyGould and The Hollywood Reporter).

I hope you'll find the book useful and reliable, despite its unofficial nature. Naturally, the inevitable errors and omissions are mine. When you find them, contact me at jh@jhandel.com and let me know where I went astray.

## SUMMARY OF CONTENTS

### Part I – Overview

| | |
|---|---:|
| About the Author | 1 |
| 1. Introduction | 2 |
| 2. The Residuals Chart | 19 |
| 3. Media, Markets, Unions and More | 22 |
| 4. Residuals Formulas | 52 |

### Part II – Cell by Cell Analysis

| | |
|---|---:|
| 5. Made for Theatrical | 66 |
| 6. Made for Free TV | 70 |
| 7. Reuse in Supplemental Markets | 81 |
| 8. Made for Pay TV and Home Video | 84 |
| 9. Made for Basic Cable | 94 |
| 10. Theatrical Use of TV and Home Video Product | 100 |
| 11. New Media Reuse of Traditional Product | 103 |
| 12. Made for New Media | 113 |

### Part III – Additional Topics

| | |
|---|---:|
| 13. Residuals Calculation | 128 |
| 14. Separated Rights and Similar Reuse Provisions | 141 |
| 15. Other Entertainment Residuals and Reuse Payments | 145 |
| 16. Commercials | 148 |
| 17. Economics | 150 |
| 18. Payment Mechanics | 154 |
| 19. International and Linguistic Issues | 157 |
| 20. Recent History | 160 |
| 21. Policy Issues | 162 |

### Part IV – Reference

| | |
|---|---:|
| Appendix: Sources and Contracts | 177 |
| Index | 185 |
| Residuals Chart | 188 |

## ROADMAP

Chapters 1-4 explain the residuals system in broad strokes. Chapters 5-12 describe the various residuals formulas in detail, cell by cell, using the format described on p. 64. The remaining chapters cover a range of other topics. See the detailed roadmap on p.6.

You'll find a copy of the chart at the end of the book – two pages that summarize the formulas, one page of contract cross-references and one page explaining the abbreviations used in the chart and book. All of the information on the chart is also provided, in greater detail, in the body of the book.

A separate pdf is available at no cost at jhandel.com/residuals, and poster size versions are available at www.cafepress.com/residuals. See pp. 20 and 191 for notes on interpreting the chart and certain aspects of the book.

# DETAILED TABLE OF CONTENTS

## Part I – Overview

About the Author .................................................. 1
1. Introduction ..................................................... 2
   A. What are Residuals? ................................. 2
   B. Precise Definition ...................................... 3
   C. Reuse Patterns .......................................... 3
   D. Residuals Formulas ................................... 4
   E. Why are There Residuals and Why are They So Complex? ........................................... 6
   F. Detailed Roadmap of the Book ................. 6
   G. Conventions Used in the Book and Chart 7
   H. Who Receives Residuals? ......................... 7
   I. Who Pays Residuals? .................................. 8
   J. The Role of the Unions ............................... 9
   K. The Contract ................................................ 9
   L. Interpreting the Contracts ....................... 10
   M. Compensation and Context .................... 12
   N. License Fees and Royalties .................... 14
   O. History in a Nutshell ................................. 15
2. The Residuals Chart ..................................... 19
   A. Constructing the Chart ............................ 19
   B. Interpreting the Chart .............................. 20
3. Media, Markets, Unions and More ........... 22
   A. Overview and Definitions ........................ 22
   B. Made-For Media ....................................... 26
   C. Reuse Markets .......................................... 38
   D. Guilds/Unions ............................................ 46
   E. Dates ........................................................... 50
   F. Other Variables ......................................... 50
4. Residuals Formulas ..................................... 52
   A. What Initial Compensation Covers ....... 52
   B. No Residuals .............................................. 54
   C. Percentage Residuals .............................. 55
   D. Fixed Residuals at 100% ......................... 59
   E. Fixed Residuals – Run by Run Declining Percentage ........................................................ 61
   F. Fixed Residuals – Year by Year Declining Percentage ........................................................ 61
   G. Fixed Residuals – A Closer Look at the Residual Base .................................................... 62
   H. AFTRA Exhibition Day Residuals .......... 63
   I. Hybrid Formulas ......................................... 63
   J. Unique Pay TV and Home Video Formulas ............................................................ 64
   K. Unique Theatrical Reuse Formulas ....... 64
   L. Specified Dollar-Amount Residuals ...... 64
   M. Format of Chapters 5-12 ........................ 64

## Part II – Cell by Cell Analysis

5. Made for Theatrical ..................................... 66
   A. Theatrical to Theatrical .......................... 66
   B. Theatrical to Free TV and Foreign TV . 67
   C. Theatrical to Domestic Basic Cable ..... 69
6. Made for Free TV .......................................... 70
   A. Free TV to Network Primetime ............. 70
   B. Free TV to Other Than Network Primetime ......................................................... 72
   C. Free TV to Foreign TV ............................. 78
   D. Free TV to (Domestic) Basic Cable ...... 80
7. Reuse in Supplemental Markets .............. 81
   A. Theatrical and Free TV to Pay TV ........ 81
   B. Theatrical and Free TV to Home Video 82
   C. History of Reuse in Supplemental Markets ............................................................. 83
8. Made for Pay TV and Home Video ........... 84
   A. Overview of Pay TV & Home Video to Pay TV & Home Video ............................................ 84
   B. DGA Pay TV and Home Video to Pay TV 85
   C. SAG-AFTRA Pay TV and Home Video to Pay TV ................................................................ 86
   D. WGA Pay TV to Pay TV ........................... 87
   E. DGA Pay TV and Home Video to Home Video ................................................................... 88
   F. SAG-AFTRA Pay TV and Home Video to Home Video ...................................................... 89
   G. WGA Pay TV to Home Video ................. 90
   H. WGA Home Video to Pay TV and Home Video ................................................................... 91
   I. IATSE and AFM Pay TV and Home Video to Pay TV and Home Video ............................ 91
   J. Pay TV and Home Video to Free TV and Foreign .............................................................. 92
   K. Pay TV and Home Video to Domestic Basic Cable ....................................................... 93
   L. History of Made for Pay TV and Home Video ................................................................... 93
9. Made for Basic Cable .................................. 94
   A. Basic Cable to Domestic Basic Cable ... 94
   B. Basic Cable to Network Primetime ...... 96
   C. Basic Cable to Other than Network Primetime ......................................................... 97

    D. Basic Cable to Foreign TV ..................... 98
    E. Basic Cable to Supplemental Markets . 99
    F. History of Made for Basic Cable ........... 99

10. Theatrical Use of TV and Home Video Product ........................................ 100

11. New Media Reuse of Traditional Product ................................................... 103
    A. Theatrical, TV and Home Video to eRental ................................................... 103
    B. Theatrical to Electronic Sell-Through (EST) ...................................................... 104
    C. TV and Home Video to Electronic Sell-Through (EST) .................................. 105
    D. Theatrical to Ad-Supported ................. 107
    E. TV and Home Video to Ad-Supported 108
    F. History of New Media Reuse and of Made-For New Media ............................. 112

12. Made for New Media ...................... 113
    A. Derivative and Original New Media to Consumer Paid ......................................... 113
    B. Derivative New Media to Ad-Supported 115
    C. Original New Media to Ad-Supported 118
    D. Derivative and Original New Media to Free TV ................................................... 119
    E. Derivative and Original New Media to Foreign TV ............................................... 120
    F. Derivative and Original New Media to Supplemental Markets ............................. 121
    G. Derivative and Original New Media to Domestic Basic Cable ............................... 122
    H. Derivative and Original New Media to Theatrical .............................................. 123
    I. Experimental New Media .................... 124
    J. High Budget SVOD to Subscription Consumer Paid New Media Platform ........ 127
    K. High Budget SVOD to Other Consumer Paid 127
    L. High Budget SVOD to Ad-Supported . 127
    M. High Budget SVOD to Traditional ..... 127
    N. History of Made-For New Media ........ 127

## Part III – Additional Topics

13. Residuals Calculation ................... 128
    A. Date .................................................... 128
    B. Budget ................................................ 128
    C. Waivers ............................................... 129
    D. Signatory Status ................................. 129
    E. Allocation Among Members ................ 129
    F. Proration ............................................. 132
    G. Allocation Across Markets and Products 133
    H. Crediting / Offset / Application of Excess 133
    I. Buyouts ............................................... 133
    J. Pension and Health ............................. 134
    K. Commissionability ............................... 135
    L. Dues .................................................... 137
    M. Taxes .................................................. 137
    N. Coogan Accounts ................................. 139
    O. Charitable Donation ............................ 139
    P. Unemployment Benefits ...................... 139
    Q. Payroll Company Fees ........................ 140
    R. Contingent Compensation .................. 140

14. Separated Rights and Similar Reuse Provisions ............................................. 141
    A. Introduction ........................................ 141
    B. What Are Separated Rights? .............. 141
    C. Publication Rights Payments ............. 142
    D. Dramatic Stage Rights Payments ....... 142
    E. Theatrical Sequel and Spinoff Payments 142
    F. Spinoffs ............................................... 142
    G. Series Sequel Payments ..................... 142
    H. Residuals on Series Sequel Payments (Separated Rights Residuals) .................... 142
    I. Adapters Royalty ................................ 143
    J. Remakes ............................................. 143
    K. Foreign Remakes ................................ 143
    L. Other Reuse of Literary Material ....... 143
    M. Merchandising .................................... 143
    N. Character Payments ........................... 143
    O. Script Publication Fee ........................ 143
    P. DGA Series Bonus ............................... 143
    Q. History ................................................ 143

15. Other Entertainment Residuals and Reuse Payments ..................................... 145
    A. Non-Primetime Scripted Programming 145
    B. Excerpts (Clip Fees) ............................ 145
    C. "Unscripted" Programming ................. 145
    D. Interactive Media (Videogames) ......... 145
    E. Animation ........................................... 145
    F. Industrials .......................................... 146
    G. Music from Other Sources .................. 146
    H. Soundtrack Albums ............................ 147
    I. Foreign Levies .................................... 147
    J. Live Stage ........................................... 147

    K. Copyright Royalty Tribunal Monies ... 147
    L. AGICOA Monies .................................. 147
**16. Commercials ......................................148**
    A. SAG-AFTRA........................................ 148
    B. AFM ..................................................... 148
    C. History................................................. 149
**17. Economics ..........................................150**
    A. Total Entertainment Residuals .......... 150
    B. Comparisons ....................................... 150
    C. WGA West Data in Detail .................. 151
    D. SAG Data in Detail............................. 151
    E. Commercials Data ............................. 151
    F. Aggregated SAG Data ........................ 151
    G. IATSE/MPIPHP Data.......................... 151
    H. AFM/FMSMF Data.............................. 151
    I. Historicals .......................................... 151
    J. Pattern Bargaining Multiplier Effect . 151
    K. Theatrical Trends in Home Video....... 152
    L. Trends in Network Primetime Reruns152
    M. Residuals Vs. Total Compensation ..... 152
    N. Writer's Case Study............................ 153
**18. Payment Mechanics ......................154**
    A. Due Dates............................................ 154
    B. Prepayment........................................ 154
    C. Payment Obligations.......................... 155
    D. Residuals Deposits............................. 155
    E. Workflow ............................................ 155
    F. Payment Statistics............................. 155
    G. Small Check Rules............................. 155
    H. Beneficiaries....................................... 156
    I. Unlocatable Recipients....................... 156
    J. Grievance and Arbitration ................. 156
    K. Tri-Guild Audits ................................. 156
**19. International and Linguistic Issues ....................................................................157**
    A. International Issues for U.S. Persons 157
    B. Canada ................................................ 158
    C. United Kingdom ................................. 158
    D. Australia ............................................. 158
    E. New Zealand ...................................... 158
    F. Other Countries.................................. 159
**20. Recent History ..................................160**
    A. 2007-2009 Negotiating Cycle ............. 160
    B. 2010-2011 Negotiating Cycle ............. 160
    C. 2013-2014 Negotiating Cycle ............. 160
**21. Policy Issues.....................................162**
    A. Strikes, Technology and Residuals..... 162
    B. Residuals Pro and Con ........................ 164
    C. Solving the Fight over Union Residuals 166
    D. Dump Residuals ................................. 169
    E. Recoupment Based Residuals............. 170
    F. Reforming Residuals .......................... 174

# Part IV – Reference

Appendix: Sources and Contracts.......177
Index..................................................................185
Residuals Chart .........................................188

For row by row discussion, see pp. 26 *ff.* For column by column discussion, see pp. 38 *ff.*

| Reused in: / Made for: | Theatrical | Free TV Network Primetime | Free TV Syndication or Non-Primetime | Foreign | Supp.Mkts. Pay TV | Supp.Mkts. Home Video | Domestic Basic Cable | New Media Consumer Pd eRental | New Media Consumer Pd EST | New Media Ad Supported |
|---|---|---|---|---|---|---|---|---|---|---|
| Theatrical | p. 66 | p. 67 | p. 67 | | p. 81 | p. 82 | p. 69 | p. 104 | p. 104 | p. 107 |
| Free TV | p. 100 | p. 70 | p. 72 | p. 78 | | | p. 80 | p. 103 | p. 105 | p. 108 |
| Pay TV | p. 100 | p. 92 | p. 92 | p. 92 | p. 84 | p. 93 | | p. 103 | p. 105 | p. 108 |
| Home Video | p. 100 | p. 92 | p. 92 | p. 92 | p. 84 | p. 93 | | p. 103 | p. 105 | p. 108 |
| Basic Cable | | p. 96 | p. 97 | p. 98 | p. 99 | p. 94 | | | | |
| Deriv. NM | p. 123 | p. 119 | p. 119 | p. 120 | p. 121 | p. 122 | p. 113 | | | p. 115 |
| Orig. NM | p. 123 | p. 119 | p. 119 | p. 120 | p. 121 | p. 122 | p. 113 | | | p. 118 |
| Exper. NM | p. 124 | | | | | | | | | |
| HB SVOD | p. 127 | p. 127 | p. 127 | p. 127 | p. 127 | p. 127 | p. 127 | p. 127 | p. 127 | p. 127 |

# ABOUT THE AUTHOR

Jonathan Handel practices transactional entertainment and technology law at TroyGould in Los Angeles and is a contributing editor for The Hollywood Reporter, where he covers entertainment labor, law and other matters. He is also a former computer scientist and was involved in local politics for over a decade.

Handel is the author of several other books: THE NEW ZEALAND HOBBIT CRISIS, which tells the dramatic story of an attempt to unionize actors on *The Hobbit*; HOLLYWOOD ON STRIKE!, which chronicles and analyzes the Hollywood writers strike of 2007-2008 and the ensuing Screen Actors Guild stalemate that lasted through mid-2009;, and the 345 page ENTERTAINMENT LABOR: AN INTERDISCIPLINARY BIBLIOGRAPHY.

Handel is an adjunct professor at USC Gould School of Law and Southwestern Law School, where he teaches courses on the entertainment unions and other topics. He has also been an adjunct professor at UCLA Law School. Handel has previously worked as a talent lawyer; as associate counsel at the Writers Guild; and as a litigator.

Handel is a member of the Academy of Television Arts and Sciences, and was named by the Daily Journal as one of the top 100 lawyers in California in 2008. He has also been profiled by the Los Angeles Business Journal and in the book *social.lawyers* by Jayne Navarre.

A magna cum laude graduate of Harvard College in applied math and computer science, Handel worked in the computer industry before attending Harvard Law School. He graduated from law school cum laude in 1990, and then clerked on the U.S. Court of Appeals for the Fifth Circuit. During 1993, while a litigation associate at a Los Angeles firm, he concurrently served as a federal Associate Independent Counsel (special prosecutor).

Handel's writing has been published in the *Los Angeles Times, Variety, The Hollywood Reporter, Billboard, Campaigns & Elections, Los Angeles Business Journal, Daily Journal, The Huffington Post*, Forbes.com and IMDB.com.

Handel has appeared as a commentator on entertainment and technology legal issues and on Hollywood guilds over 850 times in international, national and local television, radio, print and online media, including ABC, CBS and NBC nightly news programs, the *New York Times, Wall Street Journal, Los Angeles Times, Variety, Hollywood Reporter*, NPR, BBC radio, local television and radio, Canadian television, wire services, *The Economist* and *Entertainment Weekly*.

Handel is also the author of a short book for technology executives, entitled HOW TO WRITE LOIS AND TERM SHEETS. His article on trademark registration for movie titles was selected as a cover article of Los Angeles Lawyer Magazine, and his law review article *Uneasy Lies the Head that Wears the Crown: Why Content's Kingdom is Slipping Away*, which discusses the struggle between content and technology, appeared in the Vanderbilt Journal of Entertainment and Technology Law.

Handel has moderated and appeared on panels and presented seminars on the entertainment industry to professional audiences in Los Angeles, Park City (at the Sundance Film Festival), Nashville (at Vanderbilt Law School), Taiwan, and Havana. For several years, he taught a film appreciation and screening class of approximately 400 students for UCLA Extension.

# 1. INTRODUCTION

"Begin at the beginning," said the King of Hearts in *Alice in Wonderland*, "and go on till you come to the end: then stop." We'll worry about the end when we get there, but since this is a book about a perplexing topic, no doubt Lewis Carroll would approve if we start with a question: what are residuals?

## A. What are Residuals?

If you work in film or television – or even if you simply live in Los Angeles – you probably already know what residuals are, at least in broad strokes. They're union-negotiated payments that writers, actors, directors and others receive – from a studio, producer or distributor – when a movie, TV show or Internet production is rerun or is reused in different media.

The word "residual" sounds unassuming, like yesterday's leftovers, but these are pretty tasty treats: entertainment residuals amount to over $2 billion per year. (Chapter 17 has details.)

> We interrupt this book for a commercial announcement! Actors and musicians also get residuals for *commercials*, to the tune of roughly $700 million per year. That's in addition to the $2 billion figure, for a total of around $2.7 billion. This book focuses on entertainment, but commercial residuals are discussed in Chapter 16.

There are many different types of reruns and reuse that trigger residuals. For instance, a movie can be released on DVD/Blu-ray, then on pay TV (such as HBO), and the Internet in a download-to-own fashion such as on iTunes. It could also be released on a subscription service such as Netflix, or on a basic cable channel such as FX, or on foreign television. Each of these reuses generate residuals.

Similarly, a broadcast TV show can be rerun on network primetime, or on syndication, basic cable, Internet streaming (such as Hulu) and so forth. Broadcast TV shows also get released on iTunes or DVD/Blu-ray. Again, residuals will result.

Shows that are initially made for pay TV or basic cable can also be reused in the above ways. So too with direct-to-video movies. There are residuals for these reuses too.

Likewise, programs that are made for "new media" (the guild/union term for Internet, cell phones and subscription video on demand (SVOD) services like Netflix) also are rerun in those media, resulting in residuals.

Sometimes new media programs are reused in other ways too. For instance, consider 2008's *Dr. Horrible's Sing-Along Blog.* The Joss Whedon production was initially made available via free streaming on Hulu. But that was just the beginning.

The program was later released on iTunes (paid download), Netflix (streaming via consumer-paid subscription), Blu-ray disc and, in 2011, on Amazon Video on Demand under a paid streaming-to-own model (you pay once and have the perpetual right to stream the program).

That's an uncommonly broad spectrum of reuses for a short-form Internet production. All of them can generate residuals.

Even in traditional media, some reuse patterns are uncommon. For instance, a pay TV program is seldom reused on broadcast TV. Nonetheless, there are residuals formulas that apply when such reuse happens.

And a good thing too, because it actually did, during the Writers Guild strike of 2007-2008, when CBS ran edited episodes of *Dexter,* a serial killer drama that normally aired on a CBS-owned pay TV channel, Showtime.

Yes, the writers' strike truly made a bloody mess of the primetime schedule.

*Dexter* is also on Netflix and on Nuvo, a basic cable network targeted at the Latino market. Residuals will result from each of these deals.

Here's another rarity: basic cable shows aren't often sold into broadcast syndication. They seem more likely to keep running on their original home stations – as FX's *The Shield* had continued to do – or even to be licensed to another basic cable station, which is the path *The Shield* took beginning in March 2012, when it began airing on SpikeTV.

Nonetheless, broadcast syndication turns out to be a home for at least one basic cable show: in 2011, TV Land's *Hot in Cleveland* scored just such a sale. And yes, there's a residuals formula for that.

Even more unlikely is the possibility that a TV program of any sort would be released theatrically. Here again, though, there's a residuals formula. It would apply if, for instance, a TV movie gets a theatrical deal. Coming soon to a theater near you? Don't hold your breath.

## B. Precise Definition

Here's a more precise definition of residuals:

- Union-negotiated payments . . .

- . . . from an employer (such as a producer, ad agency or advertiser), studio or distributor . . .

- . . . to or for the benefit of writers, actors (principal performers), directors, musicians or crew . . .

- . . . that are made when union-covered movies, TV shows, new media productions, commercials or certain other productions are rerun (which can be in the same medium the project was made) for or are reused in different media.

## C. Reuse Patterns

The fourth prong of the definition of residuals refers to different types of projects (movies, TV shows, etc.) and talks about them being rerun in the same medium, or reused in a different medium.

Implicit in this phraseology are two concepts:

- an audiovisual product can be made in the first instance for a particular medium (which this book calls the made-for medium), such as theatrical motion picture, free TV (broadcast TV), pay TV or the Internet,

- and it can then be used or reused in a variety of different media or markets (commonly called the reuse market), such as theatrical exhibition, network primetime, syndication, foreign TV, pay TV, DVD/Blu-ray or the Internet.

The two concepts are independent of each other. For instance, when *Dexter* runs on pay TV (e.g., Showtime), both the made-for medium and the reuse market are pay TV. However, when it was released on network primetime television (CBS), the reuse market was network primetime, while the made-for medium was still pay TV.

Or consider a feature film: the made-for medium is theatrical, and typical reuse markets include pay TV (the movie plays on pay per view and HBO, say), home video, consumer paid new media (Netflix, iTunes), basic cable, domestic free TV (broadcast), foreign broadcast and more.

The made-for medium is often called the "primary market," but this term is somewhat freighted: the studios have reserved the right to assert at some later date that the primary market encompasses several reuse markets – for instance, that the primary market for theatrical motion pictures also includes home video. It seems clearer, at least at present, to use the albeit inelegant) term "made-for medium."

Each combination of a specific made-for medium and a specific reuse market is referred to in this book as a reuse pattern.

The residuals system recognizes essentially 9 made-for media and at least 10 independent reuse markets. That means there are at least 90 different reuse patterns within the focus of the residuals chart and most of this book.

## D. Residuals Formulas

Residuals formulas vary widely, and as you might expect, the applicable formula depends in part on the reuse pattern. In addition, they vary from union to union.

**%** Some formulas are based on a percentage of gross receipts. That may make these **percentage residuals** sound like the sort of deal that a movie star has when he or she gets a percentage of gross as part of a backend deal (a participation). However, they're not really comparable. For one thing, residuals are smaller percentages, such as 3.6%, rather the range of 5% to 20% that one sees in typical gross participations. And, with residuals, those already small percentages are shared among multiple actors, for instance, whereas a top star's 15% participation, say, is not shared. Also, critically, gross participation deals include a percentage of theatrical rentals (the portion of box office receipts that flow to the studio). Residuals do not.

**$** Other residuals formulas are based indirectly on the union's minimum wage scales. This is the case with network TV reruns, for instance. These are called **fixed residuals**, because they have no relation to the producer's gross receipts.

There are charts in the contracts with dollar figures from which such residuals can be calculated. However, "fixed residuals" is a bit of a misnomer, since the charts generally change from year to year.

The charts are not reproduced in this book, since they'd quickly become obsolete. Thus, you'll find few actual dollar figures in the book. Instead, you'll find cross-references that will enable you to find the charts in the union contracts.

There are other kinds of residuals formulas too. Some are hybrids of percentage and fixed residuals, while others are based on different factors altogether. All of these are discussed later in the book.

➔ Notably, there are no residuals based on net (rather than gross) profits. During WGA negotiations in 2007 the studios proposed tying all residuals to a form of net profits (see p. 170). Writers were outraged, since this would have reduced total residuals significantly; in addition, studio net profit accounting is widely distrusted. As a result, the proposal managed only to add fuel to the fire that turned into the 2007-2008 Writers Guild strike.

Five unions participate in residuals, representing directors, writers, actors, crew and musicians: the Directors Guild of America (DGA), Writers Guild of America (WGA), the performers' union SAG-AFTRA,[*] the crew union IATSE[†] and the American Federation of Musicians (AFM).

Here they are at a glance:

| Union | Abbr. |
|---|---|
| Directors Guild of America | DGA |
| Writers Guild of America | WGA |
| Screen Actors Guild - American Federation of Television and Radio Artists | SAG-AFTRA |
| The former Screen Actors Guild (legacy SAG) | SAG or L-SAG |
| The former American Federation of Television and Radio Artists (legacy AFTRA) | AFTRA or L-AFTRA |
| International Alliance of Theatrical Stage Employees | IATSE |
| American Federation of Musicians | AFM |

SAG and AFTRA merged in 2012 to form SAG-AFTRA, but their overlapping TV contracts didn't merge until July 1, 2014. For preexisting shows that remain on the air, it is necessary to refer to older SAG or AFTRA agreements separately.

We sometimes shorthand this with phraseology such as "SAG/AFTRA" in instances where the SAG and AFTRA contracts are similar. Other times we refer simply to SAG and AFTRA, or for clarity, to Legacy-SAG (L-SAG) and Legacy-AFTRA (L-AFTRA). In contrast, SAG-AFTRA means SAG-AFTRA commencing July 1, 2014.

---

[*] Screen Actors Guild – American Federation of Television and Radio Artists.
[†] International Alliance of Theatrical Stage Employees.

Different unions can have different formulas for the same reuse pattern, which means there could theoretically be at least 450 different residuals formulas – i.e., 5 unions times 90 reuse patterns. In fact, there could be more, because – as we discuss later – reuse pattern and union aren't the only variables that determine the applicable formula.

Thankfully, though, the different unions often – though not always – use similar formulas for a given reuse pattern.

For instance, when a movie is licensed to broadcast television (say, ABC), the DGA residuals formula is 1.2% of the license fee that the producer receives. The WGA formula is identical (i.e., 1.2%); the SAG-AFTRA formula is 3 times as much, or 3.6%;[*] the IATSE formula is 4.5 times as much, or 5.4%; and the AFM formula is simply 1%.

These ratios, and the AFM 1%, almost always hold true for percentage residuals. Sometimes the DGA residual will be 2%, or 1.5%, or some other figure, but the ratios (DGA 1x, WGA 1x, SAG-AFTRA or SAG/AFTRA[†] 3x, IATSE 4.5x and AFM 1%) almost always hold true, except in the frequent instances where IATSE or the AFM don't get any residuals at all.

Fixed residuals don't display the 1x, 1x, 3x, 4.5x pattern. Parallelism there is usually more indirect.

In any case, these relationships are referred to as being *in pattern*, with the opposite being *out of pattern* (when there is a pattern, but with deviations) or *no pattern* (when the different unions' formulas diverge altogether).

➔ In this book, out of pattern or no pattern situations are often denoted with *italics*.

The tendency towards pattern is a result of a negotiating process called *pattern bargaining*. The above the line (DGA, WGA and SAG-AFTRA) contracts are usually three years in duration, and are often timed to expire at roughly the same date. During each contract negotiating cycle, the studios (represented by the AMPTP) seek to negotiate first with the union that is perceived as easiest to negotiate with. In recent years, this has generally been the DGA, though SAG and AFTRA went first in the 2010-2011 negotiating cycle.

Studio negotiators then attempt to have the other unions accept the same or parallel terms regarding such key terms as wage increases[‡] and residuals formulas. Although there's no law or rule that requires the other unions to adhere to pattern, they usually do, because of the friction that refusal to follow pattern generates within and between the unions and between unions and management. In at least one instance, this friction is formalized by a contract provision: the WGA has a provision in its agreement, Article 15.A.3.a, that gives it the right to reopen negotiations with the studios if the DGA or SAG (now SAG-AFTRA) is granted out of pattern residuals for reuse of theatrical motion pictures on broadcast television. But even in the absence of such a provision (referred to as a "reopener"), a major deviation from pattern would be likely to anger the union(s) that had negotiated first.

There are also similarities between certain reuse patterns within each union. For instance, if a basic cable program is rerun on pay TV (F6), the residuals formula is the same as the one used when a free TV show is rerun on pay TV (F3). Color coding makes these parallels readily apparent.

Another fact that reduces the number of residuals formulas from the potential 450 formulas is that in many reuse patterns, as mentioned, IATSE and AFM don't participate in residuals at all.

All of these factors save us from the theoretical blizzard of 450 separate formulas. They reduce the complexity to something more manageable: about 20 categories and 40 to 75 distinct formulas, depending on how you count. Manageable is obviously a relative term.

Nonetheless, the similarities are numerous enough that the key formulas can be summa-

---

[*] L-SAG's and L-AFTRA's ratios, 3x, is the same as SAG-AFTRA's.
[†] "SAG/AFTRA" means "L-SAG and L-AFTRA."

[‡] Directors', writers' and actors' wage rates are very different, but the percentage increase in wages in a given year tends to be the same – e.g., if the directors get a 3% wage increase in a particular year, the writers and actors also likely to get 3% bumps that year.

rized in a single color-coded chart, rather than six separate ones. Granted, it takes two pages and some tiny fonts and narrow margins to cram all of the information into a single chart. I had to update my eyeglass prescription. You might too.

You may have noticed that there are actually four pages to the chart. The third one provides references to the sections of the union agreements in which the actual formulas appear, and the fourth is a table of abbreviations.

Adding to the complexity of the residuals system, many of the formulas have changed over time. Movies and TV programs created under previous versions of the union contracts continue to be reused, generally under the formulas that were then in effect, which adds to the number of formulas in use today.

➔ Sometimes, however, *current* formulas apply to reuse of older product. For instance, older product reused in new media is subject in some instances to the formulas that were introduced in 2008.

This book focuses primarily on current formulas, but describes past formulas in History sections of relevant chapters. If you are looking at older product, you should be sure to start by obtaining a copy of the union agreement(s) it was produced under. Some earlier versions of the residuals chart are available at jhandel.com/residuals.

And this is not even to mention such critical matters as proration, allocation, dues assessments and agent commissions on residuals, and pension and health (P&H) issues, which are dealt with in Chapter 13. All of these vary by union; in many cases by reuse pattern; and in a few cases even by an actor's city of residence.

## E. Why are There Residuals and Why are They So Complex?

You might be asking why there are residuals at all and why the formulas are so complex. Some of this is addressed in Subsection O below (history) and Chapter 21 (policy issues). Another reason for the complexity is that the underlying economics of the various reuse patterns vary dramatically – that is, the formulas and business models by which producers make money differ. Many of the residuals formulas reflect these differences.

## F. Detailed Roadmap of the Book

Let's pause the discussion for a moment to describe the format of the rest of this book.

● The remainder of this chapter outlines additional basic facts about residuals.

● Chapter 2 describes the residuals chart, which is the core reference for most of this book.

● Chapter 3 provides detail on made-for media, reuse markets, unions and other key determinants of which formula is used for a given reuse pattern.

● Chapter 4 describes each of the key formulas in detail – with a few exceptions: formulas that are used in only one or two cells of the chart are deferred to Chapters 5-12.

● Within Chapter 4, Section 4.M describes the structure of Chapters 5-12.

● Chapters 5-12 consist of sections that describe each of the reuse patterns. Each section describes a particular cell of the chart, which in some cases encompasses several essentially identical reuse patterns. These chapters cover key scripted entertainment programs – i.e., scripted product made for theatrical, primetime free TV, pay TV, home video, basic cable or new media (including high budget SVODv programs made for services like Netflix).

● The remaining chapters of the book discuss other subjects related to residuals, including other factors that affect payment amounts (Chapter 13), separated rights fees (Chapter 14), daytime and other entertainment product (Chapter 15), commercials (Chapter 16), economics (Chapter 17), payment mechanics (Chapter 18), international issues (Chapter 19), recent history (Chapter 20) and policy issues (Chapter 21).

# 1. Introduction – 7

- **The References** section includes details on the relevant union and guild agreements, including a list of current agreements, a table giving the locations of the new media sideletters, and charts that break down the coverage of the agreements.

> Flip to p. 177 and take a quick look.

- **The front matter**, as you've probably already seen, includes a variety of informative material.

- **The end matter** includes a discussion of references used in preparing the book, an Index and a table of abbreviations.

- **At the end of the book** is a copy of the chart. You can also download at no cost a standalone and potentially more up-to-date copy (in the event of changes post-publication) at jhandel.com/residuals.

> You'll want to read all of Chapters 1-4 in order to effectively use Chapters 5-12.

## G. Conventions Used in the Book and Chart

Cells, and references to cells, are color coded as shown on p. iv. Row and column headings of the chart are in yellow, as are references to them, e.g., A2-A9 and B1-K1. So too are references to entire rows or columns, e.g., row 6 or column 3. The top left cell of the chart is reddish: A1.

Chapter and section headings are in green and have a background that's color coordinated with the type(s) of residual formula discussed, if any (otherwise, the background is orange). References to chapters and sections are in green. Page references within the book are in dark purple. References to other documents – such as union contracts – are in normal black text (see p. 177 for information on obtaining union contracts).

URLs are in blue. Key terms are introduced in **bolded green**. ➔ Unexpected information gets a red arrow.

Red-boxed text indicates important advice.

Informational charts are in orange and blue.

Out of pattern or no-pattern items are in *italics*.

See p. 20 for an explanation of grid coding (C2, etc.) and the last page of the chart for abbreviations.

## H. Who Receives Residuals?

Now let's return to the substantive discussion of residuals. We've been referring somewhat generally to the recipients of residuals. More precisely, the following people and entities receive residuals – so long as the project is created by a signatory to their union's collective bargaining agreement:

- **Credited writers**. The basic principle is that "residuals follow credits" – i.e., that credited writers, and only credited writers, receive residuals.

That means that writers who did not receive credit on a project receive no residuals.[*] Also, writers of source material, such as a novel upon which a screenplay is based, do not receive residuals. (The novelist might negotiate for a share of gross or net profits, but that's a contract matter that has nothing to do with the WGA or residuals.)

- **Directors,** and sometimes other DGA members: the unit production manager, the first assistant director and the key second assistant director.

- **Actors** – more specifically, principal performers and also stunt coordinators – whose performances are used in the project. No residuals if you end up on the cutting room floor. Principal performers means anyone except background performers (extras), unless they are upgraded to principal.

- **"Participating musicians,"** which means musicians whose music is used in the project or, in

---

[*] They do receive their initial compensation however – i.e., their up-front fee.

the case of on-camera musicians, whose performance is used in the project.

These subjects are addressed in further detail on p. 129. Also worth noting:

- → Non-union members and dues paying non-members (aka agency fee payers or "financial core members") who work on a union-covered project and fall under the above categories receive residuals. This is required by applicable labor law and/or the union contracts. For instance, when a non-WGA writer writes, co-writes or sells a screenplay or teleplay under guild jurisdiction, he receives residuals just as if he were a Guild member.

- In some cases, the union pension and/or health funds receive a portion of residuals; or they may receive additional amounts on top of residuals; or neither. It varies. See p. 134.

- → IATSE crew members do not individually receive residuals, but the IATSE-affiliated pension and health funds do.

- IATSE and AFM participate in residuals in far fewer reuse patterns than the other guilds. See p. 49.

- → The above people and entities receive residuals in perpetuity.

- → Even the estates, and the designated beneficiaries, of the above people, and the beneficiaries of beneficiaries, etc., receive residuals in perpetuity – with the exception of AFM (musicians union) residuals, which stop after beneficiaries of beneficiaries (referred to as BOBs). This is discussed more on pp. 129 and 155.

## I. Who Pays Residuals?

We mentioned at the beginning of the chapter that residuals are paid by "the studio, producer or distributor." Who is it exactly?

In the case of a movie, producers usually create a subsidiary – a single-purpose entity – for the purpose of producing the movie. That entity becomes a union signatory – it signs the union or guild agreement. That obligates it to comply with a wide range of requirements – the agreements run to hundreds of pages – one of which is the requirement to pay residuals.

In the case of a television series, the show may be produced directly by the production company itself, in which case the production company will be a signatory. Note that these companies are separate entities from the networks. For instance, AMC's *Mad Men* is actually produced by Lionsgate, who probably would prefer us to call it Lionsgate's *Mad Men*.

Even where a single media conglomerate produces programs for its own network, as is often the case with broadcast networks, the TV production operation and the network are usually set up as two separate subsidiaries.

So, whether we're talking movies or TV, the signatory entity – the production company – bears the obligation to pay residuals. That entity is typically referred to in the union agreement as Company, Employer or Producer, depending on the union.

But the producer may not be the only one on the hook. A single purpose entity that produces a small independent film may not have other assets. The unions may be concerned that the company won't pay, so it may require a guarantee from a parent company or even a personal guarantee from the owner. Nothing like having your house on the line to make sure you pay up.

On the other hand, the residuals obligation can be transferred to the studio or distributor. This may happen as a matter of course with a major studio or it may be a matter of vigorous negotiation when foreign distribution rights in an independent movie are sold to distributors in various territories. Sometimes distributors refuse to sign an agreement – called an assumption agreement – by which they would undertake the residuals obligation. There's a federal statute that attempts to transfer the obligation anyway, but whether it's effective internationally is difficult to know.

See p. 154 for more information on payment obligations, due dates and more.

## J. The Role of the Unions

Residuals are a product of the union or guild agreement and certain related documents. ➔ That means that non-union projects don't pay residuals.

Thus, if a project is produced by a company that is signatory to the Writers Guild agreement, then residuals will be payable to the credited writers; if not, they won't. Don't come crying to me when they tell you the check isn't in the mail.

And know too that companies can be signatory to one union's agreement without being signatory to another's. An invitation to work on "a union picture" is like a plane ticket to "Paris" – you might end up in Paris, Texas.

Concretely, a movie might written by a non-WGA writer, directed by a non-DGA director, shot with non-IATSE crew, scored with non-AFM musicians, but cast with SAG-AFTRA actors under a SAG-AFTRA contract. In this case, the production entity will probably be signatory to the SAG-AFRA agreement but not the WGA's, DGA's, IATSE's or AFM's. The actors will get residuals but the writer(s), director and musicians won't.

In case you were wondering, the distinction between "union" and "guild" is stylistic. There's no legal difference. All of the above entities are unions.

Another important organization is the Alliance of Motion Picture and Television Producers (AMPTP), which represents the studios and producers. When the unions negotiate their key theatrical and television contracts, this is the organization they negotiate with. Although it has "Producers" in its name, the actual members are the six major studios (Disney, Fox, Paramount, Sony, Universal and Warner Bros.) plus MGM (essentially for historical reasons, because it once was a major studio) and CBS. (The other broadcast networks are siblings of studios: ABC/Disney, FOX/Fox and NBC/Universal.)

Those companies are the ones at the bargaining table. Other companies – big ones like Lionsgate as well as smaller ones – that sign on to the union agreements are referred to as "signatories" or "authorizers." They become bound by the union agreement even though they played no part in the negotiation. It's essentially a take it or leave it arrangement for them.

## K. The Contract

And speaking of contracts . . . Being a union project isn't necessarily enough to trigger residuals. It also depends on the particular union contract. Each of the unions has numerous contracts.

Some of these relate to commercials and other non-entertainment product, but even within our core focus – movies, TV and new media – a single union may have multiple agreements. You'll find details starting on p. 177.

In addition to offering its standard armoire of contracts, each union will cut individual deals to one degree or another. These may be called waivers, customized letters of adherence, one production only (OPO) deals or the like.

This bespoke approach was once particularly prevalent in made for basic cable product. AFTRA, for instance, used a set of four negotiable template agreements in that field, rather than a standardized contract.

Those templates, and certain other union agreements, aren't collectively bargained at all. Rather, they're what are called promulgated agreements, meaning that the union has simply issued and offered them to producers. Some are negotiable; others aren't.

As with clothing, so too with contracts: sometimes the right choice is neither hand-tailored nor off the rack. In that case, the unions take a semi-custom approach, cutting a modified deal for a category of producers.

Thus, for instance, there are sideletters that modify the residuals provisions for half-hour programs in syndication, or for "supersized episodes" – shows that are deliberately bulked up a few minutes beyond their stated half-hour or one-hour length – or for pilots or new series. Sideletters generally appear towards the end of the union contract.

There are even special rules in some cases for holiday specials, but only certain holidays qualify. Felicitously, my favorite – Halloween – is on the list.

In addition, there are special accommodations for broadcast networks that don't quite have the viewership of ABC, CBS or NBC. So, for instance, there may be special discounts for The CW. There used to be for Fox too, until that network began to kick sand in the faces of what used to be the Big Three. Fox kept hold of its deal for rather a while longer, but began paying full boat around 2003.

Yet another wrinkle is expired contracts. The union agreements generally come up for renewal every three years. If negotiation doesn't result in an agreement on a new contract before the old one expires, then union members may continue to work under the terms of the old agreement.

When a new contract is finally achieved, some of its terms – such as increases in minimums – may be retroactive. Then again, they may not. It all depends on the agreed deal, and residuals calculations can be affected.

Sometimes, of course, strikes occur. When this happens, the union may offer interim agreements (WGA terminology) or Guaranteed Completion Contracts (GCC) (SAG-AFTRA terminology) that bind the signatory to whatever terms are ultimately reached for the new deal. For these companies, product produced before the effective date of the new agreement may nonetheless be subject to it.

Even absent a strike, effective dates can be confusing. Some provisions are effective upon ratification, but other times they're retroactive to the date the negotiators reached agreement – or, occasionally, to some date further in the past. Other provisions have effective dates in the future.

Further confusing things is the way subsequent agreements may refer to effective dates. For instance, suppose a 2008 agreement establishes a new residuals formula and says "This formula is effective for product whose principal photography commenced on or after June 1, 2008."

Now suppose that a contract renewal is negotiated in 2011 with a contract term beginning June 1, 2011, and the formula is unchanged. The above sentence might be left as is, since it's still true.

Or, it might be changed to read "This formula is effective for product whose principal photography commenced on or after June 1, 2011." That's true too, but it might be misinterpreted as signifying that the rule is different for earlier product. You'd have to go back to earlier contracts to see.

And, suppose instead that the formula *is* changed in 2011. Now the sentence "This formula is effective for product whose principal photography commenced on or after June 1, 2011" does indeed mean that earlier product is subject to a different rule.

Occasionally, the contract will be more explicit, and may even spell out the formulas that apply to older product. Usually not though.

## L. Interpreting the Contracts

Union and guild agreements don't always mean what they seem to, for a variety of reasons:

- **Navigational Difficulties:** It's often difficult to determine whether you're reading the right contract, or the latest version, or the proper subsection. Some contracts are for "film," some for "theatrical film," or "television film," "video" or "tape," a set of distinctions that even in the past weren't always obvious and are now meaningless. Some of these agreements stand alone, while others function as an amendment, supplement or sidecar to others.

Once you find the right contract, you have to find the correct version. We've already noted that reusing content sometimes means referring to old contracts and sometimes to current ones, since the contracts are renegotiated every three years or so, but there's a more prosaic issue as well: the new language may remain uncodified for years, available only in one or more free-standing Memoranda that have to be read in conjunction with the underlying contract. There's a guide to all this on p. 177.

The contracts themselves are hundreds of pages, structured – if that's the word – as a jumble of Articles, Sections, Exhibits, Appendixes, Schedules, Sideletters and Supplements in an almost random order that differs from union to union. Some of these provisions have no contemporary relevance – union agreements are like Roach Motels: contract clauses check in, but they (often) don't check out.

In other cases, the most critical provisions have been deported to some contractual Siberia towards the back of the book. The entire new media framework, for instance, is jammed into two sideletters buried at the end of the union agreements, making the provisions hard to find and even harder to cite to (see p. 181). And in traditional media, some sideletters have a significant economic impact, while others are meaningless. There are also unpublished sideletters, some of which are in fact published.

Concretely, a motion picture that's made under the DGA, WGA, SAG-AFRA, IATSE and AFM contracts is governed by documents totaling about 2000 pages in length. The residuals provisions are scattered among those pages in no particular order.

- **Numbering Confusion**: Paragraph numbering can go many levels deep, and it's often hard to figure out where you are except by tediously paging backwards. For instance, there's a paragraph labeled "(2)" on a page of the WGA Agreement. But what's it a subparagraph of? We go back a page and discover an "1." So, it's "1(2)." But what's *that* a subparagraph of? Page back some more, and then again and again and you might complete the puzzle – or you might lose your page or get caught in another tangle of subparagraphs, or simply forget why you were looking at that paragraph in the first place.

- **Definitional Delirium**: Defined terms in Hollywood union and guild agreements are often not capitalized, which means that you don't always know whether you're reading English or legalese. Adding to the confusion, terms may be redefined in different sections of the contract, which can make it tough to interpret cross-references. Terms don't always mean what you'd think – for instance, a "motion picture" is not necessarily a movie that get shown in theaters – and some, even critical terms such as "original new media," aren't defined at all.

Bizarrely enough, contract provisions sometimes reference defunct companies, abandoned business practices, forgotten television programs and even such idiosyncratic matters as "the responsibilities and functions . . . during 1977 (of) Samuel Arkoff, Ron Miller, Marvin Mirisch, . . . Cardon Walker, Alan Ladd, Jr., John Calley, and Daniel Melnick." (See WGA MBA Art. B.1.a.(2).)

Sadly, some of those individuals are dead, and the others may no longer remember their job descriptions from decades ago, or care to.

Even more anachronistic, by the way, are some of the MBA's provisions regarding screen credit. There, for instance, we learn that "*From a Saturday Evening Post Story by*" is an acceptable credit – do they have an iPad edition? – and that notices regarding credit can be sent by telegraph or telegram (is there a difference?), among other means. No allowance for Candygrams though. It's truly a long walk down memory lane.

- **Arbitration Decisions**: Disagreements about the union contracts sometimes lead to arbitration, and the arbitrator's decision can affect the interpretation of the contract. They're supposedly non-precedential – but are routinely treated as though they are. Unfortunately, decisions are generally not publicly available. However, I've obtained some of them (thank you, confidential sources!) and cite them in this book where relevant.

- **Unresolved Disagreements**: Other times, disagreements about the contracts don't lead to arbitration, either because an appropriate case hasn't arisen, or because the parties would rather settle the matter than risk an adverse precedent – especially since that result might displease other studios affected by it or, because of pattern bargaining, other unions. In any case, a lack of resolution leaves the issue uncertain.

- **Custom and Practice**: Some matters have become the subject of custom and practice in the industry, even where the contract doesn't explicitly address a subject or, perhaps, in contradiction of a contract provision.

- **Related Contracts:** Some matters relating to residuals aren't addressed in the collective bargaining agreements at all, but instead in the agreements that producers sign with related organizations such as the pension and health plans. Another example is the agreements that talent and literary agents sign with the unions. These specify which residuals are commissionable, which affects the amount that the union member ultimately receives.

## M. Compensation and Context

Residuals are paid in addition to other compensation received by the union member. To put them in context, it's helpful to outline the structure of compensation that talent, crew and musicians receive.

This can be somewhat difficult, for two reasons: (a) the union agreements and related documents are complex and (b) most talent and some crew and musicians have individual contracts (technically referred to as personal services agreements, or PSAs) in addition to the union agreements.

### Union Agreement vs. Individual Deal

This dual-agreement structure – union agreements plus individual contracts – is unusual. Indeed, it is essentially unique to entertainment and sports.

How do these overlapping PSAs and union agreements relate to each other? For our purposes, the answer is straightforward: Union members, and their individual contracts, cannot waive provisions of the union agreement, unless the union agreement expressly permits this or the union itself grants a waiver. This was established in a Supreme Court case (*J L Case Co. v. NLRB*, 321 U.S. 332 (1944)) and is also explicit in some of the union and guild agreements, such as Art. 9 of the WGA Agreement (MBA).

However, individual agreements can generally provide for better terms than the union agreement – also known as overscale terms – but cannot provide for lesser or worse terms. Thus, a movie star's personal services agreement will provide for million-dollar salaries even though the SAG-AFTRA wage scales are far lower or require that the star's credit appear in extra large type even though the union agreement is silent on the matter.

However, even though it is technically possible to negotiate overscale residuals – that is, more lucrative residuals formulas than the ones in this book – no one ever does. As a matter of business practice, residuals are never negotiated.

### Above the Line (Talent) Compensation

The compensation paid to or for the benefit of writers, directors and actors may include the following:

- **Guaranteed compensation:** Guaranteed compensation (personal services agreement terminology) aka initial compensation (union and guild terminology); for certain work, such as voiceover or commercials, this is also referred to as session fees. Whatever the name, this is base salary – the money that talent is paid at the time they perform work. The compensation for a single movie or TV episode can range from union minimum (scale) – or sometimes a floor of scale plus 10% for the agent's commission – to about $15-$20 million per movie for a very small number of top movie stars. A decade ago, some stars even commanded $25 million, but everyone's cutting back these days. Most talent, of course, earns far less.

- **Overtime:** Non-star actors receive overtime payment if a production day or week goes beyond a certain number of hours. Actors making above a certain dollar amount aren't eligible for overtime. Nor are writers.

- **Meal penalties:** If actors aren't fed on time, they're paid a small amount of compensation for this violation of the union agreement, called a meal penalty.

- **Forced call:** If actors aren't allowed a certain time period after the end of one workday and the beginning of the next (their call time), this is referred to as a "forced call" or "invading the rest period" and a significant payment is due.

- **Wardrobe**: If a performer supplies wardrobe items, he or she may be entitled to a small payment.

- **Other adjustments for extras**: Extras (more formally referred to as "background actors") are entitled to additional compensation for wet, snow and smoke work, hazardous work, the wearing of body makeup, hairpieces or beards or the furnishing of pets, vehicles or personal accessories. (Extras do not receive residuals, however, unless they've been upgraded to principal performer.)

- **Deferments**: Talent may received deferred payments, which are not surprisingly called deferments. These may be triggered by various success criteria – achieving a certain level of gross receipts, box office grosses, an Oscar nomination, etc. Sometimes deferments are essentially bonuses. On other occasions, such as for low-budget movies, potions of base salary may be deferred.

- **Participations**: Talent at certain levels may receive percentage compensation, more informally called backend compensation or "participations," defined in terms of the producer's gross receipts or net profits, with many complex adjustments. Net profits (now usually called "defined proceeds") usually amount to zero – this is the much dreaded "Hollywood accounting" – but gross profits are usually worth something, and often are quite large. Flip back to p. 4 for a discussion of the differences between residuals and participations.

- **Separate pot**: Star talent may also receive separate participations in – i.e., separate income flows from – merchandising, soundtracks or other ancillary sources. This is sometimes referred to as receiving merchandising, etc. in a "separate pot."

- **Perqs**: Star actors or directors (and less often writers) may receive a variety of perqs. These can include larger trailers, first class air travel (when the movie or television show is being shot in a different city) for the star and one or more companions, and all sorts of other benefits.

- **Residuals**: All talent, no matter how large or small their wages, receive residuals under the union agreements, subject to the limitations discussed starting on p. 7..

- **Other union payments**: Talent may receive other union-mandated reuse payments, as described in Chapters 14 and 15.

- **Pension and health**: Employers make contributions on each union member's behalf to the union-affiliated pension and health plans, referred to as P&H, H&R (health and retirement) or PH&W (pension, health and welfare). The amounts contributed are a percentage of earnings – including, in many cases, a percentage of residuals, as discussed on p. 134.

- **Social Security**: Generally, employers contribute on the employee's behalf to Social Security and other government-mandated benefits.[*] (Talent are considered employees, not independent contractors.) Residuals are subject to Social Security.

- **Corporate benefits**: In television work, some writers and directors are on staff. If so, they may receive corporate benefits similar to those that large companies in other industries offer.

### Below the Line (Crew) Compensation

The compensation paid to or for the benefit of crew members – cinematographers, editors, hair and makeup people, and even truck drivers – generally includes the following:

- **Wages**: These are usually paid at scale – i.e., the amounts specified in the union agreements – but some department heads have significant reputations and abilities and thus command overscale.

- **Overtime**: This can be very lucrative. In a few cases, overtime is calculated at an amazing six times the scale rate. Overtime is often referred to as "golden time" or "golden hours."

- **Kit rental**: Many below the line workers own some of the tools of their trade, such as cameras, lights, makeup kits and the like. If the production chooses to use the worker's equipment (particularly common on small independent movies), the production will usually pay a rental fee, referred to as "kit rental" or "box rental."

- **Meal penalties**: See discussion above.

---

[*] We leave aside the issue of loan-out corporations.

- → **Residuals**: Crew residuals are paid to the IATSE-affiliated pension and health fund, not to the crew member.

- **Pension and health**: In addition to the residual payments, P&H payments are made by the employer based in part on wages and in part on hours worked.

- **Social Security**: See discussion above.

### Musicians' Compensation

The compensation paid to or for the benefit of musicians generally includes the following:

- **Session fees**: This the terminology for musicians' base salary.

- **Overtime**: See discussion above.

- **Cartage**: If a musician uses private transportation and carries her instrument, a small fee is payable to the musician for cartage, i.e., for transporting the instrument.

- **Music licensing fees**: Music royalty streams can be very complex. They're mandated by copyright law, not the unions, and are briefly discussed in the next section.

- **Residuals**: See discussion above.

- **Pension and health**: See discussion above.

- **Social Security**: In an odd wrinkle, even though residuals are subject to Social Security, employers do not contribute to Social Security on musicians' behalf with respect to residuals. Instead, for reasons that are unclear, musicians effectively pay both the employer's share and employee's share of Social Security calculated on residuals (see p. 137).

### Other

Some areas of motion picture and television are not unionized, and therefore the workers in these areas do not receive residuals for their work. Such workers include visual effects workers (workers who create computer graphics imagery, CGI), composers and lyricists, producers, executives, and production assistants. There were unsuccessful efforts in the past to unionize composers and lyricists, and there are ongoing efforts, so far unsuccessful, to unionize VFX workers.

## N. License Fees and Royalties

To put residuals in context, it's also helpful to distinguish fees that are required as a result of copyright law. These have nothing to do with the entertainment unions (at least in the U.S.) and are not discussed in this book, other than in this section.

Section 106 of the Copyright Act(17 U.S.C.) gives copyright owners the exclusive right to reproduce, distribute, publicly perform, and publicly display, and create derivative works from, works that are subject to copyright.

Among the works subject to copyright are scripts, movies, TV programs, new media productions, musical compositions (i.e., words and lyrics) and songs (i.e., the recorded performance of a musical composition).

Thus, reuse of clips from or whole copies of such works, or of scripts, generally requires permission from the copyright owner, unless such reuse falls under the fair use doctrine or is permitted by law for other reasons.

Such permission is usually not free: it generally requires paying fees, which may be flat fees, per-unit royalties, or fees calculated as a gross or net percentage or in other ways.

For instance, if a movie producer wants to incorporate a clip from another movie, she needs permission from the other studio. If permission is granted, the studio will probably charge a fee, as well as requiring the producer to pay the guild clip usage fees discussed on p. 145 (and obtain any other necessary permissions).

Likewise, if a television producer wants to use a song, she has to get permission and pay a license fee. If a nightclub owner wants to play a song from a movie (or anywhere else), he needs permission and has to pay a fee.

Obtaining permission for clips and music is referred to as clearing the material. It's often a time-consuming and costly process.

Music clearance is particularly complex, and may involve paying fees to the record label, performers (who are often paid via performing rights societies such as ASCAP, BMI and SESAC), music publishing companies and/or an organization called SoundExchange. (For a nearly comprehensive chart of music fees, see Fig. 6.2 in Hal Vogel, ENTERTAINMENT INDUSTRY ECONOMICS (9th ed. 2014).)

As another example, if a cable network wants to run a movie, it needs to license the movie from the copyright owner – usually, a studio – and pay a license fee. This may seem obvious, but it's a result of copyright law. The studio will have to pay residuals based on the license fee, unless it requires (as a condition of the deal) that the cable network pay the residuals.

## O. History in a Nutshell

You may be wondering how and when residuals started and how they grew to encompass a wide range of reuse patterns.

It's easiest to start with a chart showing the date each reuse pattern became subject to residuals. Here's the snapshot:[*]

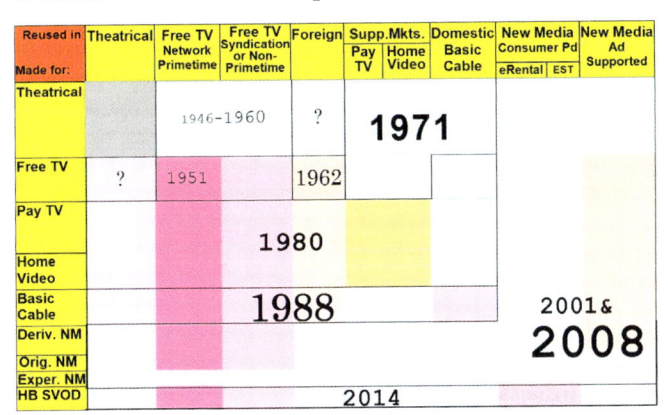

| Reused in → Made for: ↓ | Theatrical | Free TV Network Primetime | Free TV Syndication or Non-Primetime | Foreign | Supp. Mkts. Pay TV / Home Video | Domestic Basic Cable | New Media Consumer Pd eRental / EST | New Media Ad Supported |
|---|---|---|---|---|---|---|---|---|
| Theatrical | | 1946-1960 | | ? | **1971** | | | |
| Free TV | ? | 1951 | | 1962 | | | | |
| Pay TV | | | **1980** | | | | | |
| Home Video | | | | | | | | |
| Basic Cable | | | **1988** | | | | **2001 & 2008** | |
| Deriv. NM | | | | | | | | |
| Orig. NM | | | | | | | | |
| Exper. NM | | | | | | | | |
| HB SVOD | | | | 2014 | | | | |

The first date on the chart is 1946 (for some theatrical to free TV, cells C2-C3), but the story is even older. Although very little has been written on residuals history – indeed, very little has been written on residuals at all[†] – an unpublished master's dissertation[‡] on AFRA (AFTRA without the "T," because there was no commercial television then) reveals that, in 1933, prior to AFRA's formation, a subgroup of the stage actors' union Actors Equity known as Radio Equity proposed the first residuals.

The context was a National Recovery Administration hearing on a proposed Code of Fair Competition for the radio industry, one of many that the NRA was promulgating across various industries, pursuant to the 1933 National Industrial Recovery Act, a key piece of New Deal legislation.

At a hearing that year,[§] Radio Equity proposed a Code that included wage minimums and then this reuse provision: "Art. IV(I)(d)(5). Rebroadcast[**] on same working day 1/2 check extra. / Rebroadcast on another working day full check extra. / Recorded broadcast[††] 1/2 check extra" (emphasis added).[‡‡]

That appears to require a 50% residual – the same amount that would be due if the performers were required to do a repeat live broadcast on the same day as the original broadcast.

---

[*] The new media dates reflect that there were fragmentary new media residuals provisions starting in 2001, but the full structure didn't arrive until 2008, in the wake of the 2007-2008 WGA strike.
[†] See my book ENTERTAINMENT LABOR: AN INTERDISCIPLINARY BIBLIOGRAPHY (2013) for a comprehensive list.
[‡] William Franklin Becker, *The American Federation of Radio Artists: The Formation of the Los Angeles Local* (Masters thesis, UCLA, 1974) (WorldCat OCLC No. 320047000) (UCLA SRLF (Southern Regional Library Facility) Barcode D0005200159).

[§] See Becker, pp. 27, 28, 53-55.
[**] A "rebroadcast" presumably meant a repeat live performance of the same material, such as on the same day for a different time zone. Cf. Rita Morley Harvey, THOSE WONDERFUL, TERRIBLE YEARS: GEORGE HELLER AND THE AMERICAN FEDERATION OF TELEVISION AND RADIO ARTISTS 40 (Southern Illinois Univ. Pr., 1996) (asserting that "practice of 'live repeats,'" as contrasted with recording, continued until 1946.
[††] A "recorded broadcast" probably meant the broadcast of a recording (or perhaps the recording of a broadcast).
[‡‡] Becker, p. 55.

Ultimately, the final Code – which one scholar criticizes as management-centric* – did not include the reuse provisions.† But it might not have mattered anyway. Within two years, the Supreme Court struck down the NIRA and with it went all the Codes of Fair Competition.‡

But the concept of residuals didn't die. Two years further on, in 1937, AFRA was formed, superseding Radio Equity and standing beside SAG, which had been formed in 1933. Residuals weren't an issue for SAG, because in the absence of commercial television or home video there was as yet no way to reuse movies.

AFRA, on the other hand, was concerned, because actors' performances of radio programs could be recorded even then, and reused. That meant that actors could be forced to "compete against themselves" – that is, a recorded version could be used in place of hiring, and paying, the actors to give multiple performances on different dates or at different times on the same date for multiple time zones.

A 1941 AFRA radio agreement§ appears to be the first to include reuse fees. AFRA's fear was that the ability to record and reuse programs on transcription discs – essentially, oversized phonograph records used by radio stations and radio networks – meant that actors would be deprived of the opportunity to perform and get paid for additional live work when stations wanted to broadcast the same program in different time zones, for instance.

Simply put, the union view was that recording technology meant that the actor was competing against himself or herself for work. Hence the requirement in the first Transcription Code that if the program sponsor "repeats the use of the same recording, the artist shall receive for each such repeated use, a fee equal to the compensation paid for the original performance."** There were additional residuals for foreign reuse.††

The AFM (musicians union) shared AFRA's concern. The union had seen around 30,000 live musicians at movie theaters around the country lose their jobs when talkies arrived, so the organization was quite wary of recorded music and technological displacement. An assertive and controversial president, James Petrillo, led the union into two strikes against the radio and recording industries, the so-called Recording Bans of 1942-44 and 1948.

Interestingly, the early arguments for residuals do not appear to have referenced the reuse payments that book authors receive, i.e., royalties. Perhaps the parallels weren't seen as strong enough: actors and musicians aren't authors and radio broadcasts aren't tangible items. Phonograph records are, but in any case, the lack of research on the topic makes it difficult to draw conclusions. (Even the history of book royalties is little-researched.)

Regardless, union concern heightened in the mid- and late-1940s as commercial television drew nearer. SAG and the AFM, for instance, negotiated agreements with movie producers that flatly prohibited the producers from licensing their films to television (i.e., the C2-D2 reuse patterns). Beginning in 1946, a series of negotiations, strikes and lawsuits involving the Screen Writers Guild (the WGA's predecessor), SAG, AFRA/AFTRA and AFM focused on three tracks: residuals for theatrical films reused on free TV (see historical details on p. 67), free TV to free TV reruns (p. 71), and commercials residuals (p. 149).

During the 1950s, the above the line unions achieved residuals for free TV reruns, and SAG, AFTRA and AFM obtained commercials residuals. SAG got smaller studios to agree to pay residuals for theatrical motion pictures played on free TV starting with the 1952 Monogram Pictures deal, but major studios remained elusive.

---

* See Dennis W. Mazzocco, *Radio's New Deal: The NRA and U.S. Broadcasting, 1933–1935*, 12(1) J. RADIO STUDIES 32-46 (2005).
† See *Code of Fair Competition for the Radio Broadcasting Industry* (11/27/33), available at https://archive.org/details/codeoffaircompet8464unit and *Amendment to Code of Fair Competition for the Radio Broadcasting Industry* (3/23/35), available at https://archive.org/details/amendmenttocodeo2489unit.
‡ See *Schechter Poultry Corp. v. United States*, 295 U.S. 495 (1935).
§ AFRA Code of Fair Practice for Transcriptions and Recordings for Radio Broadcasting Purposes (1941) (on file with author)..

** *Id.* at 2; see also Sec. V.5 (similar).
†† See *id.*, Sec. V.7.

A turning point came with 1960 strikes by both the WGA and SAG, in which the two unions won residuals for reuse of movies on TV. They also achieved establishment of employer-funded pension plans.

The quid pro quo was that residuals were granted only for so-called Post-'60's: movies made after a certain date in 1960. The unions renounced residual claims for older movies.

That fact rankles a few old-time SAG-AFTRA members even today and leads them to bitterly charge conflict of interest on the part of then-SAG president Ronald Reagan, who – along with his agent *and employer*, MCA/Universal head Lew Wasserman – played a key role in the settlement of the strike. Both had also played a significant part in residuals developments earlier in the decade as well.

The WGA settled its strike a few month early with MCA, cutting a deal which gives the WGA alone residuals on 1948-1960 Universal movies, in addition to Post-'60s from all studios.

In any case, by 1961, the DGA, IATSE and AFM had also achieved residuals for reuse of movies on TV, and the principle of residuals was broadly established.

The system has continued to grow in the more than half-century since then, as you can see by examining the History Grids included throughout this book. The Grids and other historical material appear as part of the sections on various reuse patterns and in a few other places:

| History Grid or Other Item | Cell | Pg. |
|---|---|---|
| Reuse on Fox | Row 3 | 40 |
| Reuse on The CW | Row 3 | 40 |
| Theatrical to free TV & foreign | C2-E2 | 67 |
| Theatrical to basic cable | H2 | 69 |
| Free TV to network primetime | C3 | 71 |
| Free TV to other than network PT | D3 | 77 |
| Free TV to foreign | E3 | 78 |
| Free TV to basic cable | H3 | 80 |
| Supplemental markets | F2-G3 | 83 |
| Pay TV and home video product | C4-H5 | 93 |
| Basic cable product | C6-H6 | 99 |
| Theatrical reuse of TV / HV product | B3-B6 | 102 |
| New media reuse of trad'l product | I2-K6 | 112 |
| New media product | B7-K10 | 112 |
| Separated rights and similar reuse | na | 143 |
| Interactive media (videogames) | na | 145 |

| History Grid or Other Item | Cell | Pg. |
|---|---|---|
| Commercials | na | 149 |
| Recent history chapter | na | 160 |
| Essay on strikes, tech & residuals | na | 162 |
| ENTERTAINMENT UNIONS AND GUILDS: AN INTERDISCIPLINARY BIBLIOGRAPHY (lists historical articles) | na | 192 |
| HOLLYWOOD ON STRIKE! (re NM) | I-K, 7-9 | 192 |

Below is a unified chronology of key events. The chart includes all above the line industry-wide motion picture, television and commercials strikes since the formation of the unions.

The year shown is when the applicable residual was first established, unless otherwise noted. However, the year given is usually when a strike or negotiating cycle began, and is not necessarily when a particular union signed a deal or a change became effective.

The indication that a particular union struck is not meant to attribute "credit" for a contract gain to that union. Most of the modifications below came from an interplay of multiple unions, companies and other bargaining entities.

| Date | Pg. | Cells | Unions | Reuse Pattern or Event |
|---|---|---|---|---|
| 1933 | 71 | na | Radio Equity | Radio |
| 1939 | 71 | na | AFRA | Radio |
| 1946-60 | 67 | C2-E2 | all | Theatrical to free TV (WGA, SAG strikes) |
| 1951-52 | 71 | C3 | all | Free TV to free TV |
| 1952 | 149 | na | AFM, SAG, AFTRA | Commercials (SAG strike) |
| 1953 | 143 | na | WGA | Series sequel pmts & separated rts. residuals |
| 1960 | 67 | C2-E2 | All | Theatrical to free TV |
| 1962 | 78 | E3 | [All] | Free TV to foreign |
| 1971 | 83 | | F2-G3 | Supplemental markets |
| 1974 | 71 | C3-D3 | SAG | Free TV to free TV (perpetuity) |
| 1977 | 71 | C3-D3 | WGA | Free TV to free TV (perpetuity) |
| 1978 | 149 | na | SAG, AFTRA | [tbd] (commercials strike) |
| 1980 | 93 | C4-H5 | all | Pay TV/HV (SAG/AFTRA strike) |
| 1981 | 93 | C4-H5 | DGA | Pay TV/HV [tbd] |
| 1984 | 93 | C4-H5 | [all] | Pay TV/HV [tbd] |
| 1985 | 93 | C4-H5 | WGA | Pay TV/HV [tbd] (strike) |
| 1988 | 99 | C6-H6 | all | Basic cable (WGA strike) |
| 1988 | 149 | na | SAG, AFTRA | Commercials cable |

| Date | Pg. | Cells | Unions | Reuse Pattern or Event |
|---|---|---|---|---|
| [tbd] | 39 | Row 3 | all | Fox (discount) |
| 2000 | 149 | na | SAG, AFTRA | [tbd] (commercials strike) |
| 2001 | 112 | I-K, 7-9 | all | New media made-for & reuse (fragmentary) |
| 2001 | 39 | Row 3 | all | Fox @ 100% |
| 2001 | 143 | na | WGA | Script publication fee |
| 2001 | 99 | C6-H6 | WGA | BC (Sanchez) increased |
| 2001 | 78 | E3 | [all] | Free TV to foreign (perpetuity) |
| [tbd] | 39 | Row 3 | all | UPN/WB (discount) |
| 2007-2009 | 112 | I-K, 7-9 | all | New media (full) (WGA strike & SAG stalemate) |
| 2010 | 71 | C3 | all | Network PT freeze |
| 2013-14 | 127 | Row 10 | all | High budget SVOD |

As you can see, battles over residuals have continued to be hard-fought and often trigger costly strikes. The essay on p. 162 explores this further.

The most recent of these disputes was the 2007-2008 WGA strike and the 2008-2009 SAG stalemate, both of which centered on new media. The resulting new media formulas significantly increased the size and complexity of the system.

For more history, see pp. 160 & 162; the History Grids; the old contracts (see list on p. 183; my book HOLLYWOOD ON STRIKE! (c0vers 2007-09) and the articles and other materials on residuals listed in my book ENTERTAINMENT LABOR: AN INTERDISCIPLINARY BIBLIOGRAPHY.

# 2. THE RESIDUALS CHART

The chart is a key tool for understanding residuals. This chapter takes a closer look.

## A. Constructing the Chart

Since residuals depend on the made-for medium and the reuse market – and since any combination of the two is possible – a good way to summarize the residual system is a chart, in which each row is a different made-for medium and each column is a different reuse market:

Since five or six different sets of union agreements have residuals, one might expect to need six charts (one chart each for DGA, WGA, SAG (or SAG-AFTRA), AFTRA, IATSE and AFM):

However, as we've discussed, there are significant similarities between the formulas used by the various unions. Also, the formulas in adjacent cells are sometimes similar or identical.

By combining some neighboring cells, and exploiting the inter-union patterns, it's possible to collapse six charts into one:

But when text is added, the result is daunting:

In addition, it's not easy to discern patterns in the formulas. The solution is to add color:

And voila – the chart was born. (Later I added another row, for high budget SVOD, a 2013-2014 development discussed later.)

## B. Interpreting the Chart

### Rows and Columns

The rows of the chart correspond to made-for media:

| Made for: | Description |
|---|---|
| Theatrical | This row applies to product made for initial theatrical release (i.e., theatrical motion pictures). |
| Free TV | Product (such as 1/2 hr., 1 hr., or TV movies) made for free TV (network primetime, non-primetime, or non-network). |
| Pay TV | Product made for pay TV (such as HBO, Showtime, etc.). |
| Home Video | Direct-to-video product (such as direct-to-DVD movies). |
| Basic Cable | Product made for basic cable (such as FX, AMC, etc.). |
| Deriv. NM | Derivative new media (NM based on traditional media). |
| Orig. NM | Original new media (i.e., made for new media such as Internet). |
| Exper. NM | Experimental new media (i.e., low-budget, non-union original NM). |

And the columns correspond to reuse markets:

| Column | Description |
|---|---|
| Theatrical | This column applies to theatrical exhibition of any type of product (incl. rarely, product made for TV, HV, or NM). |
| Free TV Network Primetime | This column applies to network primetime broadcast of any type of product. |
| Free TV Syndication or Non-Primetime | This column applies to broadcast of any type of product in syndication or during non-primetime. |
| Foreign | Foreign free TV & basic cable. Also, ad-supported foreign streaming of TV & HV. |
| Supp. Mkts. Pay TV | U.S. and foreign pay TV exhibition |
| Supp. Mkts. Home Video | U.S. and foreign release on home video |
| Domestic Basic Cable | Exhibition on U.S. basic cable channels. |
| New Media Consumer Pd (eRental/EST) | Release via paid rental or subscription new media. |
| New Media Ad Supported | Electronic sell through. / Exhibition on free to the consumer, ad supported new media. |

### Four Pages

There are four pages to the chart. Page 1 summarizes virtually all of the key residuals formulas for traditional scripted product; page 2 is a continuation of page 1 and summarizes the formulas for scripted new media product; and page 3 provides cross references to the union agreement contract sections that specify the formulas. (Finding the actual contracts – and especially the new media sideletters – can be difficult, so finding aids appear at the end of this book, beginning on p. 177.) Page 4 has notes and abbreviations.

### Cross References

Each cell can be referenced by its coordinates, as in a spreadsheet: columns (including the left-hand column of row labels) are lettered A through K and rows (including the top row of column labels) are numbered 1 through 9.

If the chart were a simple grid, the scheme would look like this: [tbd HB SVOD below and previous]

| Reused in:<br>Made for: | Theatrical<br>A1 | Free TV Network Primetime<br>B1 | Free TV Syndication or Non-Primetime<br>C1 | Foreign<br>E1 | Pay TV<br>F1 | Home Video<br>G1 | Basic Cable<br>H1 | eRental<br>I1 | EST<br>J1 | Ad Supported<br>K1 |
|---|---|---|---|---|---|---|---|---|---|---|
| Theatrical | A2 | B2 | C2 | D2 | E2 | F2 | G2 | H2 | I2 | J2 | K2 |
| Free TV | A3 | B3 | C3 | D3 | E3 | F3 | G3 | H3 | I3 | J3 | K3 |
| Pay TV | A4 | B4 | C4 | D4 | E4 | F4 | G4 | H4 | I4 | J4 | K4 |
| Home Video | A5 | B5 | C5 | D5 | E5 | F5 | G5 | H5 | I5 | J5 | K5 |
| Basic Cable | A6 | B6 | C6 | D6 | E6 | F6 | G6 | H6 | I6 | J6 | K6 |
| Deriv. NM | A7 | B7 | C7 | D7 | E7 | F7 | G7 | H7 | I7 | J7 | K7 |
| Orig. NM | A8 | B8 | C8 | D8 | E8 | F8 | G8 | H8 | I8 | J8 | K8 |
| Exper. NM | A9 | B9 | C9 | D9 | E9 | F9 | G9 | H9 | I9 | J9 | K9 |

However, because some cells are merged, the labels are actually as follows:

| Reused in:<br>Made for: | Theatrical<br>A1 | Free TV Network Primetime | Free TV Syndication or Non-Primetime | Foreign | Pay TV | Home Video | Basic Cable | eRental | EST | Ad Supported |
|---|---|---|---|---|---|---|---|---|---|---|
| Theatrical | | B2 | C2 to E2 | | F2 & F3 | G2 & G3 | H2 | | J2 | K2 |
| Free TV | | | C3 | D3 | E3 | | | H3 | I2 to I6 | | K3 to K6 |
| Pay TV | B3 to B6 | | C4 | to | E5 | F4 | G4 | H4 & H5 | | J3 to J6 | |
| Home Video | | | | | | F5-G5 | F5-G5 | | | | |
| Basic Cable | | | C6 | D6 | E6 | F6-G6 | | H6 | | | |
| Deriv. NM | B7-B8 | | C7 | to | E8 | F7-G8 | | H7-H8 | I7-J8 | | K7 |
| Orig. NM | | | | | | | | | | | K8 |
| Exper. NM | | | | | B9-K9 | | | | | | |
| HB SVOD | | B10 | C10 | to | E10 | F10-G10 | | H10 | I10-J10 | | K10 |

It's better in color, of course:

| Reused in:<br>Made for: | Theatrical<br>A1 | Free TV Network Primetime | Free TV Syndication or Non-Primetime | Foreign | Pay TV | Home Video | Basic Cable | eRental | EST | Ad Supported |
|---|---|---|---|---|---|---|---|---|---|---|
| Theatrical | | B2 | C2 to E2 | | F2 & F3 | G2 & G3 | H2 | | J2 | K2 |
| Free TV | | | C3 | D3 | E3 | | | H3 | I2 to I6 | | K3 to K6 |
| Pay TV | B3 to B6 | | C4 | to | E5 | F4 | G4 | H4 & H5 | | J3 to J6 | |
| Home Video | | | | | | F5-G5 | F5-G5 | | | | |
| Basic Cable | | | C6 | D6 | E6 | F6-G6 | | H6 | | | |
| Deriv. NM | B7-B8 | | C7 | to | E8 | F7-G8 | | H7-H8 | I7-J8 | | K7 |
| Orig. NM | | | | | | | | | | | K8 |
| Exper. NM | | | | | B9-K9 | | | | | | |
| HB SVOD | | B10 | C10 | to | E10 | F10-G10 | | H10 | I10-J10 | | K10 |

A reference to a single portion within a merged cell (such as to F2, which is part of F2-F3) means the discussion relates only to that portion of the merged cell. Also, references can encompass multiple columns, multiple rows or both, such as F4-G4, H4-H5 or C7-D8.

## Merged Cells

Merged cells, such as F6-G6 (two columns merged), B3-B6 or F7-G8 (two columns and two rows merged) are used where the same or similar formulas apply to several reuse patterns. Almost all of the cells in row 8 are merged with those in row 7; the sole exception is K8. All of the cells in row 9 are merged into a single cell.

## Divided Cells

Several cells are divided in unusual ways:

• A1 is not exactly divided but includes a boxed note in yellow that indicates the date and version number of the chart. You can visit jhandel.com/residuals to check for a more recent version.

• F1-G1 have a merged heading (Supplemental Markets) and separate subheadings (Pay TV and Home Video).

• Likewise, I1-J1 have a merged heading (New Media – Consumer Paid) and separate subheadings (eRental and EST).

• C2-E2 on the full-size copies of the chart is divided horizontally in order to accommodate several notes that apply to row 3 and column C. This division does not appear on the small versions of the chart that appear as navigational aids at the beginning of each section of Chapters 5-12.

• F5 and G5, which cover home video to pay TV and to home video, are merged into a single column, but then are divided horizontally. This is because of the complexity and interrelations of the formulas in the area of pay TV and home video to pay TV and home video. See Chapter 7.C.

• I10-J10 is divided horizontally to reflect the treatment of high budget SVOD on the original and affiliated subscription consumer pay platforms versus on other pay platforms.

## Notes that Appear on the Chart

When reading a cell, you'll want to look in several additional parts of the chart for notes that may apply. Sometimes a cell is self-contained, or has explicit cross-references. But in addition:

• Look first at cells that are one or two cells to the right or left.

• Also check the row and column headings (A2-A9 and B1-K1).

• C2-E2 has some notes for row 3 and column C.

• F6-G6 has a note for row 7.

• The book's discussions of each cell, found in Chapters 5-12, also include text from other cells that have relevant notes.

• The legend on the fourth page of the chart (p. 191) has notes that apply to all cells.

# 3. MEDIA, MARKETS, UNIONS AND MORE

As we've discussed, the residuals formula that applies in any given situation is determined by a set of factors:

- The medium a project was made for.
- The reuse market – i.e., the medium that the project is being reused in.
- The particular guild or union, since the formulas vary by union or guild.
- The date the project was written or produced, since the formulas have changed over time.
- Certain other variables.

This chapter starts with an overview, then takes a closer look at each of the above factors.

## A. Overview and Definitions

For purposes of most of this book, we assume the product is scripted live action and is not low-budget; and we assume that television content is *not* daytime soap operas (which are released with a new episode every day).

The reason for these assumptions is two-fold: our focus is on the major types of content; and the residuals formulas, if any, for other content are quite different. Such other types of product are discussed in Chapter 15.

### Made-For Media

As categorized by the residuals system, there are nine distinct types of media a project can be made for. The chart has a row for each one. These represent the intended initial use of the product.

The nine types of media are:

1. **Theatrical:** A theatrical motion picture.

2. **Free TV:** A television program intended for initial release on broadcast television.

3. **Pay TV:** A television program intended for initial release on a pay TV channel or via pay-per-view.

4. **Home Video:** Product intended for initial release on a physical home video device, such as videocassette, DVD or Blu-ray.

5. **Basic Cable:** A television program intended for initial release on a basic cable channel.

6. **Derivative New Media:** A production which is intended for initial release on the Internet or mobile devices (such as cell phones) and which is based on a traditional TV series (or, in some cases, a theatrical motion picture).

7. **Original New Media:** A production which is intended for initial release on the Internet or mobile devices and which is neither a derivative new media program nor an experimental new media program.

8. **Experimental New Media:** A production which is intended for initial release on the Internet or mobile devices, and which is not derivative new media, and (a) whose budget falls below certain thresholds and (b) whose use of union personnel falls below certain thresholds.

9. **High Budget Subscription Video On Demand (SVOD) Programs:** A derivative new media or original new media program above a certain budget level and minimum length that is intended for initial release on a subscription consumer pay new media platform such as Netflix or Amazon Prime.

### Reuse Markets

The residuals system recognizes over a dozen distinct reuse markets. This book covers the eleven most important ones. The chart has a column for each of the eleven except one (discussed below). The types of reuse markets are similar to the type of media that a project can be made for, but are not identical.

The eleven important reuse markets are:

1. **Theatrical:** Exhibition in movie theaters.

2. **Free TV – Network Primetime:** Exhibition on a broadcast network during primetime.

3. **Free TV – Other than Network Primetime:** Exhibition on broadcast television other than network primetime – in other words, either on non-network TV or on network TV during a daypart (i.e., time of day) other than primetime.

4. **Foreign:** Exhibition in another country on broadcast television or basic cable. Also included is foreign ad-supported availability of TV or home video product. (See below for definition and discussion of ad-supported services.)

5/6. **Supplemental Markets:** For historical reasons, pay TV and home video are referred to as "supplemental markets." This is because they were seen as supplementing the existing theatrical and free TV markets for theatrical motion pictures (movies).

    5. **Pay TV:** Exhibition on a U.S. or foreign pay TV channel or via U.S. or foreign pay-per-view.

    6. **Home Video:** Domestic or foreign release on a physical home video medium, such as DVD or Blu-ray (or videocassettes).

7. **Basic Cable:** Exhibition on a domestic basic cable channel.

8. **Consumer Paid New Media – eRental:** Release on the Internet or mobile platforms, where the consumer pays on either a subscription basis or a per-program basis and receives the right to view the program for a fixed and limited period of time or a fixed number of viewings.

9. **Subscription Consumer Pay New Media Platform:** Release on an Internet-based platform for which the consumer pays a subscription fee, such as Netflix or Amazon Prime.

➔ Note that there is no column in the chart for reuse market #9. That's because subscription consumer pay new media platforms are treated as eRental (reuse market #8, i.e., col I) for most purposes. For instance, when a theatrical movie is reused on Netflix, we look at cell I2. Only with high budget SVOD (I10) does the concept of subscription consumer pay new media platforms come into play.

10. **Consumer Paid New Media – Electronic Sell Through (EST):** Release on the Internet or mobile platforms, where the consumer pays for right to view the program without limitations as to time or number of viewings.

11. **Ad-Supported Services:** Release on the Internet or mobile platforms or other devices, where the consumer does not pay and, instead, advertising accompanies the program, or ad-supported VOD services on cable, satellite or equivalent telephone company (telco) systems. One exception: foreign ad-supported availability of TV or home video product is treated as foreign reuse, not as ad-supported reuse.

### Categorization

As you can see from the above, the categorizations of made-for media and reuse markets are – confusingly – not entirely congruent. There are several key differences:

● **Free TV** is one of the made-for media. However, there is no single free TV reuse market. Instead, there is a **network primetime** reuse market and an **other than network primetime** reuse market. Jointly, these can be called free TV, but they're separate markets *with different formulas*.

● **Foreign TV** is a reuse market but not a made-for medium. See p. 157 for discussion of product made for initial foreign exhibition.

● **Pay TV and home video** are called **supplemental markets** when they're reuse markets, but this term is usually not used with reference to product made for pay TV or home video.

Thus, we might refer to "movies, TV programs or Internet productions reused in supplemental markets," but we would generally not speak of "product made for supplemental markets" or "pay TV or home video product reused in supplemental markets."

That's because pay TV is the *primary* market for a pay TV show; in this instance, it doesn't "supplement" anything. Ditto for home video: when a direct to video movie is released on video, that's its primary market.

● **New media** – the entertainment union/guild term for the Internet and cell phones – is subdivided differently when examined as a made-for medium or as a reuse market.

♦ As a made-for medium, new media is categorized into derivative new media productions (new media shows based on existing traditional TV shows, for instance), original new media productions and experimental new media productions (low-ish budget non-derivative productions that use few or no union personnel).

♦ As a reuse market, new media is divided into consumer paid platforms and ad-supported platforms. The consumer-paid category is subdivided into eRental and electronic sell through (EST, meaning purchase as opposed to rental).

● Internet-based platforms (over the top, or OTT platforms) are called high budget SVOD as a made-for medium and either eRental or subscription consumer pay new media as a reuse market.

The table below compares the categorization of made-for media and reuse markets.

| Concept | As a Made-For Medium | As a Reuse Market | |
|---|---|---|---|
| Theatrical | Theatrical (row 2) | Theatrical (col B) | |
| Domestic Broadcast TV | Free TV (row 3) | Network Primetime (col C) | As reuse markets, collectively can be called Free TV |
| | | Other Than Network Primetime (i.e., network non-PT or syndication) (col D) | |
| Foreign Free TV | NA | Foreign TV (col E) | |
| Pay TV | Pay TV (row 4) | Pay TV (col F) | As reuse markets, collectively called Supplemental Markets |
| Physical Home Video | Home Video (row 5) | Home Video (col G) | |
| Basic Cable | Basic Cable (row 6) | Basic Cable (col H) | |
| New Media (as made-for medium) other than streaming video | Derivative New Media (row 7) | | |
| | Original New Media (row 8) | | |
| | Experimental NM (row 9) | | |
| New Media (other than streaming video) as reuse market | | Consumer Paid – eRental (col I) | |
| | | Consumer Paid – EST (col J) | |
| | | Ad-Supported (col K) | |
| OTT streaming video | High Budget SVOD (row 10) | Subscription Consumer Pay NM Platform (I10l) | |

## The Term "Motion Picture"

The union and guild agreements are opaque, and among the sources of confusion is the term "motion picture." Surprisingly, the word doesn't mean what it seems.

➔ In the agreements, "motion picture" means either (a) a theatrical motion picture or (b) **a television motion picture**. Thus, a "motion picture" is not necessarily what people would normally think.

And it gets worse.

➔ A "television motion picture" means either (a) **an episode of a TV series (or miniseries)** or (b) a TV movie. So, here too, a "television motion picture" is not necessarily what you'd expect.

A "theatrical motion picture," however, *is* what most people would expect, i.e., a movie that is intended to be shown first in movie theaters. The terminology just sounds redundant.

To add to the confusion, new media productions (including programs made for streaming services like Netflix) are not a subcategory of motion pictures at all, or at least not clearly so.

Direct to home video productions are also ambiguous. The union and guild agreements treat them very similarly to pay TV products, which are television motion pictures. In the chart, note that the cells in Row 4 (made for pay TV) are all merged (or virtually so) with those in Row 5 (made for home video). However, the contract language does not explicitly say that direct to video products are a species of motion picture.

### The Word "Dramatic"

Another term that exemplifies this Humpty Dumpty-like practice of making words mean whatever one wants is "dramatic." The guild agreements, it turns out, are heavy on drama, light on comedy.

Now that might be exactly what you expected, but you still may be perplexed by the constant references to "dramatic programs" in the contracts. Where are the rules for comedies . . . the residuals, minimums, working conditions and more?

Well, you're looking right at them, bucko.

➜ That's because "dramatic programs" include comedies. The phrase doesn't mean drama at all: it essentially means "scripted programs."*

And yes, there are scripts of a sort for reality TV, and even game shows and late night shows,† but that's not what we're talking about. "Dramatic programs" are conventional scripted programs and TV movies.

### The Term "Television Film"

As if "television motion picture" isn't bad enough, we also need to decipher "television film," a phrase that appears in the title of older editions of one of the AFM agreements and some older agreements from other unions.

By now, you've guessed that this doesn't refer to TV movies. But it doesn't really refer to physical film either – not anymore, that is.

It did once: a "television film" agreement covered television programs shot on film, in contrast to agreements with "tape" in their name, which related to television programs shot on videotape.

Nowadays, however, most television programs are shot on digital media – the camera output is recorded directly to a hard drive, or a memory card, or perhaps digital tape, although even that is pretty long in the tooth. Very little is shot on film, and nothing on old-style analog videotape.

So the rule of thumb is this: "television film" in the title indicates free TV primetime dramatic programs and "tape" means daytime shows, especially serials (soap operas) and unscripted fare such as talk shows, game shows and perhaps sports and/or reality shows.

Those "tape" category programs historically were indeed shot on videotape – or played live – while some of the "film" category were historically shot on film and some on videotape. So there's a rough and ready sense to the distinction. Sort of.

### The Term "New Media"

You might be tempted to point out that "new media" won't be new forever. In fact, if you're 25 or under, it probably is just "media" to you. And one day most or all made-for media or reuse markets may fall into the new media category.

So what will new media be called in 10 years? Probably the same thing. After all, "modern art" is more than a half-century old. We'll just have to live with terminology that will soon be as obsolete as the technology it runs on today.

As noted above (and discussed further below), new media comes in several types: original new media, derivative new media, experimental new media, and high budget subscription video on demand (SVOD) programs. The last of these (such as Netflix) look like TV, but they're considered new media.

### The Term "Interactive Media"

Another term to watch out for is "interactive media." This means videogames, and should not be confused with "new media," which means the Internet and mobile phones.‡

---

* Also noteworthy: the WGA term "comedy-variety program" does not mean situation comedies, it means shows like *Saturday Night Live* and *The Tonight Show*. See MBA App. A Art. 1.C.22.
† The host of a game show doesn't just make up his patter on the spot. It's actually scripted. So are a late night host's jokes.

---

‡ Except in the case of the SAG-AFTRA Commercials Agreement, where the Internet is called "Internet" and "new media" means commercials made solely for cell phones.

Of course, there are games that run on new media. So, yes, those are interactive media products made for new media – and so much for eliminating confusion.

### The Terminology in this Book

To avoid confusion, this book tries to avoid most of the above terminology. Instead, you'll see plain-language terms like "movie," "TV series," and "TV program" (meaning a TV episode or a TV movie).

We use "product" or "project" to signify a movie, TV episode or TV movie (whether free TV, pay TV or basic cable), miniseries, straight to video production or new media production.

"Television" or "TV" without an adjective means product made for free TV, pay TV or basic cable – any kind of TV other than daytime serials (soap operas) and perhaps excluding non-serialized daytime programs too. In this book, "television" or "TV" does not include home video; instead, we mention home video explicitly when necessary. (In contrast, in the union agreements, "television" sometimes implicitly includes home video.) And "television" or "TV" doesn't include high budget SVOD product.

"Traditional product" means non-interactive scripted live action product made for theatrical, TV or home video, as opposed to new media.

## B. Made-For Media

The next nine subsections describe the different types of made-for media in more detail. They're followed by a subsection that points out some ambiguities in the concept of made-for media.

It's helpful to refer to the chart as you read these subsections.

### Theatrical

#### Chart Reference

Row 2.

#### Definition

A theatrical motion picture – i.e., a movie that is intended to be shown in a movie theater before it is any released in other media such as pay TV, DVD/Blu-ray, etc.*

#### Business Background

Studios these days tend to make large-scale "tentpole" movies – movies intended to be blockbusters – far more often than smaller, adult-oriented films. Larger films generally result in more DVD/Blu-ray sales and larger license fees for television exhibition. That in turn can translate to higher residuals for the actors who appear in such films.

#### Types of Residuals

Theatrical exhibition of theatrical motion pictures never generates residuals. This is true even if the movie is rereleased theatrically, or plays an extended run (*The Rocky Horror Picture Show* has been playing for decades, for instance) or is released theatrically in foreign territories.

Reuse of theatrical motion pictures in other media does generate residuals. It's always a percentage residual.

#### Who Participates

All five applicable unions (AFM, DGA, IATSE, SAG-AFTRA, WGA) participate in residuals when theatrical movies are reused. SAG-AFTRA's participation is via the SAG agreement, since the AFTRA doesn't cover theatrical product.

#### Pattern Analysis

Pattern is maintained with little or no deviation. *One exception is the WGA treatment of Universal Studios movies made between 1948-1960, as noted below.*†

---

* See DGA BA Paras. 1-201, 1-202; WGA MBA Art. 1.A.2; SAG CBA Secs. 1.A, 5.2.D(2); IATSE BA Sec. XVII; AFM Basic Theatrical Motion Picture Agreement (hereinafter "AFM Theatrical Agt.") Sec. 1. Some of these sections define "motion picture" (see p. 24) but fail to define "theatrical motion picture."

† *Italics* are used in the book and chart to indicate out of pattern or no pattern situations.

## Date Restrictions

To generate residuals, a movie must be a so-called Post-'60 picture; otherwise, there are no residuals. This means that the movie has to have commenced principal photography on or after certain 1960 date cutoffs, which vary by union. A movie that satisfies one union's date cutoff but not another's will generate residuals for members of the first union but not the second.

The date cutoffs are: DGA 5/1/60; WGA 6/13/60; SAG 2/1/60; IATSE, AFM 1/31/60. ➔ *In a deviation from pattern, post-1948 Universal movies also generate WGA residuals even if they are pre-1960; that is, they're treated as Post-'60s.* [*]

➔ All of these date cutoffs refer to commencement of principal photography, even the WGA's. In contrast, other date cutoffs found in the WGA MBA usually refer to the date that a screenplay or teleplay was written.

As discussed on p. 15, the 1960 dates result from the terms of settlement of the 1960 WGA and SAG strikes. During that same strike, the WGA reached an earlier settlement with Universal's parent company, MCA, which resulted in the 1948 date.

Later date cutoffs apply to some new media exploitation.

## Chapter References

● Chapter 5: Reuse of theatrical product in most traditional media (B2-E2, H2).

● Chapter 7: Reuse of theatrical product in supplemental markets (F2- G2).

● Chapter 11: Reuse of theatrical product in new media (I2- K2).

## Free TV

### Chart Reference

Row 3.

### Definition

A television program intended for initial release on over the air (OTA) broadcast television.[†] Free TV means TV that is broadcast for free over the air (OTA), even if most people actually pay to receive it on a cable or satellite system (or on a telephone system like Verizon FIOS or ATT U-verse). Free TV stations usually have channel numbers between 2 and 83, inclusive.[‡] Many are affiliates of the major broadcast networks: ABC, CBS, The CW, FOX or NBC.

Note that this is a single category that encompasses network primetime product, network non-primetime, and non-network. Such product is all categorized as free TV. Contrast this with the definitions of reuse markets below, in which such distinctions are made.

The program can be a series episode, a miniseries episode or a TV movie.

For residuals purposes, daytime serials – five day per week soap operas – are treated differently than other television product. For that reason, such product is discussed only in Section 15.A.

### Business Background

A couple of business trends are worth noting, because they have decreased the dollar amount of residuals that participants have been earning in recent years. One trend, which began around a decade ago or more, is that off-network syndication – which is subject to a fixed residual at a declining percentage (D3) – has increasingly been replaced with basic cable syndication, where a (probably smaller) percentage residual (H3) applies.

More recently, network primetime reruns have declined or disappeared for many shows, with reuse shifting to ad-supported platforms such as Hulu. This change has replaced a large fixed residual at 100% (C3) with a much smaller hybrid formula (K3). See p. 152 for a discussion.

---

[*] I don't know the exact cutoff date in 1948.

[†] See DGA BA Para. 1-202; WGA MBA Art. 1.A.1; SAG TV Agt. Sec. 1; IATSE BA Sec. XVIII(a); AFM Basic Television Motion Picture Agreement (hereinafter "AFM Television Agt.") Sec. 1. The AFTRA Netcode does not define free television.

[‡] See http://en.wikipedia.org/wiki/North_American_television_frequencies.

## Types of Residuals

Free TV residuals vary widely according to reuse market: fixed residuals at 100% for network primetime broadcasts (C3), fixed residuals at run by run declining percentages for network non-primetime or non-network broadcasts (so-called "other than primetime" reuse) (D3), hybrid residuals for foreign reuse (E3), a very different set of hybrid residuals for ad-supported reuse (K3) and percentage residuals for most other reuse (F3-J3). In the almost nonexistent instance that free TV product is released theatrically, the residuals are unusual (B3).

## Supersized Episodes

[tbd]

## Who Participates

All above the line unions participate.

IATSE and AFM receive residuals only for reuse in supplemental markets (F3-G3) and consumer-paid new media (I3-J3), except that AFM receives AGICOA residuals on foreign reuse (E3). See p. 41 for explanation of AGICOA.

## Pattern Analysis

The fixed residual formulas (the free TV to free TV formulas (C3-D3) and a portion of the hybrid foreign TV formulas (E3)) differ amongst the unions. However, because they are similar or analogous to each other, they are considered to be in pattern.

Above the line pattern is generally maintained in percentage residuals (F3-J3).

## Date Restrictions

"Exhausted" free TV product does not generate residuals in any reuse markets. Exhausted product means free TV product that is no longer subject to residuals when played on free TV.

Current free TV product never gets exhausted, because residuals are payable in perpetuity. However, this wasn't always the case. Product prior to July 1, 1971 only generated residuals for a limited number of runs – the number grew from contract to contract until the system that prevails today was instituted, in which there is no limit on the number of residual-bearing runs. If the product has already passed the applicable threshold, it's said to be exhausted. Most pre-7/1/71 free TV product is probably exhausted today.

On consumer paid platforms (I3-J3), various hard dates generally apply (presumably in addition to, not instead of, the exhaustion test), regardless of exhaustion. Product that is older than the applicable date cutoff (which varies by union) does not generate residuals, even if it is not exhausted.

## Chapter References

● **Chapter 6:** Reuse of free TV product in most traditional media (C3-E3, H3).

● **Chapter 7:** Reuse of free TV product in supplemental markets (F3- G3).

● **Chapter 10:** Theatrical reuse of free TV product (B3).

● **Chapter 11:** Reuse of free TV product in new media (I3- K3).

# Pay TV

## Chart Reference

Row 4.

## Definition

A television program intended for initial release on a pay TV channel or via pay-per-view.[*] The program can be a series episode, a miniseries episode or a TV movie. Pay TV means premium networks such as HBO (and its companion network, Cinemax), Showtime (and its companion network, The Movie Channel), Starz and Epix that can be purchased individually[†] as a supplement to more or less any tier of cable, satellite or telco (FIOS / U-verse) service.

---

[*] See DGA BA Paras. 20-101, 20-103; WGA MBA Art. 1.A.4, App. B Sec B.2; SAG TV Agt. Secs. 1, 78(a)(3); AFTRA Netcode Ex. E Sec. 1.C. The IATSE and AFM agreements do not define made for pay television.

[†] The networks can't literally be purchased individually; for instance, HBO is actually a package of multiple networks, including HBO, HBO2, HBO Family, etc. But conceptually, they are regarded as a single offering, "HBO," which one can choose to purchase as an add-on to whatever tier of cable, satellite or telco service one has subscribed to.

### Business Background

At first, a made for pay TV program was usually a movie. That is, a network such as HBO would show theatrical movies and made-for-HBO movies, but wouldn't show TV series.*

However, starting with the success of HBO's *Sopranos*, which premiered in 1999, the made for pay TV business shifted to be primarily television series.

### Types of Residuals

Pay TV residuals vary widely according to reuse market, but generally parallel free TV residuals (see preceding subsection). An exception: Residuals for pay TV product rerun on pay TV or released on home video (G4-H4) are very complex, and differ widely from union to union.

### Who Participates

DGA, WGA, SAG-AFTRA, L-SAG and L-AFTRA participate in residuals for made for pay TV product. IATSE does not, except when such product is used on consumer paid platforms (I4-J4). AFM does not, except when such product is reused on free TV or foreign (C4-E4), or consumer paid platforms (I4-J4).

### Pattern Analysis

There is no pattern when pay TV (or home video) product is reused in pay TV or home video (F4-G5). Pattern is generally maintained in other reuse patterns, with some variations for DGA when pay TV (or home video) product is reused on free TV or foreign (C4-E5) and with differences between the unions in ad-supported reuse (K4-K5).

### Date Restrictions

[tbd]

### Chapter References

- Chapter 8: Reuse of pay TV product in most traditional media (C4-H4).

- Chapter 10: Theatrical reuse of pay TV product (B4).

- Chapter 11: Reuse of pay TV product in new media (I4-K4).

## Home Video

### Chart Reference

Row 5.

### Definition

Product intended for initial release on a physical home video medium, such as DVD or Blu-ray or, in an earlier era, videocassettes.† Typically, such product would be a direct-to-video movie.

Such physical media, or devices, are sometimes referred to in entertainment contracts as "videograms." If product were to be released on a memory chip (such as a USB stick), this would probably also be deemed to be home video, though the union definitions may not be clear on this point.

### Business Background

Product made for home video – often referred to as "direct to video" or "direct to DVD" – is usually very low budget movies with washed up stars and dull plots. These don't usually sell very well. Sometimes, though, direct to video movies are sequels to successful theatrical movies (often, movies for children), in which case the washed up stars and dull plots may nonetheless sell very well.

### Types of Residuals

Home video residuals vary widely according to reuse market, but generally parallel pay TV residuals (see preceding subsection). Residuals for home video product released on pay TV or on home video (G5-H5) are mostly similar or identical to residuals for pay TV product rerun on pay TV or released on home video.

### Who Participates

Same as with pay TV product (see preceding subsection).

---

* Indeed, HBO's corporate name is "Home Box Office, Inc."

† See DGA BA Paras. 20-101, 20-102; WGA MBA Art. 1.A.4, App. B Sec B.1; SAG TV Agt. Secs. 1, 78(a)(2); AFTRA Netcode Ex. E Sec. 1.B. The IATSE and AFM agreements do not define made for home video.

## Pattern Analysis

Same as with pay TV product (see preceding subsection).

## Date Restrictions

[tbd]

## Chapter References

- **Chapter 8:** Reuse of home video product in most traditional media (C5-H5).

- **Chapter 10:** Theatrical reuse of home video product (B5).

- **Chapter 11:** Reuse of home video product in new media (I5- K5).

# Basic Cable

## Chart Reference

Row 6.

## Definition

A television program intended for initial release on a basic cable channel.* The program can be a series episode, a miniseries episode or a TV movie. Basic cable means cable channels/networks† that are neither free TV nor pay TV. Examples are FX, AMC, USA, Bravo, TBS and many others, including channels such as ESPN and CNN that may have little or no scripted fare.

## Business Background

Original production for basic cable has grown dramatically since the success of FX's *The Shield* (premiered 2002).

However, the medium nonetheless remains more wild and wooly than free TV for network primetime. Production budgets are lower, audiences, though growing, are almost always smaller (and this was uniformly true when the basic cable residuals formulas were initially adopted), and ad rates (the fees that channels charge advertisers) are lower than in broadcast (or, at least, are certainly lower than network primetime rates).

As a result, studio/production company revenues, although probably growing, are usually lower than for broadcast television. Also, basic cable episodes are usually rerun many more times than broadcast television episodes are. These factors led the producers to seek, and guilds and unions to agree to, lower residuals in most cases (as well as other concessions).

## Types of Residuals

Basic cable residuals vary widely according to reuse market, but somewhat parallel free TV residuals (see p. 28). However, this is not necessarily the case when basic cable product is rerun on free TV (C6-D6).

Also, when basic cable product is rerun on basic cable (H6), there are a choice of formulas. None of these parallel the free TV to basic cable formula (H3), but one of the formulas is similar to free TV product playing in syndication (D3).

## Who Participates

- **DGA, SAG-AFTRA, L-SAG and L-AFTRA** receive basic cable residuals.

- **IATSE and AFM** don't. [check AFM basic cable to supplemental markets]

## Pattern Analysis

The situation is complicated.

There is a pattern in use of a basic cable program on basic cable (H6), but with significant deviations. Several of these – the DGA, SAG-AFTRA and L-SAG formulas, one of the two alternate WGA formulas, and two of L-AFTRA's – are fixed residuals formulas that decline run by run. The formulas are identical to each other and work the same way as when free TV product is reused on other than network primetime (D3), although the percentages are much lower: they start at 17% and decline run by run to a floor of just 1.5%.

This is referred to as the "Sanchez formula," referring to the show (*Sanchez of Bel Air,* premiered 1986) with which the formula was first used.

---

* See DGA BA Para. 1-203; WGA MBA Art. 1.A.3; AFM Basic Cable Television Agreement (hereinafter "AFM Basic Cable Agt.") Sec. 1.A. The SAG, AFTRA and IATSE agreements do not define basic cable.

† "Cable channel" and "cable network" are interchangeable.

One deviation from pattern is that the WGA also offers an alternate, referred to as the "Hitchcock formula" (from *Alfred Hitchcock Presents,* the remake that premiered in 1985).

In addition, L-AFTRA offered two completely different formulas as an alternative, and also negotiated project by project modifications.

There is very little pattern in basic cable to free TV (C6-D6).

Pattern is generally maintained in other reuse patterns (B6, E6, F6-G6, I6-J6 and K6). Notably, AFM basic cable product reused on ad-supported platforms (K6) participates in residuals even though other AFM TV and home video product reused on ad-supported platforms does not.

As discussed in Section 3D, the different guilds and unions take varying contractual approaches to basic cable:

- **DGA, WGA and SAG-AFTRA** include basic cable in their main collective bargaining agreements. There are residuals only for high-budget basic cable product. That's a relative term, and each of the two guilds uses a different threshold.

- **L-SAG** used a standalone agreement, which it negotiates directly with the eight member companies of the AMPTP rather than the AMPTP itself, which is a somewhat technical distinction. [check high budget vs. low.]

- **L-AFTRA** offered four template agreements, two of which mirror the L-SAG basic cable agreement, and two of which use a residuals approach that is similar to some of those in the Netcode front of book.* The latter can result in lower residuals or even no residuals. L-AFTRA also negotiated accommodations to these agreements which could further reduce residuals.

---

* "Front of book" refers to the portion of the AFTRA Netcode (television agreement) that covers scripted daytime programming (such as soap operas and original syndication) and other scripted programming with the exception of network primetime, CW primetime or basic cable. (Front of book also covers non-scripted programming, but such programming is outside the scope of this book.) In contrast, "Exhibit A" refers to the portion of the Netcode that covers network primetime programming. Finally, "Exhibit E," although less often referred to, covers programming made for pay TV and home video.

Not surprisingly, the latter two L-AFTRA templates were controversial. The union argued that such concessions were needed to keep basic cable production in the U.S. Vocal and *sotto voce* critics within SAG disagreed and contended that AFTRA simply made cut-rate deals in order to increase its market share of basic cable at SAG's expense.

The disagreements were bitter and public from about 2006 through 2008, a period when SAG's Hollywood branch and AFTRA were at each others' throats. Dueling magazine articles in fall 2007 laid out each union's case against the other on basic cable, pension and health plans and other matters. The political winds shifted dramatically and ultimately the two unions merged.

## Date Restrictions

[tbd]

## Chapter References

- **Chapter 9:** Reuse of basic cable product in most traditional media (C6-H6).

- **Chapter 10:** Theatrical reuse of basic cable product (B6).

- **Chapter 11:** Reuse of basic cable product in new media (I6- K6).

## Derivative New Media

### Chart Reference

Row 7.

### Definition

A production which is intended for initial release on the Internet or mobile devices (such as cell phones) and which is based on a traditional TV program (or, in some cases, a theatrical motion picture).† Typically, this would be a webisode (web episode) of an Internet series (or a mobisode of a mobile phone-based series) that functions as a spinoff of an existing TV series.

---

† See DGA BA Made for NM SL § A; WGA MBA Made for NM SL § 2; SAG Made for NM SL § B; AFTRA Netcode Ex. A Made for NM SL § B; AFTRA Netcode Front of Book Made for NM SL § B; IATSE BA Made for NM SL § C; AFM Theatrical/TV Made for NM SL § C. The AFM sideletter on derivative new media based on basic cable does not define "derivative new media." For nomenclature and location of the new media sideletters, see p. 181.

Such spinoffs are sometimes released between seasons of the underlying TV series and sometimes are released during the season.

Most of the contracts refer to the traditional production as the "Original Production,"* but that's confusingly similar to "Original New Media Production," which is what new media productions are called if they're neither derivative nor experimental. For that reason, this book uses the terminology "underlying product" or "underlying program" to refer to the product on which the new media production based.

The exact definition of derivative new media varies slightly between the various guilds and unions. There are three sets of differences in the definitional language.

## Underlying Program Types

One set of differences relate to the possible underlying program types.

For instance, a new media production based on a basic cable series is considered to be an example of derivative media by most guilds/unions, but not by SAG-AFTRA. The latter union would consider such a production to be an example of "original new media," a category which is discussed in the next subsection of this book.

In contrast, a new media production based on a free TV series is considered to be an example of derivative media by all of the guilds and unions.

Here are the qualifying underlying program types in the various definitions of derivative new media:

### Derivative New Media Definition Qualifying Underlying Program Types

| Basis | DGA | WGA | †SAG-AFTRA | Legacy-AFTRA | IATSE | AFM |
|---|---|---|---|---|---|---|
| Theatrical | | | X | | | |
| Free TV | X | X | X | X | X | X |
| Pay TV | X | X | X | X | X | |
| Hm Vid | | | X | X | | |
| Basic Cbl | X | X | | | X | X |

## Covered Status of Underlying Program

Another set of differences between the unions relates to whether the underlying product has to have been produced under the union's jurisdiction or not.

For instance, suppose that *Wind, Moon and Stars* is a non-WGA program, but that the producer now wants to use a WGA writer to create a new media series based on the show. Thus, the new media series will have to be a covered show. Will it be classified as derivative new media or original new media?‡

Analogous examples could be posited for the other unions. Here are the rules, based on the definitional wording:

- **DGA:** The definition of "derivative new media" makes no reference to the covered status of the underlying product. Therefore, it would seem that the underlying product need not have been covered product – and, perhaps, that the underlying product need not even have been eligible for coverage under a DGA agreement.

---

* The AFM made for new media sideletter to the Theatrical and Television Agreements uses the term "source production."

† Also Legacy-SAG.
‡ This example assumes that the new media show has a relatively high budget, so that is not classifiable as experimental new media. See p. 36.

- **WGA:** The underlying program need not be WGA-covered, as long as it is a type of program covered by the MBA.* Thus, in the example, the new media series based on *Wind, Moon and Stars* is indeed derivative new media.

- **SAG-AFTRA and L-SAG:** The underlying program has to have been covered under the SAG CBA or TV Agreement.

- **L-AFTRA Ex. A and Ex. E:** The underlying program has to have been produced under Netcode Exhibit A, under the WB/UPN Supplement or under Section 2.A.(1) of Netcode Exhibit E.

- **AFTRA Front of Book:** The definition of "derivative new media" makes no reference to the covered status of the underlying product. Therefore, it would seem that the underlying product need not have been covered product – and, perhaps, that the underlying product need not even have been eligible for coverage under an AFTRA agreement.

- **IATSE:** The underlying program has to have been covered under the IATSE Basic Agreement. Also, in particular, an underlying program does not qualify is if was covered under the IATSE Videotape Agreement, or covered by the IATSE Digital Agreement as to which the rates and conditions of the Videotape Agreement apply.

- **AFM derivative new media based on free TV:** The underlying program has to have been covered under the AFM Television Agreement. The underlying program can be live action or animated, but not a documentary.

- **AFM derivative new media based on basic cable:** The sideletter on basic cable new media discusses derivative new media based on underlying basic cable programs, but does not define "derivative new media." Thus, there may be some uncertainty as to whether the underlying product must have been covered.

### Nature of the Derivative New Media Production

A final set of differences in the definitions appears to refer to the nature of the new media production itself. Here are the various definitional restrictions:

- **DGA:** No restriction.

- **WGA:** The derivative new media production must be "included among the types of motion pictures traditionally covered by the MBA." Thus, for example, if the underlying program is a sitcom, but the new media production is a reality competition show, then the new media production would probably not be derivative new media,† because reality competition shows are not covered by the MBA.‡

- **SAG-AFTRA or L-SAG:** No restriction.

- **L-AFTRA Ex. A and Ex. E:** The derivative new media production must be "the same type of program as the program on which it is based." Thus, for instance, a web series based on a theatrical movie would probably not be derivative new media.§

- **AFTRA Front of Book:** No restriction.

- **IATSE:** The derivative new media production must be "otherwise included among the types of motion pictures traditionally covered by the Basic Agreement."

- **AFM derivative new media based on free TV:** The derivative new media production must be a "dramatic production," which for purposes of the sideletter means "live action or animated productions of a dramatic nature, including situation comedies, but excluding documentaries."

- **AFM derivative new media based on basic cable:** As noted above, the sideletter on basic cable new media does not define "derivative new media." Thus, there may be some uncertainty as to whether any restrictions should be inferred as to the nature of the new media production.

---

* See footnote on p. 7 of http://www.wga.org/uploadedfiles/contracts/newmedia12.pdf.

† It would therefore be original new media or experimental new media, depending on budget level and personnel employed. See p. 36.

‡ In contrast, game shows are covered by the MBA, so a game show based on a sitcom would be covered. Thus, the example above is a narrow one.

§ It would therefore be original new media or experimental new media.

### A Note Regarding AFTRA

You'll notice that each of the bulleted lists above have two bullet points for AFTRA. That's because AFTRA has two sets of new media sideletters, one set corresponding to the Netcode front of book and the other to Netcode Exhibit A. Each set consists of two sideletters – one for made for new media product and the other for reuse of traditional product on new media platforms. Thus, there are a total of four AFTRA new media sideletters.

In addition to the differences highlighted above, there are various other differences between derivative new media based on the Netcode front of book as opposed to based on Exhibit A. However, those differences are beyond the primary scope of this book, since Netcode front of book (daytime soaps, game shows, and more) is outside the scope of the book.*

### A Note Regarding AFM

There are also two bullet points (in each list) for AFM. This is because AFM has what one might call one and a half sets of new media sideletters, i.e., a total of three sideletters. However, to make matters even more confusing, these sideletters are duplicated in multiple places.

Specifically, (a) the Theatrical Agreement has a Made for New Media Sideletter and a New Media Reuse Sideletter; (b) the Television Agreement has a Made for New Media Sideletter and a New Media Reuse Sideletter which appear to be identical to those included with the Theatrical Agreement;† and (c) the basic cable agreement has a single sideletter that encompasses both derivative new media based on basic cable product and new media reuse of basic cable product.

There are various differences between AFM derivative new media based on free TV and AFM derivative new media based on basic cable.

In particular, AFM derivative new media based on basic cable participates in residuals when reused on free TV (C7-D7), basic cable (H7) and ad-supported platforms (K7), whereas AFM derivative new media based on free TV does not.

Also, in supplemental markets (F7-G7), basic cable based derivative new media product participates at 3.6% of gross rather than the AFM's more common 1% of gross formula, which is what applies to free TV based product.

The same 3.6% vs. 1% distinction is true of reuse on consumer-paid platforms (I7-J7). In addition, AFM free TV based derivative new media product in that reuse pattern is subject to tests that can preclude residuals, whereas AFM basic cable based new media product is not.

### Business Background

Several years ago, a few TV series had derivative new media spinoffs, but almost none do today. Derivative new media turns out to be a bit of a backwater, at least for the time being.

### Types of Residuals

Derivative new media released to pay TV, home video or basic cable (F7-H7) generally parallels free TV released to those media. Residuals for other release patterns vary widely.

### Who Participates

All above the line unions (DGA, WGA, SAG-AFTRA, L-SAG and L-AFTRA), and AFM derivative new media based on a basic cable series, participate in residuals in all reuse patterns except theatrical (B7) and foreign (E7). These latter two reuse patterns appear to be residual-free, although this is open to dispute.

IATSE, and AFM derivative new media based on a free TV series, participate only for reuse in supplemental markets (F7-G7) and (with some unusual restrictions) for reuse on consumer paid platforms (I7-J7).

### Pattern Analysis

The definitions do not exhibit a pattern.

As to the formulas, there's no pattern in reuse on free TV (C7-D7). In reuse on ad-supported platforms (K7), there is a pattern, but with deviations. Other areas are generally in pattern,

---

* As a reminder, in terms of television, this book focuses primarily on scripted product made for primetime.
† Indeed, the Made for New Media Sideletter to the Theatrical Agreement even includes the provisions on derivative new media, notwithstanding the fact that they define derivative new media solely with reference to underlying television shows, not theatrical movies.

except for deviations in the treatment of AFM derivative new media based on a basic cable series.

➜ Although not specifically relevant to residuals, there is a noteworthy deviation from pattern regarding *initial compensation* in derivative new media: *the WGA Made for New Media Sideletter has a scale of minimums for derivative new media, whereas the other unions' Made for New Media Sideletters do not.*

### Date Restrictions

[tbd]

### Chapter References

- Chapter 12: Reuse of derivative new media product in any media (row 7).

## Original New Media

### Chart Reference

Row 8.

### Definition

Strangely enough, "original new media" is not defined in the guild and union agreements. From context, however, it means a production which is intended for initial release on the Internet or mobile devices and which is neither a derivative new media program nor an experimental new media program.[*]

Because the definitions of derivative and experimental media vary by guild/union, it is possible for a project to be considered original new media by one guild or union and derivative or experimental by another.

It's also possible, of course, for a project to be covered by one union or guild (as derivative, original or experimental, as the case may be) and to be non-union as to another guild or union.

---

[*] See DGA BA Made for NM SL § A; WGA MBA Made for NM SL § 2; SAG Made for NM SL § B; AFTRA Netcode Ex. A Made for NM SL § B; AFTRA Netcode Front of Book Made for NM SL § B; IATSE BA Made for NM SL § C; AFM Theatrical/TV Made for NM SL § C.

### Business Background

In 2008, when the extensive new media provisions were added to the DGA agreement – the first agreement in which they appeared – it was generally assumed that original new media productions would be 3-5 minutes in length (so-called "webisodes" and "mobisodes")[†] and have budgets far lower than traditional television series.

That's not the way it turned out though. How much short-form professionally scripted and directed content, with professional actors, do you recall watching lately? Original new media has not proved to be economically significant, so far at least.

Instead, Internet-based services are producing long-form content, which from mid-2014 onwards is classified as high budget SVOD (see p. 36), which is a variant of derivative new media or original new media. Prior to that date, such content – an example is the Netflix series *House of Cards* – would be classified simply as original new media, but it is not clear that such content was treated as original new media in practice. For instance, *House of Cards* was produced under specially-negotiated terms that have not been publicly disclosed.

### Types of Residuals

Residuals for original new media are similar to those for derivative new media (see preceding subsection).

### Who Participates

The same as with derivative new media, but without the special distinction for AFM derivative new media based on a basic cable series.

In other words, all four above the line unions participate in residuals in all reuse patterns except theatrical (B8) and foreign (E8). These latter two reuse patterns appear to be residual-free, although this is open to dispute.

IATSE and AFM participate only for reuse in supplemental markets (F8-G8) and (with some unusual restrictions) for reuse on consumer paid platforms (I8-J8).

---

[†] "Mobisodes" is a term for episodes of a series produced specifically for viewing on cell phones.

### Pattern Analysis

Similar to derivative new media: There's no pattern in reuse on free TV (C8-D8). Other areas are generally in pattern.

### Date Restrictions

[tbd]

### Chapter References

- **Chapter 12:** Reuse of original new media product in any media (row 8).

## Experimental New Media

### Chart Reference

Row 9.

### Definition

An experimental new media production is a production which is intended for initial release on the Internet or mobile devices, and which is not derivative new media, and (a) whose **budget falls below certain thresholds** (such as $15,000 per minute) and (b) whose **use of experienced personnel falls below certain thresholds**.* These tests are discussed starting on p. 124.

### Business Background

The difference between original and experimental new media is significant: original new media productions are subject to residuals in most cases, but experimental new media productions are not subject to residuals in any scenario.

Because most professional new media productions use experienced personnel, most such productions will not qualify as experimental new media and will instead be classified as original new media.

Note that a couple of teenagers making video in their garage are not per se an example of experimental new media. The teenager-in-charge (i.e., the producer) is presumably not a guild signatories, so the project doesn't fall under the union agreement at all.

However, if one of those teenagers is actually a professional child actor – a SAG-AFTRA member – then he or she may be in violation of Global Rule 1, a SAG-AFTRA rule requiring a union contract for any work of a type covered by the union agreements.

### Types of Residuals

There are no residuals for reuse of experimental new media (row 9).

### Who Participates

No unions receive residuals for experimental new media.

### Pattern Analysis

Pattern is maintained, other than subtle and unintended differences in the phrasing of the budget test discussed in Section 12.I.

### Date Restrictions

Not applicable.

### Chapter References

- **Section 12.I:** Reuse of experimental media product in any media (row 9).

## High Budget Subscription Video On Demand (SVOD) Programs

### Chart Reference

Row 10.

### Definition

High budget SVOD (Subscription Video On Demand) programs are original new media and derivative new media productions above certain length and budget thresholds that is made for initial exhibition on a "subscription consumer pay new media platform" (see p. 43).

The latter term is not defined, but from context it means subscription video on demand platforms such as Netflix, Amazon Prime, Hulu Plus and the like – in other words, Internet-based platforms where the consumer pays a monthly or annual subscription fee,† as opposed to paying

---

* See DGA BA Made for NM SL § B; WGA MBA Made for NM SL § 1; SAG CBA/TVA Made for NM SL § C; AFTRA Netcode Front of Book Made for NM SL § C; AFTRA Netcode Ex. A Made for NM SL § C; IATSE BA Made for NM SL § B; AFM Made for NM SL § B.

† The industry (though not the union agreements) sometimes refers to these as a subset of over-the-top (OTT) services (a term which also encompasses ad-supported stream-

a la carte for the individual program (pay per view (PPV), sometimes referred to as transactional video on demand (TVOD) or just VOD).

The budget and length thresholds for high budget SVOD are as follows:

| Length (mins) | High Budget Threshold |
|---|---|
| 0-19 | Not considered high budget SVOD |
| 20-35 | $1.3 million and above |
| 36-65 | $2.5 million and above |
| 66 or more | $3.0 million and above |

As an approximate guide, these figures mean that high budget SVOD programs must be at least 20 minutes long and be budgeted at more than roughly $35,000 to $70,000 per minute.

Note that programs under 20 minutes are never considered high budget SVOD. The apparent intent is to exclude "webisodes," i.e., short (typically 3-5 min.) programs and instead encompass primarily programs that resemble conventional TV programming but are intended to be delivered initially on subscription consumer pay new media platforms.

Such programs are usually series, such as a series made for Netflix. Netflix's most prominent original show to date, *House of Cards,* would be an example – the budget for this one-hour drama was reported to be about $4 million per episode – except that it was produced before the high budget SVOD provisions were introduced, in the 2013-2014 contract cycle (effective mid-2014 for the above the line unions). The provisions are not retroactive.

In addition to series, a TV movie made for Netflix or another SVOD platform would also be a high budget SVOD program, so long as it satisfies the budget threshold in the table for programs of the applicable length.

## Business Background

Starting around 2011, Netflix began acquiring high budget, pay TV-like original programming, for the same reason that HBO had over a decade earlier: to make the service a destination for high-profile content not available elsewhere. Amazon Prime began doing likewise as well.

To be sure, most content available on Netflix and Amazon is TV series and movies that were first made for other media – theatrical movies, for instance, or TV shows that first aired on a cable network. Such content is not high budget SVOD, because it was not made for initial exhibition on Netflix or Amazon. High budget SVOD does not encompass programming made for initial exhibition on traditional platforms.

Another distinction to bear in mind: high budget SVOD is not the same as pay-per-view (PPV) pay TV services such as HBO on Demand, which allows subscribers to HBO to view some content on demand. Such PPV services are considered pay TV under the union agreements.

Further complicating matters, late in 2014, HBO, CBS, Univision and Starz each announced that they would deploy SVOD versions of their linear services. It's the beginning of what may well become a trend, allowing consumers without a cable TV subscription to subscribe to the channel and view content on Internet-connected devices.

Such services may raise questions as to how content made for those providers should be categorized. For example, a made-for-HBO series today is considered a pay TV program, because it is initially available on pay TV. However, once HBO's SVOD offering becomes available, made-for-HBO content may be released day-and-date (i.e., concurrently) on the linear platform and the SVOD platform.

Will such content be considered pay TV product or high budget SVOD product (and who will decide)? The same question arises with Starz, and similar questions with CBS and Univision (made for free TV or made for high budget SVOD?) It's too early to tell what the answers will be. Indeed, the union treatment may change over time, if (or more likely when) such SVOD services overtake their linear forebears.

---

ing services (AVOD) such as Hulu), because they arrive without the involvement of a conventional cable or satellite set top box.

### Types of Residuals

When run and rerun on their original subscription consumer pay new media platform (I10), there is a one year free window and then a year by year (not run by run) declining fixed residual. Other reuse patterns

### Who Participates

At present (early 2015), only the above-the-line unions have negotiated special high budget SVOD residuals. It is not yet known whether IATSE and AFM will seek or obtain such residuals.

### Pattern Analysis

Pattern is maintained.

### Date Restrictions

The high budget SVOD provisions became effective with the beginning of the 2014 contract cycle, which is mid-2014 for the above the line unions (DGA 7/1/14, WGA 5/2/14, SAG-AFTRA 7/1/14).

### Chapter References

- Section 12.J: Reuse of high budget SVOD product on subscription consumer pay new media platforms (I10).

- Section 12.K: Reuse of high budget SVOD product on other consumer paid platforms (I10-J10).

- Section 12.L: Reuse of high budget SVOD product on ad-supported new media platforms (K10).

- Section 12.M: Reuse of high budget SVOD product in traditional media (B10-H10).

## Ambiguities in the Made-For Medium

If the initial use of a product doesn't match the original intention, is the product is still classified as originally intended? Although the union and guild agreements are silent on this issue, the answer is usually Yes.

For instance, if a producer informs the guilds that she's making *Watching Paint Dry* as a theatrical motion picture, but later fails to get a theatrical deal and instead releases the movie straight to home video, the product usually will treated as a theatrical motion picture for residuals purposes and other matters. That can mean paying residuals on every DVD sold even though the movie never earned any theatrical revenue (and what did you expect, with a title like that?). In other words, the producer can end up paying residuals even for the initial use of the product.

The treatment may be different under a guild's low-budget agreements. For instance, under these circumstances, the WGA low-budget theatrical agreement would automatically reclassify *Watching Paint Dry* as a direct to video product.

Good news? Not necessarily – the reclassification will save money on residuals, but it voids other benefits of the low-budget agreement – notably, the right to defer payment of initial compensation. That "ka-ching" is the sound of a big bill coming due unexpectedly. (Fortunately, reclassification can be avoided if the company uses best efforts to get a theatrical deal before going the direct-to-video route.)

The union and guild agreements also don't contemplate the possibility that a product will be released concurrently ("day and date," in Hollywood parlance) on multiple platforms.

For instance, if a movie is intended for release day and date in theaters and pay per view, should it be classified as a theatrical motion picture or a pay TV product? Such a release is rare, but as release windows shrink, it may become more common or even, one day, the norm.[xxx]

## C. Reuse Markets

Below are eleven subsections describing the key reuse markets in more detail, plus an additional subsection listing several less significant reuse markets that are not otherwise discussed in the book.

### Theatrical

### Chart Reference

Column B.

### Definition

Exhibition in movie theaters.*

### Business Background

This is a very unusual reuse market for most product (B3-B9) (except, of course, for theatrical movies (B2)). For instance, very seldom would a made for TV movie obtain a theatrical release.

### Types of Residuals

Residuals in this reuse market tend to be a one-time payment of 100% or 150% of applicable minimum.

### Who Participates

All four above the line unions participate in the residual-bearing reuse patterns (B3-B6). IATSE does not. AFM participates in almost the same patterns as the above the line unions (B3-B5, i.e., not for basic cable product reused theatrically).

### Pattern Analysis

All of the applicable formulas in B3-B6 are different, yet similar, so the gestalt of a pattern is maintained (other than with respect to AFM basic cable product, B6).

### Chapter References

- Section 5.A: Theatrical reuse of theatrical product (B2).

- Chapter 10: Theatrical reuse of television and home video product (B3-B6).

- Section 12.H: Theatrical reuse of derivative and original new media product (B7-B8).

- Section 12.I: Reuse of experimental new media product (Row 9).

## Free TV – Network Primetime

### Chart Reference

Column C.

---

\* The agreements use the term "theatrical exhibition" or "exhibited theatrically," but do not define them.

### Definition

Exhibition on a broadcast network† in the U.S. and Canada‡ during primetime.§ Broadcast networks are ABC, CBS, The CW, FOX and NBC, although programming on The CW may be subject to certain discounts or other accommodations.

### Business Background

Network primetime as a reuse market is fairly empty these days. In the past you'd find reruns of current season episodes of primetime series, but today these are more often on Hulu or the networks' own websites. You'd also find reruns of theatrical movies, and sometimes still do, but these are more often found now on pay TV or basic cable. Instead, network primetime is primarily home to new episodes of scripted and unscripted series and sports.

The decline of primetime reruns of free TV shows has meant the reduction to union members of a very large fixed residual (C3). It's been replaced by a much lower fixed residual (K3).

### Types of Residuals

When theatrical product is exhibited on network primetime, a percentage residual is payable (C2). When other product is exhibited on network primetime (C3-C8, C10) the residual is usually a fixed residual at 100%.

### Who Participates

All unions participate when theatrical product is reused on network primetime (C2). The above the line unions participate when other product

---

† For definition of "network," see DGA BA Para. 1-205; WGA MBA Art. 1.A.12.1; SAG CBA Sec. 5.E(3); SAG TV Agt. Sec. 18(b)(6); AFTRA Netcode Para. 71; AFM Television Agt. Para. 15(a)(5)(iv)(B).
‡ [tbd – note re northern Mexico, etc.]
§ The agreements do not define the terms "primetime" or "prime time," with the exception of AFM Television Agt. Para. 15(a)(5)(iv)(B). The hours traditionally constituting prime time in North America are 8:00-11:00 p.m. Eastern/Pacific and 7:00-10:00 p.m. Central/Mountain on Monday–Saturday, and 7:00-11:00 p.m. Eastern/Pacific and 6:00-10:00 p.m. Central/Mountain on Sunday. See http://en.wikipedia.org/wiki/Prime_time#North_America.

is reused on network primetime (C3-C8, C10). IATSE does not,* and AFM varies.

### Pattern Analysis

Pattern is maintained when theatrical or free TV product is reused on network primetime (C2 and C3). There are deviations from pattern when pay TV and home video product is reused in network primetime (C4-C5) and large deviations or no pattern when basic cable and new media product is reused in network primetime (C6-C8, C10).

### Reuse on Fox

Reuse of all product on Fox is paid at 100% of network primetime rates, but were previously paid at a lower percentage. Here's the history:

| Date | Unions | Event |
|---|---|---|
|  |  | Residuals established at [tbd]% |
|  |  | Increased to [tbd]% |
|  |  | Increased to [tbd]% |
| 2001? | DGA | Increased to 100% eff. 7/1/03? |
| 2001 | WGA | Increased to 100% eff. 5/2/03 |
| ? | SAG/ AFTRA | Increased to 100% eff.7/1/?? |

### Reuse on the CW

Reuse on the CW (and its predecessors, UPN and the WB) was and is paid at lower rates, pursuant to a CW Supplement [for each union]

[WGA 2011 MOA p. 35]

Here's the history:

| Date | Unions | Event |
|---|---|---|
|  |  | Residuals established at [tbd]% |
|  |  | Increased to [tbd]% |
|  |  | Increased to [tbd]% |

[Made for CW reused on non-CW?]

### Chapter References

- Section 5.B: Reuse of theatrical product on free TV or foreign TV (C2-E2).

- Section 6.A: Reuse of free TV product on network primetime (C3).

- Section 8.J: Pay TV and home video product to free TV and foreign (C4-E5).

- Section 9.B: Reuse of basic cable product in network primetime (C6).

- Section 12.D: Free TV reuse of derivative and original new media (C7-D8).

- Section 12.I: Reuse of experimental new media product (Row 9).

- Section 12.M: Reuse of high budget SVOD product in traditional media (B10-H10).

## Free TV – Other than Network Primetime

### Chart Reference

Column D.

### Definition

Exhibition on broadcast television in the U.S. and Canada other than in network primetime. This can be on a broadcast network outside of primetime; or via syndication[†] or other sale for exhibition on independent stations or network affiliates during any daypart.

### Business Background

Broadcast syndication used to be common for shows that had aired for at least a certain number of seasons or episodes (such as 100 episodes). Today, however, a basic cable deal is more likely for such shows.

### Types of Residuals

When theatrical product is exhibited on other than network primetime, a percentage residual is payable (D2). When other product is exhibited on other than network primetime (D3-D8), the residual is usually a fixed residual at a run-by-run declining percentage.

---

* Whether IATSE will participate in C10 is not yet known as of this writing (early 2015).

[†] The agreements do not define "syndication," but a good definition is "the sale of the right to broadcast television and radio programs by multiple television and radio stations, without going through a broadcast network." See http://en.wikipedia.org/wiki/Broadcast_syndication. For definitions of "network" and "primetime," see the footnote on p. 39.

### Who Participates

Same as with exhibition on network primetime (see above).

### Pattern Analysis

Same as with exhibition on network primetime (see above).

### Chapter References

- Section 5.B: Reuse of theatrical product on free TV or foreign TV (C2-E2).

- Section 6.B: Reuse of free TV product on other than network primetime (D3).

- Section 8.J: Pay TV and home video product to free TV and foreign (C4-E5).

- Section 9.C: Reuse of basic cable product in other than network primetime (D6).

- Section 12.D: Free TV reuse of derivative and original new media (C7-D8).

- Section 12.I: Reuse of experimental new media product (Row 9).

- Section 12.M: Reuse of high budget SVOD product in traditional media (B10-H10).

## Foreign

### Chart Reference

Column E.

### Definition

Exhibition in outside the U.S. and Canada on broadcast television or basic cable. Also includes foreign ad-supported Internet, mobile or AVOD availability of television and home video product, but not of theatrical product.*

### Business Background

Foreign rights sales are a critical part of the motion picture and television businesses. Most movies won't get financed or greenlit without strong international interest, and many television shows are sold internationally.

In foreign rights deals for motion pictures and television programs, ad-supported Internet rights are often included, since these are viewed as the Internet equivalent of television. That's why foreign reuse of television product includes ad-supported services.†

### Types of Residuals

When theatrical product is exhibited on foreign broadcast television or foreign basic cable, a percentage residual is payable (E2). When other product is exhibited on foreign broadcast television, foreign basic cable or foreign ad-supported services (E3-E8), the residual is usually a hybrid fixed and percentage residual.

### Who Participates

Same as with exhibition on network primetime (see above). In addition, AFM receives foreign residuals based on AGICOA monies. AGICOA (agicoa.org) is a foreign rights organization that remits monies to the AFM.

### Pattern Analysis

Pattern is generally maintained.

### Chapter References

- Section 5.B: Reuse of theatrical product on free TV or foreign TV (C2-E2).

- Section 6.C: Foreign reuse of free TV product (E3).

- Section 8.J: Pay TV and home video product to free TV and foreign (C4-E5).

- Section 9.D: Foreign reuse of basic cable product (E6).

- Section 12.E: Foreign reuse of derivative and original new media (E7-E8).

- Section 12.I: Reuse of experimental new media product (Row 9).

- Section 12.M: Reuse of high budget SVOD product in traditional media (B10-H10).

---

* See p. 45 for definition and discussion of ad-supported services.

† The inclusion of foreign ad-supported Internet and AVOD services is addressed in the new media reuse sideletters' discussion of ad-supported services. See p. 111 for contract references.

## Supplemental Markets

### Chart Reference

Columns F & G.

### Definition

For historical reasons, pay TV and home video are referred to as "supplemental markets" (except when discussing reuse of product made for pay TV or home video) because they were seen as supplementing the existing theatrical and free TV markets.[*]

### Who Participates

All unions participate in reuse in supplemental markets (F2-G3, F6-G8). All four above the lines also participate when pay TV or home video product is reused in pay TV or home video (F4-G5), but [IATSE and AFM do not.]

### Pattern Analysis

Pattern is generally maintained in supplemental markets (F2-G3, F6-G8). There is no pattern when pay TV or home video product is reused in pay TV or home video (F4-G5).

### Chapter References

- Chapter 7: Reuse in supplemental markets (F2-G3).
- [tbd: add rows 4, 5, 6, 7-8]
- Section 12.I: Reuse of experimental new media product (Row 9).
- Section 12.M: Reuse of high budget SVOD product in traditional media (B10-H10).

## Pay TV

### Chart Reference

Column F.

### Definition

Exhibition on a U.S. or foreign pay TV channel or via U.S. or foreign pay-per-view.[†]

### Business Background

[tbd]

### Types of Residuals

Residuals for reuse of most types of product in pay TV are percentage residuals. The exception is that reuse of pay TV or home video product in pay TV is subject to a range of quite varying formulas.

### Other Details and Chapter References

See discussion of supplemental markets above.

## Home Video

### Chart Reference

Column G.

### Definition

Release on a physical home video medium, such as DVD or Blu-ray.[‡]

### Business Background

[tbd]

### Types of Residuals

[tbd]

### Other Details and Chapter References

See discussion of supplemental markets above.

## Basic Cable

### Chart Reference

Column H.

---

[*] See DGA BA Para. 18-102; WGA MBA Art. 51.B; SAG CBA Sec. 5.2.D; SAG TV Agt. Sec. 20(a); AFTRA Netcode Ex. D Sec. 2; IATSE BA Sec. XXVIII(a)(3); AFM Theatrical Agt. Sec. 16(a)(3); AFM Television Agt. Sec. 14(a)(3).

[†] See DGA BA Para. 18-102(b); WGA MBA Art. 51.B.2; SAG CBA Sec. 5.2.D(2); SAG TV Agt. Sec. 20(a)(2); AFTRA Netcode Ex. D Sec. 2.B; IATSE BA Sec. XXVIII(a)(3)(ii); AFM Theatrical Agt. Sec. 16(a)(3)(ii); AFM Television Agt. Sec. 14(a)(3)(ii).

[‡] See DGA BA Para. 18-102(a); WGA MBA Art. 51.B.1; SAG CBA Sec. 5.2.D(1); SAG TV Agt. Sec. 20(a)(1); AFTRA Netcode Ex. D Sec. 2.A; IATSE BA Sec. XXVIII(a)(3)(i); AFM Theatrical Agt. Sec. 16(a)(3)(i); AFM Television Agt. Sec. 14(a)(3)(i).

### Definition

Exhibition on a domestic basic cable channel.

### Types of Residuals

[tbd]

### Business Background

[tbd]

### Who Participates

All four above the line unions participate. IATSE participates only for reuse of theatrical product in basic cable (H2); same for AFM, except that AFM derivative media based on a basic cable show participates in residuals when reused on basic cable (H7).

### Pattern Analysis

Pattern is generally maintained when product is reused in basic cable, except for significant deviations from pattern when basic cable product is itself used in basic cable (H6).

### Chapter References

- [tbd rows 2-8]

- Section 12.I: Reuse of experimental new media product (Row 9).

- Section 12.M: Reuse of high budget SVOD product in traditional media (B10-H10).

## Consumer Paid New Media – eRental

### Chart Reference

Column I.

### Definition

Release on the Internet or mobile platforms, where the consumer pays on either a subscription basis (such as Netflix streaming) [xxx] or a per-program basis (such as download rental, rare business model) and receives the right to view the program for a fixed and limited period of time or a fixed number of viewings.[*]

This mode of exhibition is analogous to renting a physical DVD from a video store or kiosk.

### Business Background

[tbd]

### Types of Residuals

Percentage residuals.

### Who Participates

All unions participate.

### Pattern Analysis

Pattern is generally maintained, with variations when derivative or original new media are reused on consumer paid platforms (I7-J8).

### Chapter References

- Chapter 11: New media reuse of traditional product (I2-J6).

- Section 12.A: Reuse of new media on consumer-paid platforms (I7-J8).

- Section 12.I: Reuse of experimental new media product (Row 9).

- Section 12.K: Reuse of high budget SVOD product on other consumer paid platforms (I10-J10).

## Subscription Consumer Pay New Media Platform

### Chart Reference

Cell I10 only.

### Definition

See discussion of high budget subscription video on demand (SVOD) programs (p. 36).

Note that the term "subscription consumer pay new media platform" as a reuse market is only used with respect to High Budget SVOD product. For instance, if a high budget show made for a streaming video service is exhibited on a streaming video service (such as Netflix), then we say that a High Budget SVOD program has

---

[*] See DGA BA NM Reuse SL § 1; WGA MBA NM Reuse SL § 1.a; SAG CBA/TVA NM Reuse SL § 1.A; AFTRA Netcode Ex. A NM Reuse SL § 1.A; IATSE NM Reuse SL § 1.a;

AFM NM Reuse SL § 1(a); AFM Basic Cable Ex. B NM Reuse SL § 1A.

been exhibited on a subscription consumer pay new media platform and we reference I10* for the residual formula.

If, instead, we wish to analyze a theatrical movie (a movie that is made for exhibition in movie theaters) that is being made available on Netflix, we say that the movie is being released on an eRental platform,† not a subscription consumer pay new media platform. The residual is found in cell I2.

Likewise, if a TV series that was first produced for the FX basic cable network is made available on Netflix, we say that a basic cable show is being released on an eRental platform, not a subscription consumer pay new media platform. The residual is found in cell I6.

Note too in this example that the FX basic cable show is not a "high budget SVOD Program," regardless of its budget and regardless of the fact that it's being shown on Netflix now. The show was initially made for basic cable – that was the made-for medium in this example – whereas High Budget SVOD Programs by definition are programs (above certain budgets and lengths) that are made for a subscription consumer pay new media platform in the first instance. Re-running the FX show on Netflix does not change its identity as a show that was produced initially for basic cable.

### Business Background

See discussion of high budget subscription video on demand (SVOD) programs (p. 36).

### Types of Residuals

See discussion of high budget subscription video on demand (SVOD) programs (p. 36).

---

* We refer to I10 (I10), not I10-J10 (I10-J10), because a subscription consumer pay new media platform is a form of eRental, rather than EST, because the consumer does not own the movies she watches on Netflix. Rather, she has the right to watch them for a limited period of time – namely, the period during which she pays a monthly subscription fee to Netflix. In effect, her subscription fee allows her to rent the entire Netflix inventory, because she can watch whatever she wants

† It is eRental, not EST, for the reasons explained in the preceding footnote.

### Who Participates

At present (early 2015), only the above-the-line unions have negotiated special high budget SVOD residuals. It is not yet known whether IATSE and AFM will seek or obtain such residuals.

### Pattern Analysis

Pattern is maintained.

### Chapter References

● Sections 12.J: Reuse of high budget SVOD product (I10).

## Consumer Paid New Media – Electronic Sell Through (EST)

### Chart Reference

Column J.

### Definition

This term is not expressly defined in the agreements. However, from context, it means release on the Internet or mobile platforms, where the consumer pays for right to view the program without limitations as to time or number of viewings.‡ iTunes downloads are an example.

The agreements refer to this mode of exhibition as "paid permanent downloads," which raises the question of whether paid permanent streaming access – i.e., permanent access via "the cloud," which is one purchase option offered by Amazon Video on Demand – is also encompassed in this market/medium. Presumably so, but perhaps the matter would have to be (or has been) arbitrated.

### Business Background

At one time, EST seemed to be increasingly replacing DVD and Blu-ray purchases as a medium of choice for home viewing of movies. However, streaming (a form of eRental) and kiosk rental of DVDs and Blu-ray discs (Redbox) probably are more common now than EST.

---

‡ See DGA BA NM Reuse SL § 2; WGA MBA NM Reuse SL § 1.b; SAG CBA/TVA NM Reuse SL § 1.B; AFTRA Netcode Ex. A NM Reuse SL § 1.B; IATSE NM Reuse SL § 1.b; AFM NM Reuse SL § 1(b); AFM Basic Cable Ex. B NM Reuse SL § 1B.

### Types of Residuals

Percentage residuals modeled on home video (20% of 100% for affiliated distributors).

### Who Participates

Same as eRental – all unions participate.

### Pattern Analysis

Same as eRental – pattern is generally maintained, with variations when derivative or original new media are reused on consumer paid platforms (I7-J8).

### Chapter References

- Chapter 11: New media reuse of traditional product (I2-J6).

- Section 12.A: Reuse of new media on consumer-paid platforms (I7-J8).

- Section 12.I: Reuse of experimental new media product (Row 9).

- Section 12.K: Reuse of high budget SVOD product on other consumer paid platforms (I10-J10).

## Ad-Supported Services

### Chart Reference

Column K.

### Definition

Release on the Internet or mobile platforms, where the consumer does not pay and, instead, advertising accompanies the program (such as on Hulu (as distinguished from the pay service, Hulu Plus).*

Also, commencing mid-2014, this reuse market encompasses release on an advertiser-supported video-on-demand service ("AVOD") of a multichannel video programming distributor ("MVPD") (i.e., a cable, satellite or telco system) or "any similar service that currently exists or may hereafter be developed."

---

\* See DGA BA NM Reuse SL § 3; WGA MBA NM Reuse SL § 2; SAG CBA/TVA NM Reuse SL § 2; AFTRA Netcode Ex. A NM Reuse SL § 2; IATSE NM Reuse SL § 2; AFM NM Reuse SL § 2; AFM Basic Cable Ex. B NM Reuse SL § 2.

---

The 2008/09 agreements referred to this mode of exhibition as "ad-supported streaming," which raised the question of whether ad-supported downloads are also encompassed in this market/medium. Presumably so, but perhaps the matter would have had to be (or was) arbitrated. In any case, the 2014 agreements refer to "free-to-the-consumer, advertiser-supported service transmitted via the internet or mobile or other device," which removes the reference to streaming.

### Business Background

[tbd]

### Types of Residuals

[tbd]

### Who Participates

All above the line unions participate. IATSE and AFM participate only in theatrical to ad-supported (K2), except that AFM basic cable product (K6) and AFM derivative new media based on a basic cable series (K7) also do so.

### Pattern Analysis

[tbd]

### Chapter References

- Chapter 11: New media use of traditional product (K2-K6).

- Section 12.B: Reuse of new media on ad-supported platforms (K7).

- Section 12.C: Reuse of new media on ad-supported platforms (K8).

- Section 12.I: Reuse of experimental new media product (Row 9).

- Section 12.L: Reuse of high budget SVOD product on ad-supported new media platforms (K10).

## Other Markets

There are several other reuse markets of lesser significance, which this book does not discuss:

- In-Flight: Exhibition on airplanes in flight ✈ and ships at sea 🚢. Depending on the guild/union, this may or may not be considered a supplemental market, and may or may not be payable using the same formulas as for exhibition on pay TV.

- **Hotel:** Exhibition on hotel room pay per view systems.

- **Nontheatrical:** This term sounds like it means "anything other than theatrical" – but it doesn't. Instead, "nontheatrical" means exhibition in institutions such as schools, hospitals and prisons.

## D. Guilds/Unions

This section presents key union-specific information, including the structure of the various union contracts. (For more on that subject, see also p. 177).

### Who Participates in Residuals

Residuals look very different to above versus below the line unions.

#### Above the Line

DGA, WGA, SAG-AFTRA, L-SAG and L-AFTRA participate broadly:

#### IATSE

In contrast, IATSE participates in very few reuse patterns – and all IATSE residuals go to the P&H plans,* which may diminish their perceived importance to individual union members:

As usual, grey indicates no residuals. The * indicates that special tests apply to the indicated reuse pattern. See p. 113.

#### AFM

The AFM participates more widely than IATSE, but its percentage residual is small – typically 1% rather than the DGA's and WGA's 1.2% – and is generally shared by more people:

---

* MPIPHP – the Motion Picture Industry Pension and Health Plans.

## Media, Markets, Unions and More – 47

### AFM

| Reused in:<br>Made for: | Theatrical | Free TV Network Primetime | Free TV Syndication or Non-Primetime | Foreign | Supp. Mkts. Pay TV | Supp. Mkts. Home Video | Domestic Basic Cable | New Media Consumer Pd eRental | New Media Consumer Pd EST | New Media Ad Supported |
|---|---|---|---|---|---|---|---|---|---|---|
| Theatrical | | | | | | | | | | |
| Free TV | | | | † | | | | | | |
| Pay TV | | | | | | | | | | |
| Home Video | § | | | † | | | | | | |
| Basic Cable | | | | † | | | | | | |
| Deriv. NM | | ‡ | ‡ | | | | ‡ | * | | ‡ |
| Orig. NM | | | | | | | | | | |
| Exper. NM | | | | | | | | | | |

AFM residuals have additional limitations in some reuse patterns, as indicated the symbols:

| AFM Limitations | Page |
|---|---|
| * Special tests apply | 113 |
| † Specialized formula | 78 |
| ‡ Residuals for derivative new media if based on a basic cable program, but none if based on a free TV program | 115<br>119<br>122 |
| § No residuals if made under TV Agt. | 92 |

### DGA

The DGA has two major agreements for scripted product, the Basic Agreement (BA) and the Freelance Live and Tape Television Agreement (FLTTA). As technology has evolved, the titles have become somewhat inapt: the BA covers theatrical and primetime television product regardless of recording medium (film, tape, hard disk, memory card, etc.), while the FLTTA covers daytime product, particularly soap operas.

### WGA

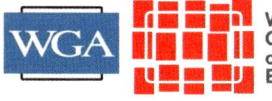

The WGA is actually two unions, WGA West and WGA East. They negotiate their studio contract jointly, so the division has little practical impact on the subject of this book. The WGA West handles residuals processing for the WGA East, as the West coast union has twice as many members as its East coast counterpart and is more Hollywood-centric.

The main WGA contract, the MBA,* is more comprehensive than the main contracts of the other unions. The latter tend to divide coverage into several contracts, whereas the MBA encompasses key scripted areas as well as daytime serials, certain thinly scripted product such as game shows, and even interactive media (video games).

Another notable fact about the WGA is that its members create scripts, not audiovisual product itself. Those scripts then get turned into audiovisual product – movies, TV shows, home video product and Internet productions. In contrast, directors, actors and crew members create audiovisual product directly.

The residuals that this book focuses on are paid for reuse of the audiovisual product, but it's also possible to reuse the scripts (or components of them) independent of the audiovisual product.

For example, a remake of a movie reuses the script but not the original movie (audiovisual product) itself. Likewise, a sequel uses elements of the script – characters, settings, tone, themes, etc. – even if it doesn't include a single second of footage from the first film or even a single line from the original script.

Even a TV series is in a sense a sequel of the script for its pilot. Indeed, the WGA views it that way.

All of these reuses generate reuse payments that are unique to writers, such as series sequel payments, separated rights residuals and more. They're discussed in Chapter 14, and are not addressed in other chapters or on the residuals chart.

Terminology warning: the WGA categorizes scripts as a type of "literary material." That term, however, does not include things that most people would consider "literary," such as books, stage plays, short stories, *New Yorker* articles and the like. None of those are "literary material." Only scripts and stories are.

---

* "MBA" stands for "Minimum Basic Agreement," the former name of the contract. It's now just called the "Basic Agreement," so BA has become a common abbreviation. However, the DGA and IATSE also have BA's, so this book uses the term MBA to avoid further confusion.

Also, "stories" does not mean ideas, pitches, concepts or what some jerk at a party reels off when he says "hey, let me tell you a funny story" and then jumps right in without waiting for you to explain that you really need to get home and file your nails.

Rather, a "story" is a fleshed-out description of characters, plot and other elements. It's essentially equivalent to a reasonably detailed treatment (the more common industry term).

However, if there is no separate treatment for a project, then the story is deemed incorporated in the script itself.

## SAG-AFTRA

As earlier noted, SAG and AFTRA merged in 2012 but until mid-2014 their key contracts remained separate (other than their commercials contracts, which merged in 2013).

There are two main SAG-AFTRA agreements that we're concerned with: the Codified Basic Agreement, or CBA, covers theatrical motion pictures and television programs, while the Television Agreement, or TVA, operates as a supplement to the CBA and relates to television programs.

In other words, for theatrical, just read the CBA.* For television, you have to read both agreements.

Unlike the Legacy-SAG TVA, the SAG-AFTRA TVA also covers basic cable, just as do the DGA BA and WGA MBA.

However, the SAG-AFTRA CBA and TVA have yet to be codified into single volumes, meaning that all that exists right now are the 2005 SAG CBA, 2005 SAG TVA, the basic cable agreement and memorandums of Agreement (MOAs) from 2005 through 2014-17. Collectively, those constitute the 2014-17 documents. See p. 181 for further discussion of this.

In addition, the Legacy-AFTRA Netcode front of book (essentially, the entire Netcode other than Exs. A & E), as updated by recent MOAs, is still in effect. See the discussion below under Legacy-AFTRA.

## Legacy SAG-AFTRA Overlap

Before looking at the Legacy-SAG and Legacy-AFTRA agreements separately, it's helpful to note where their scripted programming jurisdictions overlap:

| SAG Only | Shared Jurisdiction | AFTRA Only |
|---|---|---|
| Theatrical motion pictures | Network Primetime TV | First-run syndication |
|  | Pay TV | Daytime serials (soap operas) (not covered in most of this book) |
|  | Home video |  |
|  | Basic cable |  |
|  | New media |  |

## Legacy-SAG

As noted above, the two main L-SAG agreements are the Codified Basic Agreement, or CBA, and the Television Agreement, or TVA, plus the short basic cable agreement, which incorporates the other two agreements by reference and provides terms (including residuals) that are specific to basic cable. Thus, in Legacy-SAG, understanding basic cable means reviewing provisions in the CBA, TVA and Basic Cable agreement.

## Legacy-AFTRA

There is one main Legacy-AFTRA contract that concerns us, the Network Code, or Netcode.† As with most of these contracts, it includes a number of exhibits, sideletters and the like. Conceptually, it is often thought of as being composed of two portions: Ex. A, which covers scripted network primetime programs; and the "front of book," which covers daytime programs, non-scripted programs, non-network programs, and the like.

---

* This is an unfortunate abbreviation, since "CBA" also stands for "collective bargaining agreement." Most union agreements – including the DGA BA, WGA MBA, SAG CBA and TVA, AFTRA Netcode, and others – are collective bargaining agreements.

† The formal name is the National Code of Fair Practice for Network Television Broadcasting. Notwithstanding the name, the Netcode doesn't just apply to network programs.

This division is a bit of an oversimplification, since two other exhibits form categories of their own: Ex. D (reuse in supplemental markets) and Ex. E (product made for pay TV and home video).

Thus, Ex. D applies to both front of book product and Ex. A product. And, Ex. E product is neither front of book nor Ex. A.

The front of book is still in effect in SAG-AFTRA, for the program types listed above (which are discussed in Chapter 15 only).

The Netcode does not cover basic cable. Nor is there a single Legacy-AFTRA basic cable agreement. Rather, there are four separate basic cable contracts, or templates, each of which Legacy-AFTRA modified on a show by show (or sometimes network by network) basis.

Two of the templates are similar to the Legacy-SAG Basic Cable Agreement, while the other two are not. In particular, residuals under the first pair of templates work the same way as under the SAG Basic Cable Agreement, while the second pair of templates embody a different approach to residuals. See p. 94 for details.

## IATSE

IATSE is a union composed of specialized locals, each with jurisdiction over different types of work and/or different regions. Each local has a collective bargaining agreement, and IATSE itself has several master agreements.

However, for most of the purposes of this book, only one agreement is important: the Basic Agreement, or BA, whose scope is limited to California and a number of other western and southwestern states, thirteen total.* IATSE residuals provisions are found in the BA. There are no residuals under other IATSE agreements, such as the IATSE Area Standards Agreement (ASA), and there are few residuals provisions in the individual locals' agreements.

As noted above, all IATSE residuals are paid in a lump sum to the union's pension and health plan, not to the individual members. Individual members are not "credited" with residuals – that is, the amount of residuals does not in itself affect the amount of pension or health benefits paid to the member. Thus, residuals benefit members in a very indirect fashion, i.e., by strengthening the overall fiscal soundness of the P&H plan.

## Teamsters

The Teamsters union represents drivers, location managers, casting directors, animal handlers, various office personnel, and others. None of these people receive residuals. However, they may receive benefits from the same pension and health plan as IATSE, so Teamsters too receive an indirect benefit from residuals.

## AFM

The American Federation of Musicians represents musicians who create music for motion pictures or television programs. There are two main agreements that concern us, the Basic Theatrical Motion Picture Agreement and the Basic Television Motion Picture Agreement.

As with SAG, there is also a Basic Cable Television Agreement. In addition, there's a new media sideletter to the Basic Cable Television Agreement. It addresses derivative new media based on underlying basic cable programs. (Other forms of new media are discussed in the 2009 Memorandum of Agreement that updated the theatrical and television agreements.) That sideletter is still in draft form and is not publicly available. This book discusses its terms, but such discussion should be understood as being of an interim nature and is dependent on the final outcome of negotiations.

Unlike the above the line unions, the AFM does not generally handle residuals. Rather, an organization called the Film Musicians Secondary Markets Fund (FMSMF) collects and processes residual payments from producers and distributes them to film and television musicians. (See AFM Basic Theatrical Motion Picture Agreement Ex. A and AFM Basic Television Motion Picture Agreement Ex. A.) The Fund was established in 1972.

---

* Alaska, Arizona, California, Colorado, Idaho, Montana, Nevada, New Mexico, Oregon, Texas, Utah, Washington and Wyoming.

One exception: in the unlikely event of theatrical release of free TV, pay TV or home video product (B3-B5), I am told that the AFM would collect and distribute those moneys; or allow and direct the Producer to make and distribute those payments to musicians through a signatory company or authorized payroll service. The FMSMF would not handle those payments.

## E. Dates

The residuals formulas have changed many times over the years. In general, the applicable formula is the one that was in effect when the screenplay was written (for WGA residuals) or the episode or movie was produced (commencement of principal photography).

Nonetheless, as previously mentioned, sometimes current formulas rather than past ones apply to reuse of older product. For instance, although the current new media reuse formulas were introduced in 2008, older product reused in new media are subject to these formulas. Cutoff dates apply, however, so some older product is not subject to new media reuse residuals.

The contracts may sometimes be ambiguous if a formula changes in mid-stream: for instance, while a screenplay is being written or while a program is being produced. There are no doubt customs and practices, and perhaps arbitration decisions, on these questions.

In general, the formulas discussed in this book apply to product written or produced as of the book's copyright date unless otherwise noted. Historical information is provided where available.

## F. Other Variables

Other variables that can affect the choice of applicable residuals formula include:

- **Budget:** Low-budget productions may not be subject to residuals in some cases. (There are different definitions of budget level depending on the union and the made-for medium.) See p. 128.

- **Program Length:** Formulas sometimes differ for one-hour TV shows as opposed to half-hours, or for long-form programs (say, 90 minutes or more) versus half-hour or one-hour episodes.

- **Daypart:** Residuals for programs made for or reused during the daytime or late night – i.e., outside of primetime – may be different than those for primetime. See p. 145.

- **Frequency:** Formulas are usually different for stripped serials – shows, such as soap operas, that televise a new episode every day as opposed to once a week. This book does not discuss such shows, except briefly starting on p. 145.

- **Pilots:** Formulas sometimes differ for pilots. See p. [tbd].

- **New Series:** Formulas sometimes differ for all or a portion of the first season of a new series. See p. [tbd].

- **Quasi-Networks:** For over a decade, residuals for shows on FOX were less than the three major broadcast networks, in recognition of the network's then-lower budgets and ad revenue. This is no longer true, but is still the case with the CW. See p. 40.

- **Choice of Contract or Residuals Formula:** In several contexts, producer have – or had – choices:

    1. Producers can choose one of three approaches to WGA basic cable residuals. See p. 94.

    2. Under AFM practice, made for home video product can be produced under the theatrical or the television contract, with different residuals resulting. See p. [tbd].

    3. Prior to merger of the SAG and AFTRA TV contracts in mid-2014, producers were able to choose to produce network primetime

shows under the Legacy-SAG TV Agreement or under Exhibit A of the Legacy-AFTRA Netcode. There are no differences in the residuals formulas themselves, but Legacy-AFTRA fixed residuals (such as C3-E3, K3) are generally about 3.5% higher than Legacy-SAG's (see p. [tbd] for explanation).*

4. Prior to merger of the SAG and AFTRA TV contracts in mid-2014, producers were able to choose to produce made for pay TV product or made for home video product (such as direct to video movies) under the Legacy-SAG TV Agreement or under Exhibit E of the Legacy-AFTRA Netcode. There is a slight difference in the residuals formulas. See p. 89.

5. Legacy-AFTRA offered four different basic cable templates, with different residuals formulas. See p. 95.

● **Waivers**: The unions and guilds sometimes grant individual waivers of certain requirements. SAG-AFTRA refers to these as "one production only" deals, or OPO.

---

* This difference actually applies to a wide range of reuse patterns – C3-E6, C7-D8 and K3-K6.

# 4. RESIDUALS FORMULAS

In the previous chapter, we examined the various factors that determine the choice of residuals formula. In this chapter, we take a closer look at the types of formulas.

● Section A examines what initial compensation covers – in other words, what uses the studio or producer can make before residuals are triggered at all. This varies by reuse pattern and is fundamental to understanding the way the formulas work once they kick in.

● Sections B-L survey the various types of formulas. The amount of detail in the sections varies somewhat. For instance, where a formula is used repeatedly throughout the book (such as percentage residuals), the discussion is more detailed, so that the same details won't have to be repeated throughout Chapters 5-12 as each reuse pattern is examined. On the other hand, formulas that are used in only one or two reuse patterns receive less focus in this chapter and are discussed in greater detail when the applicable reuse pattern is examined.

● Section M is a prelude to the next portion of the book: it explains the format used in Chapters 5-12, which examine each reuse pattern in the chart, cell by cell.

## A. What Initial Compensation Covers

Producers pay initial compensation (also referred to as upfront or guaranteed compensation) to writers, directors, actors, musicians and crew who work on a project. What does the producer get for his money? Or, to put it another way, what uses can a producer make of a project – such as a movie, TV program or new media production – before residuals kick in?

The virtually tautological answer is that the "initial use" of the project is residual-free. The reason for this is that initial compensation is deemed to cover not just the production of the project, but also its initial use.

But what constitutes the initial use? The answer depends on the made-for medium, and sometimes on other factors. (Doesn't it always?)

➜ Regardless of the made-for medium, the producer always gets some sort of residual-free initial use in the reuse market that corresponds to the made-for medium, e.g., cells B2, C3 or D3, F4, G5, H6, I7-J8 and I10 – roughly speaking, the cells along the diagonal of the table.

In addition, the producer may *also* get some residual-free use in other markets as well. This is particularly likely to be the case in two contexts: (a) some reuses of made for pay TV product in home video (G4) and made for home video product on pay TV (F5) may be residual-free, depending on the union; and (b) reuse of current-season TV programs and new home video product on ad-supported new media (K3-K6) starts with a multi-day residual-free window.

Let's take a closer look at what initial compensation covers in various reuse scenarios.

### Entire Market

Sometimes the producer gets an entire market without having to pay residuals – in other words, the entire reuse pattern is residual-free. The simplest example is theatrical use (or reuse) of a theatrical movie (B2). No residuals are ever due for such use: as discussed on p. 26, the movie can be played over and over again in theaters domestically and abroad, for decades on end, with no residuals.

The free market doesn't even have to be the initial market. For instance, it appears that there are no residuals for foreign television broadcasting of derivative and original new media (E7-E8).

### Runs

Sometimes the free period is measured in runs. For instance, a free TV program can only be aired once on free TV. After that, residuals will be due for any additional free TV broadcasts, whether network primetime (C3) or not (D3). So the producer gets one residual-free run.

What is a "run"? It's basically the right to air a program once in any given city.

More precisely, a made-for free TV product which has been telecast not more than once in any city in the United States or Canada is considered in its first run. It doesn't matter whether the run is in network primetime or not.

A made-for free TV product which has been telecast more than once but not more than twice in any city in the United States and Canada is in its second run.

A similar test applies in determining when a made-for-free TV product is in its third and succeeding runs.

The simplest example is that a show that has aired once in most cities in the U.S. is in its first run (so long as it hasn't aired twice anywhere). Such a show is in its first run. An example would be a network primetime broadcast of a show.

Here are some more subtle examples: a show that has aired once in Los Angeles but has not aired in any other city in the U.S. is in its first run. A show that's aired twice in Tucson but has not aired even once anywhere else is in its second run. A show that's aired five times in Fargo, three times in Topeka and once in every other media market in the country is in its fifth run. If it then airs once more in Topeka, it's still in its fifth run.

The first run is the initial run and is residual-free. That's what initial comp covers. The second run – which is the first rerun – will trigger residuals. If the second run is in network primetime, the formula in cell C3 will apply; if it's not, then we look to D3.

## Units of Product

There are other metrics too. Suppose you release *Valley of the Dudes* as a straight to video potboiler, knowing there's no chance you'd get a theatrical release. Luckily, you manage to move a boatload of discs, ensuring us the chance to see a sequel. What does initial compensation cover?

For DGA and SAG-AFTRA purposes, the residual-free period – the "initial use" – is measured in terms of the number of units sold. Residuals don't kick in until 100,000 bored gay stoners have scooped up your masterpiece. See cell G5. After that, the DGA residual is 2% of gross, while the SAG-AFTRA figure is 3 times that amount.

## Gross Break

And what about the WGA residual for *Valley of the Dudes*? There, the free period is measured in dollars not donuts. That is, the producer doesn't pay residuals until after her gross receipts have exceeded a specified threshold, referred to as a **gross break** or **gross plateau**. At that point, a 2% of gross formula kicks in.

## Time Period

In other instances, time is the measuring stick. Release a derivative new media production on a consumer paid new media platform (I7-J7) and you'll get a 26 week free window during which no residuals are payable. Release it on an ad-supported platform and you get 13 free weeks (K7). And if you release it on both, you get both free windows, generally speaking.

Or consider a made-for-free TV show. Yes, the producer gets one free run on broadcast television. However, she also gets a multi-day residual-free window on ad-supported new media (K3).

What does it mean to refer to a certain time period as a "free window"? Simply put, it means that no residuals are payable for the reuse made during that time period.

That means in the case of percentage residuals that any gross receipts derived from exploitation during the free window are not subject to residuals.

For instance, suppose a program generates $1,000 of gross receipts during the free window and $100 of gross receipts during a later time period. If the residual formula is 6% of gross, then the total residual will be $6 (i.e., 6% of $100), not $66 (i.e., 6% of $1,100). The $1,000 is ignored, because it was derived from exploitation during the free window.

What if the time periods aren't broken out? For instance, suppose that a producer receives a $12,000 license fee (i.e., producers gross) to cover a twelve-month period, of which the first 30 days is a free window.

In that case, the producer will have to allocate the $12,000 over the twelve months. The union would probably prefer a straight-line allocation of $1,000 per month, which means that $1,000 would be allocated to the free window and the remaining $11,000 would be subject to the 6% residual. However, the producer may assert that a disproportionate amount of viewership happens in the first month that a product is out, and argue that perhaps $2,000, $3,000 or more of the $12,000 license fee should be allocated to the free window, leaving a lesser amount than $11,000 to be subjected to residuals.

Such disagreements are probably more often resolved by compromise than by arbitration. There may be custom and practice in this area, but I'm not aware of what it is.

### Exhibition Days

Time can also work a bit differently. Here, the concept is exhibition days, which means the days on which a program is aired. Thus, if a program airs a few times on Jan. 15 and a few times on Feb. 14, that counts as two exhibition days, even though the elapsed time is 30 days.

Some formulas allow the producer a specified number of exhibition days residual-free, usually with a requirement that those days all occur within a year of each other. For instance, a formula might provide that the producer gets ten exhibition days within a year.

This is equivalent to saying that residuals kick in once ten exhibition days have occurred or a year has elapsed, whichever comes first.

Thus, for instance, if only eight exhibition days occur within the year, the producer does not get two more "free" (i.e., residual-free) exhibition days. Instead, once the year is up, the producer is out of luck if it used less than ten of its residual-free exhibition days. Those days are gone, baby.

Note that the formula does not mean that the producer can only use ten exhibition days in a year. The producer can allow the network to exhibit the program as many days as the two parties agree. But any exhibition days beyond ten will trigger residuals. The producer and network will want to negotiate the license terms and fee with this in mind.

Likewise, the producer is free to allow the network to exhibit the program for more than one year, but any such use will trigger residuals.

The exhibition day approach is seen with (1) some of the Legacy-AFTRA basic cable template formulas for basic cable reruns (see cell H6), (2) the SAG-AFTRA pay TV and home video to pay TV formula (F4-F5) and (3) the WGA pay TV to pay TV formula (F4), for instance.

As convoluted as the exhibition day approach may sound, it synchs up with cable channel business models that emphasize showing product in spurts. Since cable channels are usually nationwide, they frequently need to show episodes at least twice in a day to accommodate viewing patterns in the east and west coast time zones.

The need is less acute today, since people increasing record programs on DVR and watch at their leisure, but the exhibition day approach remains, as does the industry practice of multiple airings on a single day.

In order to avoid paying any residuals at all, producers not infrequently decide to license the network to show an episode on no more than ten exhibition days and to permit the network to show the episode only during the current television season.

## B. No Residuals

Now we begin to examine the different residuals formulas in detail.

### Formula

We start with the simplest one, which is no residuals at all or zero. This is indicated in the residuals chart as "$0" or "no residuals." (The two notations are equivalent.)

### Reuse Patterns

There are no residuals for:

- The initial use, as discussed in the preceding subsection.

- Theatrical to theatrical (B2).

## 4. Residuals Formulas and Related Matters – 55

- Original new media to ad-supported (K8).

- Many uses of derivative and original new media on consumer paid platforms (I7-J8).

- Derivative and original new media to theatrical (although there may be disagreement on this; see p. 123) (B7-B8).

- Derivative and original new media to foreign (although there may also be disagreement on this; see p. 120) (E7-E8).

- Any use or reuse of experimental new media (row 9).

- Possibly miscellaneous other circumstances.

### Pattern Analysis

Most occurrences of the no residuals situations are in pattern as to above the line unions. As to below the line unions:

- Most reuse doesn't generate IATSE residuals, other than reuse of Post-'60s (C2-G2), reuse in supplemental markets (F2-G3), reuse of traditional product on consumer-paid new media platforms (I2-J6) and certain reuse patterns for derivative or original new media.

- Most reuse doesn't generate AFM residuals other than the reuse patterns that generate IATSE residuals, and also free TV to foreign (E3) and a few other reuse patterns.

### Date Cutoffs

Reuse of older product may not generate residuals. Specifically, there are no residuals for:

- Most reuse of pre-Post-'60 theatrical product (B2-H2).

- Reuse of pre-7/1/71 theatrical product on ad-supported platforms (K2).

- Most reuse of exhausted free TV product (C3-H3, K3). See p. 28.

- Reuse of pay TV, home video and basic cable product produced prior to various date cutoffs.

- Reuse on consumer-paid new media platforms (I2-J6) of traditional product produced prior to various date cutoffs.

## C. Percentage Residuals

### Formula

These residuals are calculated as a percentage of gross receipts, which (in the case of licensing product to television or new media platforms) means the license fee that the producer received.

### Reuse Patterns

This formula is used for all reuse of theatrical product (B2-K2), all reuse in supplemental markets (F2-G3, F6-G8), all reuse in domestic basic cable (H2-H5, H7-H8) except basic cable to basic cable (H6).

### Pattern Analysis

As previously mentioned (see p. 5), percentage residuals are almost always in a lockstep pattern:

- The DGA and WGA percentages will be identical. The most common figures are 1.2% or 2%. This figure will be listed first in the particular cell, sentence or clause, without specification as to union. That is, "1.2%" would indicate that the DGA gets a 1.2% residual and the WGA also gets a separate 1.2% residual.[*]

- The SAG-AFTRA, Legacy-SAG and Legacy-AFTRA percentages will be 3 times the DGA/WGA percentage. This is indicated in the residuals chart in parentheses as ""SAG-AFTRA 3x" or "SAG/AFTRA 3x." Thus, for instance, if the DGA and WGA each get 1.2%, then SAG-AFTRA will get 3.6%.

- The IATSE percentage (if any) will be 4.5 times the DGA/WGA percentage. This is indicated in the residuals chart in parentheses as "IATSE 4.5x" or "IA 4.5x." Thus, for instance, if the DGA and WGA each get 1.2%, then IATSE will get 5.4% (because 1.2 x 4.5 = 5.4).

- The AFM percentage (if any) will be 1% (regardless of what the other unions' percentages

---

[*] The unions do not split the residual. 1.2% means they each get 1.2%, not that they each get 0.6%.

are). This will be indicated in the residuals chart (possibly in parentheses) as "AFM 1%."

● Exception: the AFM percentage (if any) for basic cable product or for derivative new media based on a basic cable TV series will usually be either (a) 3 times the DGA/WGA percentage (shown as "AFM BC 3x" or "AFM BC Deriv 3x") or (b) 3.6% (regardless of what the other unions' percentages are).

Here's an example from the chart (H2): "1.2% of gross (SAG-AFTRA 3x, IATSE 4.5x). AFM: 1% of gross." This means that the DGA residuals formula is 1.2% of gross, the WGA formula is also 1.2% of gross, the SAG-AFTRA formula is 3.6% of gross and the IATSE formula is 5.4% of gross.

### Date Cutoffs

There are no residuals for:

● Most reuse of **non**-Post-'60 theatrical product (B2-H2).

● Reuse of pre-7/1/71 theatrical product on ad-supported platforms (K2).

● Most reuse of exhausted free TV product (F3-H3). See p. 28.

● Reuse of pay TV, home video and basic cable product produced prior to various date cutoffs.

● Reuse on consumer-paid new media platforms (I2-J6) of traditional product produced prior to various date cutoffs.

### Terminology

The applicable terminology differs among (and sometimes within) the various union agreements. In general, "Producers gross," "Employers gross" and "Company's gross" mean the same thing, while "Distributors gross" may or may not mean something different.

Notably, "Producers gross" is defined in at least one place as the gross derived by the *distributor*!* That contract provision notes in an almost helpful tone that the "distributor" may or may not be the same as the "Company."

---

* See MBA Art. 15.A.3.a.

As if this isn't confusing enough, you'll also see the term "accountable receipts." It will usually be defined to either mean the same thing as one of the other "Gross" terms or to have a specified mathematical relationship to one of those terms.

### Number Mumbo-Jumbo

Some of the numbers in the book and chart don't directly appear in the union contracts. For instance, the chart's summary of the theatrical to TV formula (C2-E2) says in part "1.2% of gross (SAG 3x, IATSE 4.5x)." But if you look in the contracts for the corresponding numbers – DGA 1.2%, WGA 1.2%, SAG 3.6%, IATSE 5.4% – you won't find them.

Instead, you'll find 2%, 6% and 9%, and an instruction that an "arbitrary 40%" is to be deducted in order to cover distribution fees and expenses. Deducting 40% from something leaves 60%, of course. 60% of 2% of gross is equivalent to 1.2% of gross – or, as entertainment lawyers sometimes express it, "1.2% of 100% of gross."

So that's where the 1.2% comes from, and similarly as to the 3.6% and 5.4%. That's what the term "accountable receipts" may be used for: it's defined in some places as gross less that arbitrary 40%. But beware: the same term "accountable receipts" may mean something different in other parts of the multi-hundred page union contract. Keep your wits about you.

The AFM agreements can be even more confusing, since the 40% deduction isn't always explicitly noted. Nonetheless, AFM experts assure me that the agreement with the companies is for 1%. You can't believe everything you read,

And about that 40%: Is it really that expensive to license a movie to TV? Maybe not, but that's not your business, or mine either. The formula is what it is, unless the parties decide to renegotiate one day. In essence, the deal to today's eyes looks like "1.2% of gross," not "2% of gross less an arbitrary 40% deduction for distribution fees and expenses."

### Whose Gross?

We've been talking about gross, but whose gross are we talking about? Movies, TV shows and other entertainment product pass through a variety of hands as they generate money. Whose books should we be looking at?

# 4. Residuals Formulas and Related Matters – 57

In general, the answer is that we look at what the producer receives. So, for instance, if the producer licenses a movie to a domestic television network (C2) or sells it into syndication (C3), a lot of people will ultimately receive revenue – gross receipts – by the time the movie airs: the network, the syndication company and the local stations will all have some sort of accounting of how much they grossed from the movie.

None of those figures matter, however. The only thing that's usually relevant to the residuals calculation is how much the producer grossed: in other words, what license fee the producer obtained for the movie.

## Home Video

Now we look at a controversial and somewhat complex gross formula: the formula for home video residuals (G2-G3). You may think this of passing interest as home video revenues decline,* but it's not, since the EST formulas (J2-J6) are modeled on the home video formula.

The home video residual rate for the DGA and WGA starts at 1.5% of Producer's gross. After Producer's gross has reached $1 million, the residual rate becomes 1.8%. That higher figure then applies to all Producer's gross above the $1 million threshold. (It does not apply retroactively to the first million dollars.)

As usual, the SAG-AFTRA rate is 3 times as much (i.e., 4.5%, rising to 5.4%), the IATSE rate is 4.5 times as much (i.e., 6.75%, rising to 8.1%). The AFM percentage is 1% and does not rise at the $1 million breakpoint.

But here's the controversial part: for studios (but not for independent producers), Producer's gross is defined to mean 20% of the producer's worldwide wholesale gross. Thus, 80% of home video revenue is swept off the table before even beginning the calculation.

More precisely, that's the way the calculation works when the company has an affiliated video distribution company. Each of the studios do – for example, Warner Home Video is the entity that Warner Bros. studio uses. For independent producers and companies without a home video entity, Producer's gross is defined to mean 100% of worldwide wholesale gross.

[arb decision tbd]

Note, by the way, that for studios, $1 million in Producer's gross corresponds to $5 million in worldwide wholesale gross (because 20% of $5 million is $1 million). Thus, for studios, the first $5 million in worldwide wholesale gross is paid at the lower (1.5% / 4.5% / 6.75%) residual rate.

Let's see how the formula works with a studio example. If the worldwide wholesale gross is $100 million, then Producer's gross is $20 million (20% of $100 million). The WGA residual is $357,000 (1.5% of $1 million plus 1.8% of $19 million), the DGA residual is also $357,000, the SAG residual is $1,071,000, and the IATSE residual is $1,606,500.

Those figures add up to $3,391,500. The remainder – over $96 million – is not pure profit, of course. It covers disc manufacturing costs (these are low – well below $1 per disc), marketing, backend revenue sharing with A-list stars, and the like.

Still, even when those costs are deducted, quite a hefty haul remains. Why is the formula so seemingly studio-centric? In the early days, the logic was apparently two-fold: (a) videocassettes (which were then the technology in use) were expensive to manufacture, meaning that it made sense to set aside a large sum to cover the cost of goods, and (b) videocassettes were primarily distributed by independent distributers, who paid the studios a 20% royalty rate – the same rate paid for certain music distribution.†

Some within the guilds have long maintained that this formula is unfair, particularly since discs are far less expensive to manufacture than videocassettes initially were. Studios respond that they need the additional revenue in order to help offset losses on many movies, in an era

---

* Recall that :"home vide" means physical home video devices, specifically tapes and discs.

† Another place that the 20% figure shows up is in calculating gross receipts for purposes of gross or net profit participations. That is, only 20% of a studio's home video revenue is usually included in gross receipts for purposes of calculating gross or net participations (although some stars are able to achieve higher percentages). This development was apparently concurrent with the development of the 20% base for home video residuals.

where they say seven out of ten movies are not profitable at the box office.*

Now let's take a look at how the formula operates at a micro level. During the 2007-2008 WGA strike, writers complained that they only receive $0.04 per DVD in residuals. Is that figure correct?

Yes. In fact now, with DVD prices lower, the figure is more like three cents per DVD sold.

Here's the calculation. Suppose a movie DVD costs $12.99 from a retailer and the retailer is charging a 30% markup. That means the retailer is paying $9.99 per disc. Let's assume that money goes directly to the home video company (Paramount Home Video or whoever it might be), i.e., that there is no intermediate distributor or rack jobber taking a cut. Thus, the studio's wholesale gross is $9.99 per disc.

That means the Producer's gross is $2.00 (20% of $9.99). Multiply that by 1.5% and the result is three cents ($0.03).† That's the WGA residual; it gets split among the writers on the movie. The DGA also gets three cents, split among the director and assistant directors. SAG-AFTRA actors receive a total of nine cents, which is split among the various actors.‡ IATSE's pension and health plan receives 13.5 cents.

Of course, Blu-rays are priced a bit higher than DVDs, so the WGA residual may be around $0.04 per Blu-ray sold. But on the other hand, fewer people buy DVDs or Blu-ray discs these days. Instead they may rent them from a Redbox kiosk for $1.50 or less a night. The studios receive less money from these transactions than from a sale, and so the residual is much less as well.§

The 20% formula applies for films and televisions show made in or after 1984 or 1985 (the exact date varies by union). Earlier formulas were different; see the history grid on p. 83.

## Territoriality

"Gross" almost always means "worldwide gross."

## Intra-Company Transactions

Since the elimination of the Fin-Syn rules in the mid-1990's, production entities and broadcast television networks have been allowed to own one another. Today, all of the broadcast networks and many of the basic cable and pay TV channels are under common ownership with production entities.

That means that when a network pays a licensing fee to a producer, they may just be transferring money from one pot to another when the entire set of cookware resides in the same kitchen. Why not just lowball the license fee so that residuals – and payouts to gross and net profit participants – will be reduced?

Why not indeed. I don't want to start a food fight in a full-color forum, and there are disincentives to doing lowball deals. These include the fact that executives' bonuses may be based on how their own division performs, and the fact that snarky deals can lead to gnarly lawsuits.

Still, the unions want to be sure that the deal are done at fair market value. They obtained contract language in 2008 facilitating certain audits, but the language only applies to licensing to new media. And hovering over all of this is the argument that media consolidation itself depresses fair market value – and hence residuals – as a once-thriving independent television production business has turned into the domain of the studios and mini-majors.

## Allocation among Pictures

Rights in theatrical motion pictures are often sold in a bundle. Common scenarios are:

● **Movies to pay TV (F2):** Studios and mini-majors usually enter into multi-year output deals with pay TV channels. These deals cover most of a studio's theatrical product during the term of the agreement, though sometimes particular movies are set aside and licensed separately.

---

* Some guild members contend that at the time the 20% formula was negotiated, the studios promised they would increase it over time. However, it is not clear that there is any support for this claim.
† After $1 million in Producer's gross, the multiplier would be 1.8%, yielding a 3.6 cent residual.
‡ The split – i.e., the allocation of the residual among different members – is discussed starting on p. 129.
§ Alternately, people watch a movie online instead of buying or renting any kind of disc. In that case, new media residuals formulas apply. These are discussed elsewhere.

- **Movies to eRental (I2):** Streaming services like Netflix compete with pay TV channels and enter into output deals with the studios and mini-majors.

Often, the license fee is calculated on product by product basis (based on box office performance, for instance), in which case calculating the residual for each individual product is straightforward.

If, however, HBO or Netflix pays a blanket license fee covering multiple pictures, the studio has certainly received gross revenue, but how much should be allocated to each movie for purposes of the residuals calculation?

The answer in the guild agreements is simply that the allocation has to be "fair and reasonable." That's a common entertainment law catch-all that leaves a lot open to interpretation and arbitration.

### Allocation among Reuse Markets

Independent producers usually "sell" (i.e., license) their movies into foreign territories on an all-rights basis, meaning that a single distribution company in the territory acquires theatrical, free TV, basic cable, pay TV and home video rights, and often Internet rights as well (B2, E2, F2-G2, and possibly I2-K2).

Here, the question is how to allocate the gross receipts, particularly the non-returnable advance – generally known as the minimum guarantee, or MG – among the different reuse markets. (Usually, the MG is all the producer ever receives; overages are rare.)

Particularly critical is the weighting of the allocation between the theatrical rights, for which no residual is payable, and all the others, which are subject to residuals, albeit at varying percentages. Naturally, the producer would prefer to attribute as much of the advance as possible to the theatrical rights, while the union position is the opposite.

According to an entertainment attorney who represents many independent producers, 20% to 33% of the MG is typically allocated to theatrical, with the balance allocated equally between home video and television. An independent producer had slightly different numbers to share: 33% to 50% to theatrical, with the remainder split equally between video and TV. These were 2015 conversations; perhaps the custom and practice will change over time as physical home video continues to decline.

### Timing of Inclusion of Advances

Advances raise another question: timing. When are the advances included in gross?

Here's the answer, in language that is common to several of the union agreements:

Non-returnable advances are included in gross when a product is "available" and "identifiable" and the amount of the advance is "ascertainable."

A product is available when it first may be exhibited or otherwise exploited, or when it first may be sold or rented by a retailer.

A product is identifiable when the producer first knows or reasonably should have known that the given product is covered by a particular license or distribution agreement.

The amount of the advance is ascertainable if the advance is for one product, means of exhibition, and territory.

If the total amount of the advance is for more than one product, means of exhibition and/or territory, the producer must reasonably and fairly allocate such advance among the licensed products, exhibition markets and/or territorial markets. As each of these products, markets or territories becomes identifiable and available, the allocated portion is included in gross for that quarter.

See also the discussion of residuals deposits on p. 155.

### Exclusions from Gross

[tbd]

## D. Fixed Residuals at 100%

## Formula

With fixed residuals, the residual for each rerun is 100% of something.

That "something" – which is sometimes referred to as the "residual base" – is more or less related to the union wage scale for the work that the union member performed on the project. Typically, for the DGA and WGA, the residual base might be roughly 2/3 or more of the union wage scale for the work. Remember the difference between wage scales and actual wages: the WGA agreement might say that $35,000 is the scale (i.e., minimum) for writing a one-hour network primetime story and teleplay,* whereas the writer might actually have been paid $75,000 per his individual contract. That $75,000 figure is irrelevant. The residual for a network primetime rerun (C3) may be about $24,000, which is approximately 2/3 of the $35,000 scale figure. (See MBA Art. 15.B.1.b.2.(a) for the exact figure.)

To be clear, the residual is not calculated as 2/3 of the scale wages. Rather, the WGA MBA has tables of scale wages and tables of residuals, and it happens that the ratio of the two tables is about 2/3.

What about a one-hour series that is not for network primetime – i.e., it is for non-network (e.g., first-run syndication) or for network use in a non-primetime daypart? Here, the scale wage for a one-hour story and teleplay might be about $25,000 (see MBA Art. 13.B.7.c) but the residual might still be about $24,000 (see MBA Art. 15.B.1.b.2.(a)), which is almost as much as the initial scale wage.

For SAG-AFTRA (and Legacy-SAG and Legacy-AFTRA Ex. A), the formula is a bit different. The residual base is 100% of the actor's total actual compensation (TAC), but subject to a ceiling called the primetime residual ceiling. Thus, if scale for a day player is about $900 per day (see SAG CBA Sch. A, Sec. 2 for the exact figure) but the day player was paid $3,000 for two days' work, then her residual will be $3,000 (which is her TAC). However, if she was paid $10,000 (perhaps she's a former star doing a cameo), then her residual would be about $3,500 if that is the ceiling in the union agreement. (See SAG TVA Sec. 18(b)(1)b) for the exact ceiling.)

[tbd precise definition of TAC – excludes premium o/t, penalties, etc.]

The primetime residual ceilings vary depending on program length (e.g., half-hour vs. one hour).

Although the SAG-AFTRA, Legacy-SAG and Legacy-AFTRA formulas are the same, the actual amount of the residual for identical work will generally differ, because Legacy-AFTRA minimums are 3.5% higher than SAG-AFTRA's or Legacy-SAG's throughout most of the contract year. This is a result of the 2007-2009 bargaining cycle: AFTRA made a deal with the studios in summer 2008, but in an echo of the 2007-2008 WGA strike, SAG did not until almost a year later due to opposition and political turmoil within SAG. (See my book HOLLYWOOD ON STRIKE! for a history of this period.)

A key point to remember is that fixed residuals are completely unrelated to producers gross. Instead, there are tables of dollar figures in the union agreements that allow you to determine the residual. You can determine the residual just by looking in the guild agreement, so long as you know what the talent did – e.g., did the writer write the story and teleplay, or just the teleplay; how many days did the actor work; etc. For fixed residuals, you don't need any knowledge of how much revenue the producer derived.

## The 2010/2011 Primetime Freeze

A notable change in the 2010/2011 negotiating cycle affected the residual calculation for network primetime residuals: the calculation of those residuals was frozen in particular ways. Specifically, the DGA and WGA residual bases were frozen (i.e., not increased) for the three contract years in the cycle (2011-2014) (see discussion in Subsection G below) and the SAG and AFTRA primetime residuals ceiling did not increase.

**The freeze only applied to reuse in network primetime.** In particular, reuse in other than network primetime (D3) and in foreign (E3) was unaffected.

When product made for pay TV, home video, basic cable, derivative new media, or original new media is reused on free TV or foreign, the re-

---

* See MBA Art. 13.B.7.d(3) for the actual, exact figure.

siduals formula is often similar to the formula for use of free TV product in such markets. However, the primetime residuals freeze is apparently not intended to affect those reuse patterns (C4-C8).

### Reuse Patterns

This type of residual is used for reuse of TV, home video and derivative and original new media product on network primetime (C3-C8). See further discussion starting on p. 70.

### Pattern Analysis

Most reuse patterns are roughly in pattern, but there are significant deviations. See discussion of cells C3-C8 in Chapters 6, 8, 9 & 12.

### Date Cutoffs

No residuals for most reuse of exhausted free TV product (F3-H3). See p. 28.

### Terminology

This type of residuals is called fixed residuals, because they are defined with reference to tables in the guild agreements rather than with reference to the employer's gross receipts. As mentioned earlier, the terminology is a bit confusing, though, because those tables change over time. Also, which table is applicable, and which row and column, depends on things like the length of the program (half-hour, one-hour, etc.) and the type or amount of work the guild member did on the program.

## E. Fixed Residuals – Run by Run Declining Percentage

### Formula

The *basis* of this type of residual is similar to the fixed residuals described in the preceding subsection, but rather than being paid at 100% of something, the employer gets a discount: the percentage starts at 50%, 40% or even lower, and then declines with each rerun until a floor is reached, with all further reruns payable at the floor percentage. So, the first rerun (more formally known as the second run) might be paid at 50% of the residual base, the third run at 40% of the residual base, the fourth run at 25% of the residual base, and so on.

Also, the "something" – the residual base – is not necessarily the same as the residual base for fixed residuals at 100%. That is, for the DGA or WGA there may be a separate table to refer to.

In the case of SAG-AFTRA (and Legacy-SAG and Legacy-AFTRA Ex. A), rather than total actual compensation (TAC), the residual is based on total applicable minimum (TAM). To understand the difference, consider the day player example in the preceding section who worked two days and was paid $3,000. Although her TAC is $3,000, her TAM is only about $1,800 – that is 2 days times the scale minimum (the applicable minimum) of about $900 per day.

Note that there is never a ceiling with TAM.

As discussed in the preceding subsection, although the SAG-AFTRA, Legacy-SAG and Legacy-AFTRA formulas are the same, the actual amount of the residual for identical work will generally differ, because Legacy-AFTRA minimums are 3.5% higher than SAG-AFTRA's or Legacy-SAG's throughout most of the contract year.

### Reuse Patterns

This type of formula is used for reuse of TV, home video and derivative and original new media product in other than network primetime (D3-D8), and for basic cable to basic cable (H6). See further discussion starting on p. 72.

### Pattern Analysis

Most reuse patterns are roughly in pattern, but there are significant deviations. See discussion of cells D3-D8 & H6 in Chapters 6, 8, 9 & 12.

### Date Cutoffs

No residuals for most reuse of exhausted free TV product (F3-H3). See p. 28.

## F. Fixed Residuals – Year by Year Declining Percentage

### Formula

These residuals are similar to the run by run declining residuals described in the preceding subsection, but the percentage declines with each *year* of use until a floor is reached, with all further years payable at the floor percentage.

Note the subtle yet significant distinction between this type of formula and the run by run declining formula in the preceding subsection: in the year by year formula, the director, writer or actor gets only one payment that covers an entire year of reuse, no matter how many people view the movie or TV episode. In contrast, the run by run formula pays for each rerun.

Another difference: the year by year declining formulas use the network primetime residual base – that is, the same base used for fixed residuals at 100% (Subsection D above, not Subsection E). In the case of SAG-AFTRA and Legacy, that means that year by year declining residuals use TAC subject to a ceiling, rather than TAM.

### Reuse Patterns

This type of formula is used for reuse of high budget SVOD product on subscription consumer pay new media platforms such as Netflix and Amazon Prime (I10).

### Pattern Analysis

Pattern is maintained.

### Date Cutoffs

The high budget SVOD provisions became effective with the beginning of the 2014 contract cycle, mid-2014 for the above the line unions.

## G. Fixed Residuals – A Closer Look at the Residual Base

In the interest of simplicity, we introduced fixed residuals in the preceding three subsections without much specificity as to the residual base. Now we take a closer look.

### DGA

The DGA BA has several residual base tables for dramatic programming:

- Art. 11-101(b)(1)(i) applies to reruns in network primetime (C3) paid at 100% and to residuals for reuse of high budget SVOD product on subscription consumer pay new media platforms (I10).

- Art. 11-101(b)(2) applies to reruns in other than network primetime (D3) and a range of other contexts, such as basic cable product rerun on basic cable (H6).

- However, Art. 24-301 (instead of 11-101(b)(2)) applies for multicamera pilots and series – generally, sitcoms.

- There is a third table, in Art. 11-102(d), for foreign residuals (E3, discussed in Subsection I below), but the residual base amounts are identical to Art. 11-101(b)(2).

- There is another table, in Art. 11-101(b)(1)(ii), but it applies to non-dramatic (i.e., unscripted) programming.

The residual base amounts are on the order of 80% of the wage minimums. They usually increase each contract year by the same percentage as the DGA wage minimums do. However, in the 2010-2011 negotiating cycle, the network primetime residual (the table in Art. 11-101(b)(1)(i) was frozen, presumably due to the Great Recession, even though the minimum wage scales and other residual bases increased.

### WGA

The WGA approach to residual base for network primetime reruns (C3) has changed several times recently.

- From at least the 1980's (and perhaps earlier) through May 1, 2011, the residual base was the "applicable minimum" (AM) (and the term "residual base" was generally not used). This sounds like it refers to the scale wage table (the table of minimums) that applies to the work the writer did, but that's only partially true:

    ♦ If the writer wrote for a show that is initially exhibited in other than network primetime, the minimum wage scale is found in MBA Art. 13.B.7.a, b & c, and those tables would also be used as the applicable minimum for residuals calculation purposes.

♦ ➔ However, if the writer wrote for a network primetime show, the minimum wage scale is found in Art. 13.B.7.d(1), (2) & (3), but for residuals calculation purposes the tables found in MBA Art. 13.B.7.a, b & c are used. That is, the other than network primetime wage minimums are used for residuals purposes even though the work was done for network primetime and even though the reuse is in network primetime.

If you're wondering why, the answer is simply "because that's what they negotiated." The residual would be higher if the 7.d table was used, but that's not what the parties agreed on.

- Just as for the DGA, in the 2010-2011 negotiating cycle the network primetime residual was frozen even though the minimum wage scales increased. Thus, from May 2, 2011 – May 1, 2014, the residual base is the figures found in MBA Art. 13.B.7.a, b & c *as of May 2, 2010 – May 1, 2011*, even though the wage scales are found in the 2011-2014 version of MBA Art. 13.B.7.

- In the 2013-2014 negotiating cycle, the parties decoupled the primetime residuals provisions from the wage scales. Now, the residual base for network primetime reruns (C3) is found in the residuals provision itself (Art. 15.B.1.b.(2)(a)), without any cross-reference to Art. 13.

However, to add to the confusion, the WGA approach to other than network primetime reruns (D3) has not changed during the above time period – and it uses the MBA Art. 13.B.7.a, b & c minimums (which increase in each contract year). For these reruns, it is still necessary to cross-reference from Art. 15 to Art. 13. So, for instance, if a program was written for network primetime then reruns in syndication, the minimum wage scale is found in Art. 13.B.7.d(1), (2) & (3), but for residuals calculation purposes the tables found in MBA Art. 13.B.7.a, b & c are used.

For reuse of high budget SVOD product on subscription consumer pay new media platforms (I10), the network primetime residual base found in Art. 15.B.1.b.(2)(a) is used.

### SAG-AFTRA (and Legacy)

See discussion of TAC and TAM in the preceding subsections.

### IATSE

Not applicable. IATSE does not participate in any fixed residuals.

### AFM

Generally not applicable. Except for basic cable product (or derivative new media based on an underlying basic cable show) reused on ad-supported new media (K6-K7), AFM does not participate in any fixed residuals.

## H. AFTRA Exhibition Day Residuals

[tbd – use new color and add to color code charts]

## I. Hybrid Formulas

### Formula

Some formulas are a hybrid of fixed and percentage residuals.

### Reuse Patterns

Hybrid formulas are used with the following reuse patterns:

- Free TV to foreign (E3): various percentages of the residual base are payable as certain levels of gross receipts are achieved. Finally, after even greater gross receipts, the formula switches to a percentage of gross. See further discussion starting on p. 78.

- **Pay TV, home video and basic cable to foreign (E4-E6):** These are similar to free TV to foreign.

- **Traditional media to ad-supported (K3-K6):** These are complex formulas. They bear no relation to the foreign TV formulas, but are depicted in the same color because they too are hybrid formulas involving both fixed residual and percentage residual components.

- **Derivative media to ad-supported (K7):** This has echoes of the formula for traditional media to ad-supported (K3-K6), but it distinctly different. It is, however, also a hybrid formula.

### Pattern Analysis

The foreign reuse patterns are generally in pattern, but the new media ones have some deviations from pattern. See discussion of individual cells in the applicable chapters.

### Date Cutoffs

No residuals for most reuse of exhausted free TV product in foreign (E4-E6). See p. 28. Date cutoffs vary for new media. See discussion of individual cells in the applicable chapters.

## J. Unique Pay TV and Home Video Formulas

The formulas for pay TV and home video to pay TV and home video (F4-G5) are their own unique beasts. Several of the formulas are percentage residuals, but they depend on factors such as the number of DVDs sold or the achievement of certain levels of gross receipts. Because of these unusual factors and the fact that there is little pattern, they're coded in their own color. All of them are discussed in the applicable sections of Chapter 8.

## K. Unique Theatrical Reuse Formulas

Also unique are the formulas for theatrical release of television and home video product (B3-B6). They are discussed in Chapter 10.

## L. Specified Dollar-Amount Residuals

Several formulas are simply flat dollar amounts (e.g., $2,000 per year of reuse) that have no relation to wage scales and thus are not "fixed residuals" in the usual sense. There is no agreed terminology for these residuals, so this book calls them specified dollar-amount residuals.

## M. Format of Chapters 5-12

The next eight chapters focus on reuse patterns cell by cell. The chapter and section format is as follows:

### Chapter Format

Chapters 5-12 discuss the individual reuse patterns. Each chapter relates to a group of related cells of the chart. That generally means that each chapter discusses most of a specific row, except that there are separate chapters for several columns: supplemental markets (F2-G3), new media reuse of traditional product (I2-K6) and theatrical reuse of television and home video product (B3-B6).

Each chapter begins with an introduction and reminder of key common aspects of the reuse patterns discussed, along with cross references to the page in Chapter 3 where more details appear. The chapter heading is color coded for the types of formulas that appear in the chapter.

### Section Format

Each section discusses a single cell of the chart and contains some or all of the following subsections. Subsections are omitted where inapplicable or if the relevant information was unavailable.

- Mini Chart: A small version of the residuals chart with the applicable cell indicated by a heavy outline. Related cells are indicated with lighter outlines. You'll note that sometimes the outline thickness is a bit random or the outline appears broken. This is due to Word bugs that appear to be insurmountable.☹

- Contents of Cell (with cell reference): The text that appears in the corresponding cell of the chart, usually without alteration. See p. 191 for a table of abbreviations.

- Notes in Other Cells: A reference to, and copy of, notes relating the cell discussed in section if the notes appear in other cells.

- Explanation: An explanation of the applicable formula. The explanation is brief if the formula was thoroughly discussed in Chapter 4, which is usually the case, or detailed if not.

- Dates of Applicability: The dates of product to which the formula(s) in the cell are applicable.

- Sideletters: If there are Sideletters that affect the formula they are discussed or cross-referenced.

- No Residuals: The unions and situations under which no residuals are payable.

- Pattern Analysis: The degree to which pattern is or is not maintained.

- Related Cells: A list of the cell(s) that influenced or were influenced by the reuse pattern in the cell and the key differences, if any. For instance, the formula for reuse on EST platforms was influenced by the physical home video formula.

- Book Cross References: Page references in the book for the made-for market, reuse market, type of formula, History Grid and any other relevant discussions.

- Contract References: Abbreviated references to the sections of the collective bargaining agreements where the applicable provisions appear. See p. 177 for guides to finding the contracts and the new media sideletters and p. 191 for a table of abbreviations. The references are "pinpoint cites," so you'll want to look at adjacent contract sections for additional details.

- History: The history of the reuse pattern is discussed at the end of the section or, in some cases, at the end of the chapter.

Section and subsection headings are in the color(s) that correspond to the formulas that apply to the reuse pattern(s) summarized.

## 5. MADE FOR THEATRICAL

Theatrical exhibition of theatrical motion pictures never generates residuals. Reuse of theatrical motion pictures in other media does generate residuals – it's always a percentage residual – for all five applicable unions (i.e., no residuals for AFTRA, because AFTRA doesn't have jurisdiction over theatrical product), but only if the movie is a Post-'60 picture. *In addition, post-1948 Universal product also generates WGA residuals.* For details, see p. 26.

### A. Theatrical to Theatrical

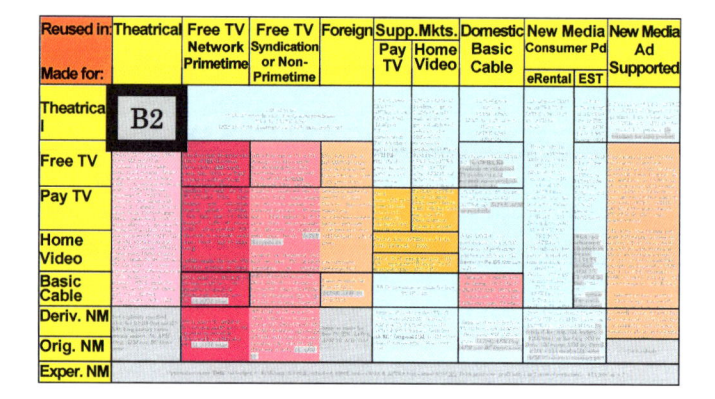

### Contents of Cell B2

No residuals (even for rereleases, foreign theatrical releases, or extended runs).

### Explanation/No Residuals

All theatrical use of made for theatrical product is considered to be an initial use (i.e., in the initial market). Thus, there are no residuals, even when the film is released in foreign theaters, and even if the film is rereleased, or runs for many years (domestically or foreign).

### Pattern Analysis

Pattern is maintained – i.e., the above explanation applies to all unions.

### Book Cross References

Made for theatrical: p. 26.
Reused in theatrical: p. 38.
What initial comp covers (entire market): p. 52.
No residuals: p. 54.

### Contract References

None. The absence of residuals is implicit in the lack of any provision for them.

## B. Theatrical to Free TV and Foreign TV

Reuse on network primetime: p. 39.
Reuse on other than network primetime: p. 40.
Foreign reuse: p. 41.
Percentage residuals: p. 55.

### Contract References

DGA BA Paras. 19-101 to 104.
WGA MBA Arts. 15.A.2, 3 (preamble), 3.a, b.
SAG CBA Sec. 5.A.
IATSE BA Sec. XIX(b)(1)-(3).
AFM Theatrical Agt. Sec. 15(b)(i)(1) & (2).

### Contents of Cells C2-E2

1.2% of gross (1.8% if "outright sale"; rarely used provision) (SAG 3x, IATSE 4.5x).

AFM: 1% of gross (1.5% if outright sale).

### Explanation

DGA: 1.2% of gross (1.8% if outright sale).
WGA: same as DGA.
SAG: 3 times this percentage (i.e., 3.6% or 5.4%).
IATSE: 4.5 times this percentage (i.e., 5.4% or 8.1%).
AFM: 1% of gross.

The "outright sale" figures are rarely used.

### No Residuals

As noted in cell A2, no residuals unless the picture is a Post-'60 *(or WGA post-1948 Universal).*

### Pattern Analysis

Pattern is maintained.

### Related Cells

This is a common formula for reuse of theatrical product and is also used for all other reuse of theatrical product on TV (F2 theatrical to pay TV and H2 theatrical to domestic basic cable) and reuse of theatrical product on Internet-based platforms that are analogous to TV (I2 theatrical to eRental and K2 theatrical to ad-supported). One difference: none of these other reuse patterns have a special provision for outright sales.

### Book Cross References

Made for theatrical: p. 26.
Post-'60 theatrical motion pictures: p. 27.

### History

| Date | Unions | Event |
|------|--------|-------|
| 1946 | AFM | Collective bargaining agreement with major studios and larger independent producers prohibits reuse of theatrical movies via television (if the movie contains music created under AFM jurisdiction) |
| 1948 | SAG | Agt. w/producers includes "stop-gap clause" re residuals |
| 1951 | AFM | 1946 agt. changed to allow reuse on TV, provided that movie is completely re-scored by a new orchestra and that a reuse fee of 5% of gross receipts be paid to a trust fund |
| 1952 | SAG | Deal with Monogram Pictures for residuals on 70 post-1948 films. See Billboard, August 9, 1952 ([tbd]). |
| 1952 | AFM | Re-scoring abolished, replaced by requirement that a fixed residual equal to 50% of 1952 scale be paid to the original musicians; 5% gross payment also continues to be required |
| 1950's | SAG | Monogram deal extended to other "poverty row" studios (i.e., non-majors) |
| 1954 | AFM | 1952 deal renewed |
| 1955 | AFM | Mid-contract, union president James Petrillo orders that the 50% scale payments be made to the trust fund rather than the individual musicians |
| 1956-1957 | AFM | Four California state lawsuits filed by AFM members against |

| Date | Unions | Event |
|---|---|---|
| | | the union: *Anderson v. AFM* (challenging diversion to trust fund of phonograph industry reuse payments previously made to the individual musicians); *Atkinson v. AFM* (challenging diversion to trust fund of the payments for TV reuse of theatrical films (noted in the previous paragraph)); *Bellmann v. AFM* (challenging requirement of 5% trust fund payment for TV reruns of TV films, see 1951 and 1956-1957 AFM entries on p. 71); and *Bain v. AFM* (challenging diversion to trust fund of radio transcription (i.e., recording) industry reuse payments); note also *Shapiro v. Rosenbaum* (1959, federal court, re phonograph record trust fund) and *Republic Productions v. AFM* (below) |
| Betw. 1955-1957 | AFM | 50% scale payments eliminated, and royalty rate increased from 5% to 6% |
| 1957 | AFM | *Republic Productions v. AFM* (federal court) seeks to end requirement of payment to trust funds; suit dismissed in 1965 |
| 1957 | SAG | Agts. w/ C & C Television Corp. and Associated Artists Corp. provide for residuals for TV broadcast of 82 post-1948 RKO movies and 12 post-1948 Warner Bros. movies |
| 1958 | AFM | Several-month strike over issue |

| Date | Unions | Event |
|---|---|---|
| | | of TV reuse of theatrical films ends inconclusively due to intra-union strife |
| 1958 | MGA | Musicians Guild of America (LA-based breakaway group from AFM) agrees with major studios to a deal with no reuse payments, in exchange for certain guaranteed employment and strict limitations on reuse; similar deal reached for reuse of theatrical movies on TV |
| 1959 | AFM | *Anderson* plaintiffs prevail in trial court |
| 1959 | SAG | "TV residuals increase 33%" (per SAG website; unclear if this is free TV reruns or TV reuse of movies) |
| 1960 | WGA | Strike regarding reuse of theatrical motion pictures on broadcast television; strike ends with agreement for residuals for Post-'60's |
| 1960 | SAG | Overlapping strike on same issue; ends on same terms as WGA |
| 1960 | AFM | *Anderson, Atkinson, Bellmann* and *Bain v. AFM* settled in plaintiffs' favor while *Anderson* is on appeal |
| [1960] | IATSE, DGA | Residuals achieved |
| 1961 | AFM | Theatrical film agreement establishes 1% gross residual payable pro rata to the musicians |
| 1960's | Various | [formula changes several times] |

## C. Theatrical to Domestic Basic Cable

| Reused in: | Theatrical | Free TV Network Primetime | Free TV Syndication or Non-Primetime | Foreign | Supp. Mkts. Pay TV | Home Video | Domestic Basic Cable | New Media Consumer Pd eRental | EST | New Media Ad Supported |
|---|---|---|---|---|---|---|---|---|---|---|
| Made for: | | | | | | | | | | |
| Theatrical | | **C2-E2** | | | | | **H2** | | | |
| Free TV | | | | | | | | | | |
| Pay TV | | | | | | | | | | |
| Home Video | | | | | | | | | | |
| Basic Cable | | | | | | | | | | |
| Deriv. NM | | | | | | | | | | |
| Orig. NM | | | | | | | | | | |
| Exper. NM | | | | | | | | | | |

### Contents of Cell H2

1.2% of gross (SAG 3x, IATSE 4.5x). AFM: 1% of gross.

### Explanation

DGA: 1.2% of gross.
WGA: same as DGA.
SAG: 3 times this percentage (i.e., 3.6%).
IATSE: 4.5 times this percentage (i.e., 5.4%).
AFM: 1% of gross.

### No Residuals

[As noted in cell A2, no residuals unless the picture is a Post-'60 (or *WGA post-1948 Universal*).] [No residuals unless picture is post-7/1/71?]

### Pattern Analysis

Pattern is maintained.

### Related Cells

C2-D2 theatrical to free TV is the model (p. 67) but with no provision here for "outright sale."

### Book Cross References

Made for theatrical: p. 26.
Post-'60 theatrical motion pictures: p. 27.
Reuse in basic cable: p. 42.
Percentage residuals: p. 55.

### Contract References

DGA BA Para. 18-102 (2nd to last para).
WGA MBA Art. 58.
SAG CBA Sec. 5.A (implicit; per Guild).
[IATSE ?]
[AFM ?]

### History

| Date | Unions | Event |
|---|---|---|
| 1971 | All (but AFTRA, na) | Residual established |

70 – Entertainment Residuals: A Full Color Guide

# 6. MADE FOR FREE TV

## A. Free TV to Network Primetime

| Reused in:<br>Made for: | Theatrical | Free TV Network Primetime | Free TV Syndication or Non-Primetime | Foreign | Supp. Mkts. Pay TV | Supp. Mkts. Home Video | Domestic Basic Cable | New Media Consumer Pd eRental | New Media Consumer Pd EST | New Media Ad Supported |
|---|---|---|---|---|---|---|---|---|---|---|
| Theatrical | | | | | | | | | | |
| Free TV | | C3 | D3 | | | | | | | |
| Pay TV | | C4 & C5 | | | | | | | | |
| Home Video | | C4 & C5 | | | | | | | | |
| Basic Cable | | C6 | | | | | | | | |
| Deriv. NM | | C7 & C8 | | | | | | | | |
| Orig. NM | | C7 & C8 | | | | | | | | |
| Exper. NM | | | | | | | | | | |

### Contents of Cell C3

One free run, then per-run: 100% of: RB (Residual Base, DGA); RB (WGA); or TAC subject to ceiling (Total Actual Comp., SAG-AFTRA). IATSE, AFM no residuals.

### Notes in Other Cells

C2-E2: C3-H3, I3-J3?, K3 are subj. to H3 note re exhausted free TV product.

H3: No . . . residuals on exhausted TV product (i.e., if network rerun residuals not still payable (generally, pre-7/1/71 product))

### Explanation

A program made for free TV gets one "free run" on domestic free TV, which can be either network primetime or not (i.e., C3 or D3). Thereafter, each network primetime run triggers a residual of 100% of the DGA residual base (RB), WGA residual base (RB, but formerly applicable minimum (AM)) or SAG-AFTRA total actual compensation (but TAC is subject to a specified ceiling).

The DGA and WGA formulas are similar to each other. Both use tables to determine the residual, although the dollar figures and table structures differ. See p. 62. SAG-AFTRA, Legacy-SAG and Legacy-AFTRA use a different approach from the DGA and WGA. The residual is the performer's total actual compensation (TAC), subject to a "primetime residual ceiling." See p. 59.

[DGA BA 11-302 re combined programs][applies to all free TV programs, maybe others too]

### Sideletters and Other Exceptions

There are several sideletters (essentially, addenda) and other provisions that provide for reduced residuals under certain circumstances. These are as follows:

[promotional launch, MBA p. 141 print, 155 pdf]

#### The CW

[Reuse on The CW is paid at a reduced percentage of network rates.] See p. 39.

BA 11-101(h) (also MyNetwork TV)

#### Supersized Episodes

[DGA SL 26]

#### Interrupted Programs

SL to 15.B.1, WGA 2011 MOA p. 32

### No Residuals

No residuals for IATSE, AFM, or exhausted TV product (the latter as noted in H3).

### Pattern Analysis

Pattern is generally maintained: the formulas are different but echo each other.

### Related Cells

D3 free TV to other than network primetime is also a fixed residual, but with declining percentages. Also, the residuals bases are different.

C4-C5 pay TV and home video to free TV are the same as C3, with slight deviation.

C6 basic cable to network primetime is the same as C3 for DGA, SAG and sometimes WGA and AFTRA.

C7-D8 derivative and original new media to free TV is related to C3-D3, but with differences in many details.

## Book Cross References

Made for free TV: p. 27.
Exhausted free TV product: p. 28.
Reuse on network primetime: p. 39.
What initial comp covers (runs): p. 52.
Fixed residuals at 100%: p. 59.
Fixed residuals – the residual base: p. 62.

## Contract References

DGA BA Para. 11-101(b)(1)(i).

WGA MBA Arts. 15.B.1.a, b(1), (2)(a), (d), (3), and SL to Art. 15.B.1.

SAG-AFTRA and L-SAG TVA Secs. 18(a), (b)(1), (3), (4).

L-AFTRA Netcode Ex. A § 3.

## History

| Date | Unions | Event |
|---|---|---|
| Note: see also related notes on p. 77 | | |
| 1933 | Radio Equity | Proposal regarding reuse fees |
| 1941 | AFRA | Transcription Code agt. requires reuse fees in radio (fixed residuals) |
| 1945 | AFM | Union forbids members from playing on live or recorded TV programs |
| 1948 | AFM | 1945 ban lifted |
| 1951 | AFM | Television film and trust agts. require 5% gross reuse fees |
| 1952 | SAG | Residuals established for small number of reruns |
| 1953 | WGA | Residuals established for up to 5 reruns |
| 1955 | SAG | Strike for increased residuals |
| 1956 | AFTRA | Residuals established |
| 1956-1957 | AFM | *Bellmann v. AFM* (challenging requirement of 5% trust fund payment for TV reruns of TV films, see 1956-1957 AFM entry in history grid beginning on p. 67) |
| 1958 | AFM | Revue Productions agt. provides for 1% payment to trust fund instead of 5%. Desilu Productions agt. provides for diminishing flat fee payments (and no percentage payments) to trust fund for runs 2-5. |
| 1958 | MGA | Musicians Guild of America (LA-based breakaway group from AFM) agrees with major studios to a deal with no reuse payments, in exchange for certain guaranteed employment and strict limitations on reuse; similar deal reached for reuse of theatrical movies on TV |
| 1959 | SAG | "TV residuals increase 33%" (per SAG website; unclear if this is free TV reruns or TV reuse of movies) |
| 1959 or 1960 | AFM | Television Film Agt. replaces 5% gross residual with fixed residuals for runs 2-7 |
| 1960 | [DGA, WGA, SAG] | Royalty Plan adopted for residuals calculation |
| 1960 | AFM | *Bellmann* settled (see 1959 and 1960 AFM entries on p. 67) for legal fees and court costs (since effectively mooted by 1959 or 1960 Television Film Agt.) |
| 1961 | AFM | TV Film Agt. w/networks established declining fixed residuals payable to musician for runs 2-6 |
| 1970 | WGA | Residuals payable for 9 reruns |
| 1974 | SAG | Residuals payable in perpetuity, rather than just two reruns; [also, fees increased 25%?] |
| 1977 | WGA | Residuals payable in perpetuity |
| 2010 | SAG | PT ceilings frozen at 2010 levels |
| 2011 | DGA, WGA | RBs and AMs frozen at 2010 levels |

## B. Free TV to Other Than Network Primetime

| Reused in: | Theatrical | Free TV Network Primetime | Free TV Syndication or Non-Primetime | Foreign | Supp. Mkts. Pay TV | Supp. Mkts. Home Video | Domestic Basic Cable | New Media Consumer Pd eRental | New Media Consumer Pd EST | New Media Ad Supported |
|---|---|---|---|---|---|---|---|---|---|---|
| **Made for:** | | | | | | | | | | |
| Theatrical | | | | | | | | | | |
| Free TV | | C3 | D3 | | | | | | | |
| Pay TV | | | D4 & D5 | | | | | | | |
| Home Video | | | | | | | | | | |
| Basic Cable | | | D6 | | | | H6 | | | |
| Deriv. NM | | | D7 | | | | | | | |
| Orig. NM | | | | | | | | | | |
| Exper. NM | | | | | | | | | | |

### Contents of Cell D3

After free run on C3 or D3 & subject to SLs: run by run declining from 50% (network) or 40% (off-net) to 5% of RB/AM/TAM (Total Applicable Min., SAG-AFTRA). IATSE, AFM $0.

### Notes in Other Cells

C2-E2: C3-H3, I3-J3?, K3 are subj. to H3 note re exhausted free TV product.

H3: No . . . residuals on exhausted TV product (i.e., if network rerun residuals not still payable (generally, pre-7/1/71 product)).

### Explanation

After one free run on domestic free TV – which can be either network primetime or not (i.e., C3 or D3) – each run on other than network primetime triggers a residual of that is a percentage of the DGA residual base, WGA applicable minimum or SAG-AFTRA total applicable minimum, TAM (with no ceiling, rather than TAC with a ceiling, as is used in network primetime residuals, C3; see below for explanation of TAM). The applied percentage declines run by run.

These residuals are much smaller than network primetime residuals (C3). They are calculated somewhat similarly, but with key differences:

- **Declining Percentages.** Network primetime residuals are paid at 100% (as described on p. 70), but other than network primetime residuals are paid according to a declining percentage scale. The percentages start at 50% (for network non-primetime reuse) or 40% (for non-network reuse) and decline to a floor of 5%, with all further reruns payable at the 5% rate:

| Run | Percent |
|---|---|
| 2 | 50%/40% |
| 3 | 40%/30% |
| 4 | 25% |
| 5 | 25% |
| 6 | 25% |
| 7 | 15% |

| Run | Percent |
|---|---|
| 8 | 15% |
| 9 | 15% |
| 10 | 15% |
| 11 | 10% |
| 12 | 10% |
| after | 5% |

Thus, for example, the 4th run (3rd rerun) is payable at 25% of the DGA residual base, 25% of the WGA applicable minimum or 25% of the SAG-AFTRA total applicable minimum.

→ The WGA always uses the other than network primetime AMs,[*] **even if the script was written for network primetime.** Thus, even though the network primetime minimum is applicable for determining the writer's minimum upfront compensation, that minimum is not "applicable" for the purposes of the residual calculation.

- **SAG-AFTRA Uses TAM (Without a Ceiling) Rather Than TAC (With a Ceiling).** The SAG-AFTRA formula uses the performer's total applicable minimum (TAM). TAM is calculated as the minimum wage amount (scale) multiplied by the time period worked. There is no ceiling, unlike the way total applicable compensation (TAC) is calculated for network primetime residuals (see p. 62).

So, for instance, if a day player works two days, her TAM is 2 times the day player minimum.[†]

- **No 2010/2011 Freeze.** The network primetime freeze (see p. 62) do not apply. This means that the DGA tables of residual bases for these reuse patterns *do* increase year by year at the same rate as wages, and that WGA residuals for these reuse patterns use the current table of applicable minimums, rather than the frozen 2010 table.

---

[*] These are found in Arts. 13.B.7.a-c, not in Art. 13.B.7.d.
[†] The minimums are found in SAG-AFTRA TV Agt. Sec. 2.

- **DGA Has Two Separate RB Tables.** Be sure to use BA Art. 24-301 (instead of Art. 11-101(b)(2)) for multicamera pilots and series – generally, sitcoms.

- **Sideletters May Apply.** The unions have agreed to a number of sideletters and other provisions that reduce residuals for this reuse pattern. These are discussed in the next subsection.

### Sideletters and Other Exceptions

There are several sideletters (essentially, addenda) and other provisions – referred to as waivers[*] – that provide for reduced residuals under certain circumstances. These are as follows:

#### One Hour Programs

Residuals are calculated differently for an episode of a one-hour network primetime program where the series has not previously been exhibited in syndication[†] (or, in the case of several guilds, has not been exhibited in syndication prior to a specified date). These provisions were intended to accommodate a decline that apparently occurred some years ago in the market for one-hour syndication.

Here are the formulas:

#### *DGA*

2.6% of gross received for exhibition of the episode in syndication until gross exceeds $400,000; thereafter, 1.75% of such gross.[‡]

The residual is subject to a ceiling of 150% of the otherwise-applicable fixed residual. Also, the residual is subject to a floor of 50% of the otherwise-applicable fixed residual, unless the series is licensed only in markets representing less than one-half of all U.S. television households, in which case there is no floor.

Eligible series are those that have not previously been exhibited in syndication (i.e., at any time); however, with respect to Fox product produced prior to July 1, 2005, the series must not have been exhibited in syndication prior to July 1, 2003.

#### *WGA*

Residuals for episodes of eligible series are computed by multiplying the fixed residual amount otherwise due by a ratio, the numerator of which is the revenue contracted for by the distributor,[§] and the denominator of which is $650,000.

The residual is subject to a ceiling of 150% of the otherwise-applicable fixed residual. Also, the residual is subject to a floor of 50% of the otherwise-applicable fixed residual, unless the series is licensed only in markets representing less than one-third[**] of all U.S. television households, in which case there is no floor.

Eligible series are those that have not previously been exhibited in syndication prior to March 1, 1988; however, with respect to Fox product, the series must not have been exhibited in syndication prior to May 2, 2002.

#### *SAG-AFTRA*

The calculation, floor and ceiling are the same as the WGA.

Eligible series are those that have not previously been exhibited in syndication prior to July 1, 2005; however, programs that were released in syndication pursuant to the same provision of the 1989, 1992, 1995, 1998 or 2001 SAG Television Agreements are also eligible. It's necessary to refer to the applicable agreement – in particular, the 1989 agreement – to see if there are other date restrictions.

Also eligible are (i) one hour dramatic series made for "late night" network broadcast which are rerun in syndication, and (ii) one-hour dramatic series made for network prime time which are rerun on late night network television, provided that all performers employed on any such episodes covered under clause (ii) which were

---

[*] This terminology is a bit confusing. The residuals are not actually waived; rather, there are substitute formulas.
[†] The language in the agreements is not a model of clarity, but appears to mean the first sale into syndication.
[‡] BA Sideletter 10 has a detailed example that explains how to allocate to each episode the appropriate portion of a series (multi-episode) license fee covering multiple years.

[§] MBA Sideletter No. 1 to Article 15.B.1.b.(2)(c) contains provisions that deal with situations where the company doesn't receive the contracted-for revenue.
[**] Not one-half, as is the case with the DGA floor.

produced after June 30, 2005 must have been employed under residual terms and conditions not less favorable than those provided under this Agreement.

"Late night" is defined as 11:00 p.m. to 6:00 a.m. in the Eastern and Pacific time zones; 10:00 p.m. to 5:00 a.m. in the Central and Mountain time zones. The TV Agreement doesn't specify how Alaska and Hawaii are treated.

### Syndication of Half-Hour Series

The half-hour syndication market also became difficult, albeit more recently (the early 2000's) than the one-hour market.

[tbd]

DGA: 11-101(b)(1)(i)(B) of the BA; p. 13 of 2008 MOA

### Supersized Episodes

See p. 70.

### Interrupted Programs

See p. 70.

### Secondary Digital Channels

In the 2013-14 negotiating cycle, a new Sideletter with percentage residuals formulas was added[*] in order to encourage licensing of product to secondary digital channels (also known as digital subchannels). Although not defined in the union agreements, these are such channels as Channel 4.2, 4.3, etc. They are secondary to and owned by the broadcaster who owns the main channel (i.e., Channel 4 in this example).[†] These channels first became possible when the U.S. transitioned from analog to digital over-the-air broadcasting in 2009, and are made possible by certain technological capabilities of digital broadcasting.[‡]

Such channels generally have very small audiences, and are often not be available on cable systems, but they are available using antennas on a rooftop or on top of or behind the TV set. They are used for various things, such as "hyperlocal" content, 24-hour news or weather, temporarily running the network feed (normally on the main channel, e.g., Channel 4) while running a local sports game on the main channel (or vice versa), running a different network (such as CW or even one of the four majors) in a market that traditionally did not have local carriage of all major networks, running a "traditional" minor network like ION or MyNetwork TV, or running one of several newer "secondary digital networks" that have arisen in the last several years.

Thus, when product made for free TV, made for pay TV or made for basic cable[§] is reused on secondary digital channels, and if certain tests are met, a percentage residuals formula applies rather than fixed residuals. The formula is:

DGA: 2% of gross.
WGA: same as DGA.
SAG-AFTRA: 3 times this percentage (i.e., 6%).

### *Tests*

This formula only applies if all of the following three tests apply:

#### 1. Fixed Residual Otherwise Payable

A fixed residual must otherwise be payable. This means that the percentage residual does not apply to exhausted product.

#### 2. Out of Production Test

The series must have been out of production for at least two or three years. Several points are notable.

● **Two vs. Three Years.** Normally, the requisite out of production period is three years. However, for any free television series consisting of sixty-eight (68) or fewer episodes or any basic cable or pay television series consisting of forty (40) or fewer episodes, the series need only have been out of production for at least two years.

● **For Series Only, Not TV Movies.** The phrase "out of production" and a later reference to "the

---

[*] In the case of the DGA, the Sideletter applies to both the BA and the FLTTA.
[†] In this context, Channel 4.1 is equivalent to Channel 4.
[‡] See http://en.wikipedia.org/wiki/Digital_subchannel.

[§] This section of the book (Section 6.B) is about reuse of free TV product. However, the Sideletter regarding secondary digital channels applies to reuse of product made for free TV, made for pay TV or made for basic cable, so we discuss all three of those kinds of product here, rather than fracturing the discussion into three different places.

series ... out of production" make clear that the percentage formula only applies to series and not, therefore, to single-episode productions, i.e., TV movies.*

- **Measured by Series, Not by Episode.** The same phrase and subsequent reference means that the series must have been out of production for two or three years rather than that the particular licensed episode must have been "out of production" for that time.†

- **Unclear When Clock Starts Ticking.** The language does not indicate how one measures the duration a series has been out of production – i.e., is it measured from the last day of principal photography of the last season, or from some other date?

### 3. Out of Exhibition (Under Fixed Residuals) Test

The product must not have been exhibited under a fixed residual formula in certain media for at least one or three years.

More specifically, the test is as follows:

- **Free TV.** The series must not have been exhibited under a fixed residual formula in syndication (except in the non-lead market)‡ (D3) or pay television (F3) for at least one or three years.

- **Pay TV Series.** The series must not have been exhibited under a fixed residual formula in syndication (except in the non-lead market) (D4) or pay television (F4) for at least one or three years.

- **Basic Cable Series.** The series must not have been exhibited under a fixed residual formula in syndication (except in the non-lead market) (D6), pay television (F6) or basic cable (H6) for at least one or three years

---

\* This is so notwithstanding DGA language referring to "Any free television or pay television dramatic motion picture," which technically is a reference to either a TV movie or an individual episode of a series. Understood as a whole, and in concert with the WGA language, the DGA language (like the WGA language) applies only to series.
† Again, there is some arguable ambiguity in one sentence of the DGA language, but not if read in context with later sentences and with the WGA language.
‡ See discussion of the term "non-lead market" below.

Several points are notable regarding the out of exhibition test:

- **One vs. Three Years.** Normally, the requisite out of exhibition period is three years. However, for any free television series consisting of sixty-eight (68) or fewer episodes or any basic cable or pay television series consisting of forty (40) or fewer episodes, the series need only have been out of exhibition for at least one year.

- **Free TV or Pay TV *Respectively*?** If free TV product is released under a fixed residual formula in syndication (except in the non-lead market) (D4) or if pay TV product is released under a fixed residual formula on pay TV (F4), the "out of exhibition" clock does not yet begin run and the series is still in exhibition for purposes of the test. However, what if free TV product is released on pay TV (F3) or pay TV product is released in syndication (D4)? There is ambiguity in the language. However, it appears that the best interpretation is that the latter two reuse patterns also count as in-exhibition, meaning that the clock has not yet begun to run.§

- **Product Made for Network is Apparently Not Subject to Out of Exhibition Restriction.** The term "non-lead market" is not defined in the union agreements. However, if "lead market" means "initial market" (i.e., what this book calls the made-for medium), then the intent of the parenthetical seems to be to carve out any free TV series that was exhibited in syndication\*\* but where syndication was not the initial market.†† The result of such a carveout is free TV series made for initial broadcast on a network (whether or not in primetime). Thus, it appears that product made for initial exhibition on network is not subject to the out of exhibition test. [reviewers?]

---

§ There are two reasons this seems the best interpretation: (1) the word "respectively" does not appear in the relevant language and (2) the language appears to be parallel to the relevant language for basic cable series, where there is no ambiguity, and where any of three kinds of release are sufficient to keep the clock running.
\*\* The language actually says "exhibited under a fixed residual formula in syndication," but all free or pay TV series exhibited in syndication are subject to fixed residuals (D3-D4) unless a negotiated waiver of some sort provides otherwise. [tbd – verify]
†† Note, however, that it is difficult to know how to interpret to out of exhibition test with respect to pay TV series.

- **"Under a Fixed Residual Formula."** The reference to a fixed residual formula seems redundant or inconsistent – hence, illogical – at first glance, because one might think that broadcasts of free, pay or basic cable series in syndication (D3, D4, D6), and broadcasts of basic cable series on basic cable (H6), are always subject to fixed residuals (making the reference to fixed residuals seemingly redundant) and that broadcasts of free, pay or basic cable series on pay TV (F3, F4, F6) are never subject to fixed residuals (making the reference to fixed residuals seemingly illogical). However, this first impression would be flawed, for several reasons: First, including the reference to fixed residuals underscores that the out of exhibition test is only intended to apply if the series has recently been exhibited under fixed residuals. Thus, the test is presumably intended to deter movement of series off of fixed residual platforms. Rather, the intent is to encourage new forms of syndication for series that might otherwise lie fallow. Second, individually negotiated waivers may have allowed series to be exhibited under percentage residuals formulas where they would ordinarily have been exhibited under fixed residuals. [reviewers – other reasons?]

- **Interaction With One Hour Formulas.** One hour free TV series exhibited in syndication (D3) are subject to fixed residuals under the WGA and SAG / SAG-AFTRA agreements, but percentage residuals under the DGA agreement.[*] That seems to mean that the out of exhibition test would apply differently under the DGA agreement than under the other two unions' agreements – except that, as noted above, product made for network may not be subject to the out of exhibition test at all.

- **Measured by Series, Not by Episode.** There is some ambiguity in one portion of the language as to whether the entire series must have been out of exhibition for one or three years rather than that the particular licensed episode must have been out of exhibition for that time. However, a later sentence makes clear that it is the series that must have been out of exhibition for the specified time.

- **When Clock Starts Ticking.** The language does not indicate how one measures the duration a series has been out of exhibition, but this would presumably be measured from the last date that an episode of the series aired under a fixed residual formula in any of the specified media.

## *Related or Affiliated Entity*

How is gross calculated? There is a fair market value-type provision: When the gross is received from a related or affiliated entity that acts as the distributor or exhibitor of the program, then the gross is measured by (a) the distributor/exhibitor's payments to unrelated and unaffiliated entities in arms' length transactions for comparable programs, or, if none, then (b) the amounts received by the employer from unrelated and unaffiliated Distributors/exhibitors in arms' length transactions for comparable programs, or, if none, (c) a comparable distributor/exhibitor's payments to comparable unrelated and unaffiliated entities in arms' length transactions for comparable programs.

For further protection, there is a floor for non arms' length transactions. The minimum DGA or WGA residuals payment for any program licensed to a related or affiliated entity is $50 for a 30 minute program, $100 for a 60 minute program, $150 for a 90 minute program, and $200 for a 120 minute program, and 3 times these amounts for SAG-AFTRA.

## *Old and New Series*

The percentage residuals formula applies to series produced under the 2014 union agreements or any prior union agreement,[†] so long as residuals would still be payable (i.e., non-exhausted product).

## *Secondary Digital Networks*

Under the WGA Sideletter but not the DGA or SAG-AFTRA ones, the percentage residuals formula also applies to licenses to certain secondary digital networks. The language is as follows:

"This sideletter shall also apply to the following secondary digital networks: Antenna TV,

---

[*] See p. 73.

[†] More precisely, any prior BA, FLTTA, MBA or SAG, AFTRA or SAG-AFTRA agreement.

## 6. Made for Free TV Product – 77

Bounce TV, Cozi TV, Live Well, ME TV, Movies!, getTV, This TV and any other similar secondary digital network so long as such secondary digital network has (i) an overall average Nielsen NTI rating (9am to 2am) of 1.0 or less (HHLD Live+ 7, as measured by the previous calendar year) and (ii) the majority of such network's broadcast station affiliates in the top 100 Nielsen markets comprising the network are not full-power primary digital channels.

"The residual formula provided under this sideletter shall not apply to any license agreement entered into more than 90 days after the end of the measuring year in which such Nielsen rating is greater than 1.0 or after a majority of such network affiliates in such markets become full-power primary digital channels.

"In no event shall Ion or MyNetworkTV qualify as secondary digital networks for purposes of applying the terms of this Sideletter."

### Canada-Only Syndication

In the 2013-14 negotiating cycle, new language was added to encourage Canada-only sales. Under the language, if a company licenses a television program for syndication only in Canada, it has the option of paying a percentage residual instead of fixed residuals.

The formula is:

**DGA:** 4% of gross.
**WGA:** same as DGA.
**SAG-AFTRA:** 3 times this percentage (i.e., 12%).

The option to use this formula is applicable for free TV product (including product made for the CW, but excluding "any other [product] made for syndication"), pay TV product and basic cable product,[tbd – add to those sections] and it applies to TV movies or series. The option applies to product produced under the 2014 union agreements or any prior union agreement,[*] so long as residuals would still be payable (i.e., non-exhausted product).

### No Residuals

No residuals for IATSE, AFM, or exhausted TV product (the latter is noted in H3).

---

[*] More precisely, any prior BA, FLTTA, MBA or SAG-AFTRA, Legacy-SAG or Legacy-AFTRA agreement.

### Pattern Analysis

Pattern is generally maintained – the formulas are different but echo each other – except in the case of some of the sideletters.

### Related Cells

Reuse of free TV product in network PT: C3.
Other reuse in other than network PT: D4-D8.
Reuse of basic cable product on basic cable: H6.

### Book Cross References

Made for free TV: p. 27.
Exhausted free TV product: p. 28.
Reuse on other than network primetime: p. 40.
What initial comp covers (runs): p. 52.
Percentage residuals: p. 55.
Fixed residuals at run by run declining %: p. 61.
Fixed residuals – the residual base: p. 62.

### Contract References

DGA BA Paras. 11-101(b)(2)-(4), 24-301, and SLs 10 & 12.

WGA MBA Arts. 15.B.1.a, b.(1), (2)(c), (d), (3), and SL to Art. 15.B.1, SLs 1 & 2 to Art. 15.B.1.b.(2)(c).

SAG-AFTRA and L-SAG TVA Sec. 18(a), (b)(2), (3), (4), SLs B, B-1 & B-2.

L-AFTRA Netcode Ex. A § 3.

### History

| Date | Unions | Event |
|---|---|---|
| See also related notes on p. 71 | | |
| 1974 | SAG | Residuals payable in perpetuity for syndication rather than buy-out at 10$^{th}$ run; fees increased 25% |
| 1977 | WGA | Residuals payable in perpetuity |
| 1988 strike | WGA | Waiver re hour-long programs in syndication |
| 2013-2014 | DGA, WGA, SAG-AFTRA | Percentage residuals formula introduced for secondary digital channels and Canada-only syndication. |

78 – *Entertainment Residuals: A Full Color Guide*

## C. Free TV to Foreign TV

### Contents of Cell E3

15%, 10%, 10% (one-time 35% for 1 hrs.) of RB/AM/TAM triggered by telecast or two GR breaks; then 1.2% gross (SAG-AFTRA 3x) after GR break. AFM: 1% of AGICOA. IATSE $0.

### Notes in Other Cells

H3: No . . . residuals on exhausted TV product (i.e., if network rerun residuals not still payable (generally, pre-7/1/71 product)).

### Explanation

**DGA:** 15% of foreign residual base is due after the first foreign telecast, then 10% of foreign residual base after a gross break, then another 10% of foreign residual base after second gross break, then 1.2% of gross in excess of a third gross break. Gross means producer's gross from foreign telecasting; foreign basic cable exhibition; and foreign ad-supported services availability of television and home video product (this latter is reuse that would be covered by K3-K6 if it were domestic).

Notwithstanding the foregoing 15%/10%/10% structure, a different structure applies for one-hour programs that are subject to the one-hour syndication sideletter (see p. 73): the entire 35% (15%+10%+10%) is payable after the first foreign telecast.

**WGA:** same as DGA, except that the other-than-network-primetime applicable minimum is used rather than a table of foreign residual bases.
➔ The other than network primetime AMs are used, **even if the teleplay was written for network primetime**. The gross breaks are the same as the DGA's.

**SAG-AFTRA:** same as the DGA, except that the total applicable minimum (TAM, see p. 72) is used rather than a table of foreign residual bases. The gross breaks are the same as the DGA's.

**AFM:** 1% of AGICOA monies (not of gross). See p. 41 for explanation of AGICOA.

### Sideletters

#### Interrupted Programs

[tbd]

#### No Residuals

No residuals for IATSE, or exhausted TV product (the latter is noted in H3).

### Pattern Analysis

Pattern is maintained.

### Related Cells

Pay TV and home video to foreign: E4-E5. Basic cable to foreign: E6.

### Book Cross References

Made for free TV: p. 27.
Exhausted free TV product: p. 28.
Foreign reuse: p. 41.
What initial comp covers: p. 52.
Hybrid residual formulas: p. 63.

### Contract References

DGA BA Para. 11-102.
WGA MBA Art. 15.B.2.
SAG TVA Sec. 18(c)(1)-(4).
AFTRA Netcode Ex. A § 3.
[AFM ?.]

### History

| Date | Unions | Event |
|---|---|---|
| 1962 | WGA | Residuals established ("Royalty Plan") |
| 1965? | SAG | Residuals established |
| 1966 | WGA | Fixed residuals established; Royalty Plan ended |

| Date | Unions | Event |
|---|---|---|
| 1968 | DGA | Residuals established |
| 1988 strike | WGA | Some gains when hour-long programs are licensed to foreign |
| 2001 | WGA | 1.2% gross provision added (perpetuity); eff. for product where writing services commenced on or after 5/2/01 |

## D. Free TV to (Domestic) Basic Cable

### Contents of Cell H3

2% of gross (SAG-AFTRA 3x). No **C3-H3, I3-J3?, K3** residuals on exhausted TV product (i.e., if network rerun residuals not still payable (generally, pre-7/1/71 product)). IATSE, AFM: $0.

### Explanation

DGA: 2% of gross.
WGA: same as DGA.
SAG-AFTRA: 3 times this percentage (i.e., 6%).

### No Residuals

No residuals for IATSE, AFM, or exhausted free TV product.

### Pattern Analysis

Pattern is maintained.

### Related Cells

**H7-H8** derivative and original new media to domestic basic cable use the same formula via cross-reference.

### Book Cross References

Made for free TV: p. 27.
Exhausted free TV product: p. 28.
Reuse on basic cable: p. 42.
What initial comp covers: p. 52.
Percentage residuals: p. 55.

### Contract References

DGA BA Para. 11-108.

WGA MBA Art. 58, also 1995 Amendment Agt. Re Release of Royalty Plan Programs to Basic Cable (last item in MBA, after all Sideletters)

SAG TVA Sec. 18.1(a).

AFTRA Netcode Ex. A § 3.

### History

| Date | Unions | Event |
|---|---|---|
| 1971 | All | Residuals established |
| 1988 strike | WGA | Residuals increased |
| tbd | DGA | Residuals increased |
| 1989 | SAG | Residuals increased |
| 1995 | WGA | Eff. 10/1/94, Art. 58 formula and allocation will apply to Royalty Plan TV programs (see 1960 entry in History grid beginning on p. 71 and Sideletter on p. 452 of 2008 MBA) |

# 7. REUSE IN SUPPLEMENTAL MARKETS

## A. Theatrical and Free TV to Pay TV

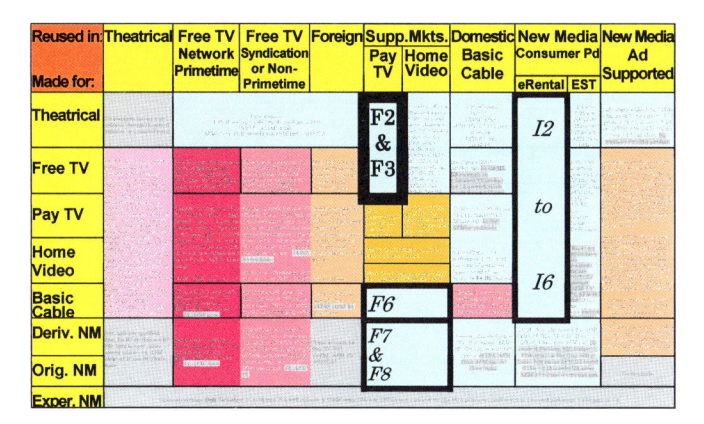

### Contents of Cells F2-F3

1.2% of gross (SAG 3x, AFTRA TV 3x, IATSE 4.5x). AFM post-7/1/71 *theatrical & TV only* (date applies for all AFM F2-G3): 1% of gross. Re non-AFM, see H3 note re exhausted free TV product.

### Notes in Other Cells

H3: No . . . residuals on exhausted TV product (i.e., if network rerun residuals not still payable (generally, pre-7/1/71 product)).

### Explanation

DGA: 1.2% of gross.
WGA: same as DGA.
SAG-AFTRA: 3 times this percentage (i.e., 3.6%).
IATSE: 4.5 times this percentage (i.e., 5.4%).
AFM: 1% of gross.

### No Residuals

As noted in cell A2, no residuals for theatrical product unless the picture is a Post-'60 *(or WGA post-1948 Universal)*. No residuals for exhausted free TV product (as noted in H3). No AFM residuals for pre-7/1/71 theatrical and TV product.

### Pattern Analysis

Pattern is maintained.

### Related Cells

Basic cable to pay TV: F6.

Derivative and original new media to pay TV: F7-F8.

Traditional media to eRental: I2-I6.

### Book Cross References

Made for theatrical: p. 26.
Post-'60 theatrical motion pictures: p. 27.
Made for free TV: p. 27.
Exhausted free TV product: p. 28.
Reuse in supplemental markets: p. 41.
Reuse on pay TV: p. 42.
Percentage residuals: p. 55.

### Contract References

DGA BA Paras. 18-101, 102, 103.
WGA MBA Art. 51.C.1.a.
SAG CBA Sec. 5.2.A(1), E(1), (2).
SAG TVA Sec. 20.1.
AFTRA Netcode Ex. D §§ 3.A, 4.A, B.
IATSE BA Sec. XXVIII(b)(1).
AFM Theatrical Agt. Sec. 16(b)(1).
AFM Television Agt. Sec. 14(b)(1).

82 – *Entertainment Residuals: A Full Color Guide*

## B. Theatrical and Free TV to Home Video

| Reused in:<br>Made for: | Theatrical | Free TV Network Primetime | Free TV Syndication or Non-Primetime | Foreign | Supp.Mkts. Pay TV | Supp.Mkts. Home Video | Domestic Basic Cable | New Media Consumer Pd eRental | New Media Consumer Pd EST | New Media Ad Supported |
|---|---|---|---|---|---|---|---|---|---|---|
| Theatrical | | | | | | **G2 & G3** | | **J2** | | |
| Free TV | | | | | | | | **J3** | | |
| Pay TV | | | | | | | | to | | |
| Home Video | | | | | | | | **J6** | | |
| Basic Cable | | | | | | **G6** | | | | |
| Deriv. NM | | | | | | **G7 & G8** | | | | |
| Orig. NM | | | | | | | | | | |
| Exper. NM | | | | | | | | | | |

### Contents of Cells G2-G3

1.5% (to 1.8%) of Producer's gross (=20% of worldwide wholesale gross if affiliated video co.; else, 100% of fee received by producer) (1.8% at $1M Prod. gross) (SAG 3x, AFTRA TV 3x, IATSE 4.5x, AFM 1% (of 20%)). See F2-F3 notes. Pre 1984/85 vary.

### Notes in Other Cells

**F2-F3:** AFM post-7/1/71 theatrical & TV only (date applies for all AFM F2-G3): 1% of gross. Re non-AFM, see H3 note re exhausted free TV product.

**H3:** No . . . residuals on exhausted TV product (i.e., if network rerun residuals not still payable (generally, pre-7/1/71 product)).

### Explanation

**DGA:** 1.5% of Producer's gross for the first $1 million of Producer's gross, and 1.8% for Producer's gross thereafter.

**WGA:** same as DGA.

**SAG-AFTRA:** 3 times these percentages (i.e., 4.5% and 5.4%).

**IATSE:** 4.5 times these percentages (i.e., 6.75% and 8.1%).

**AFM:** 1% of gross.

Producer's gross equals 20% of worldwide gross receipts received by producer for physical home video devices if producer has an affiliated home video company.* This is generally the case for the major studios, and generally not the case for non-studios.

See p. 57 for a detailed explanation of home video residuals.

### No Residuals

As noted in cell A2, no residuals for theatrical product unless the picture is a Post-'60 *(or WGA post-1948 Universal)*. No residuals for exhausted free TV product (as noted in H3). No AFM residuals for pre-7/1/71 theatrical and TV product.

### Pattern Analysis

Pattern is maintained.

### Related Cells

Basic cable to home video: G6.

Derivative and original new media to home video: G7-G8.

Theatrical to eRental: J2.

TV and home video to eRental: J3-J6.

### Book Cross References

Made for theatrical: p. 26.
Post-'60 theatrical motion pictures: p. 27.
Made for free TV: p. 27.
Exhausted free TV product: p. 28.
Reuse in supplemental markets: p. 41.
Reuse on home video: p. 42.
Percentage residuals: p. 55.
Home video residuals: p. 57.

### Contract References

DGA BA Para. 18-101, 102, 104.
WGA MBA Art. 51.C.1.b, SL to Art. 51.
SAG CBA Sec. 5.2.A(2), E(1), (3).
SAG TVA Sec. 20.1.
AFTRA Netcode Ex. D §§ 3.A, 4.A, B.
IATSE BA XXVIII Sec. (b)(2).

---

* Thus,, where there is an affiliated home video company, the $1 million Producer's gross breakpoint is equivalent to a breakpoint of $5 million in worldwide gross receipts, because 20% of $5 million is $1 million.

AFM Theatrical Agt. Sec. 16(b)(1).
AFM Television Agt. Sec. 14(b)(1).

## C. History of Reuse in Supplemental Markets

| Date | Unions | Event |
|------|--------|-------|
| 1971 | SAG, DGA, WGA | Residuals established |
| 1977 | SAG | Pay TV exhibition of TV product: 20% of residual base + 10% at gross break + 10% at 2$^{nd}$ gross break; residual base is, e.g., $100 for one day of work |
| 1980 | SAG | Pay TV exhibition of TV product: 3.6% gross |

[Note – older SAG TV product to supp mkts is in TVA 20][add to chart from EP]

# 8. MADE FOR PAY TV AND HOME VIDEO

This chapter discusses content made for pay TV services like HBO, Showtime, Starz and Epix, as well as content made for physical home video media such as DVD and Blu-ray. Note that over the top (OTT) / Internet subscription services such as Netflix, Amazon Prime and Hulu Plus are not considered pay TV. Instead, product made for these services is considered High Budget SVOD (or sometimes just Original New Media), and is discussed starting on p. xxx and p. xxx.

## A. Overview of Pay TV & Home Video to Pay TV & Home Video

As mentioned earlier in this book, the formulas for pay TV and/or home video to pay TV and/or home video are complex and unusual. Before considering them one by one in subsections B-I, it's helpful to look at a blown up excerpt from the chart. It reveals several things:

- Many of the formulas for these reuse patterns are percentage residuals. However, they don't kick in until a certain level of gross is achieved (such a threshold is referred to as a break) or until a certain number of units (copies) of a DVD/Blu-ray disc have been sold. This gives the producer a residual-free initial use.

- For pay TV reruns (i.e., pay TV to pay TV, F4), the three unions have completely different formulas. The DGA receives a certain amount per pay TV channel subscriber (called a "subscriber fee" or, more commonly, "sub fee"). This has turned out to be quite lucrative, since pay TV subscriber figures are quite high (they're in the tens of millions). SAG and AFTRA receive a percentage residual; this is the second best of the above the line unions. The WGA is in last place, and receives only a (relatively small) set dollar amount.

- The DGA treats made for home video product the same way as made for pay TV product. SAG and AFTRA essentially do likewise, with only a slight distinction. The WGA does something quite different: it aggregates the gross receipts that a made for home video product achieves in its video sales with the gross that the product achieves in its pay TV exhibition (if the product gets any pay TV exhibition). The residual is then 2% of this aggregate gross after a break is achieved.

The remainder of this chapter explains the formulas one by one. Subsections B-I address the formulas shown in this excerpt, while subsections J and K look at other reuse patterns involving product made for pay TV or for home video. Subsection L contains a history grid.

### Excerpt from Residuals Chart

| Reused in: Made for: | F/G Supplemental Markets | |
|---|---|---|
| | Pay TV | Home Video |
| 4 Pay TV | *DGA* (max=AM/yr.): Domestic cbl: sub fees % yr (+ possible 2% gross>break); PPV 2% gross>break. *WGA* domestic: fixed $/yr. for >10 exhib days or 1 yr. *SAG/AFTRA* domestic after same: 6% gross; & 2nd svc. 6% gross Foreign svc 2% gross (SAG-AFTRA 3x). *AFM:* $0 | 2% (SAG-AFTRA 3x) of gross after 100K units (*WGA, SAG:* 75K for 30/60 min. pay TV). *DGA:* if initial release is on pay TV, must also meet gross break. *AFM:* $0. |
| 5 Home Video | ... | *DGA & SAG-AFTRA:* see F4-G4. *SAG:* G5 break = 100K. *WGA:* 2% of aggregate (pay + HV) gross > aggregate gross break. |

## 7.Supplemental Markets – 85

### B. DGA Pay TV and Home Video to Pay TV

### Contents of Cells F4-F5 (DGA Portions Only)

**Cell F4:** *DGA* (max=AM/yr.): Dom cbl: sub fees % yr (+ possible 2% GR>brk); PPV 2% GR>brk. Foreign svc 2% GR.

**Cell F5:** *DGA*: see F4.

### Explanation

The residual is an amount calculated on the basis of the number of subscribers to the pay TV channel (HBO, Showtime, etc.).

[tbd]

### No Residuals

[tbd]

### Pattern Analysis

There is little pattern in F4-G5 reuse.

### Book Cross References

Made for pay TV: p. 28.
Made for home video: p. 29.
Reuse in supplemental markets: p. 41.
Reuse on pay TV: p. 42.
Reuse on home video: p. 42.
What initial comp covers (gross break): p. 53.
Percentage residuals: p. 55.
Unique residual formulas: p. 64.

### Contract References

DGA BA Paras. 20-100, 400, 600, 804, and SL 7.

## C. SAG-AFTRA Pay TV and Home Video to Pay TV

### Explanation

[tbd]

### No Residuals

[tbd]

### Pattern Analysis

There is little pattern in F4-G5 reuse.

Also, note the unusual SAG-AFTRA proration rule for under four performers.

### Book Cross References

Made for pay TV: p. 28.
Made for home video: p. 29.
Reuse in supplemental markets: p. 41.
Reuse on pay TV: p. 42.
Reuse on home video: p. 42.
What initial comp covers (exhibition days): p. 54.
Percentage residuals: p. 55.
Unique residual formulas: p. 64.

### Contract References

SAG TVA Secs. 78(c)(1)a)-c), 78(d)(5).
AFTRA Netcode Ex. E §§ 2.B, 3.A(1), 4.E.

### Contents of Cells F4-F5 (SAG-AFTRA Portions Only)

Cell F4: . . . >10 exhib days or 1 yr. *SAG-AFTRA* dom after same: 6% GR; & 2nd svc. 6% GR. Foreign svc 2% GR (SAG-AFTRA 3x).

Cell F5: *SAG-AFTRA*: see F4.

### Notes in Other Cells

H4-H5: SAG-AFTRA: <= 4 performers: 1.5% of GR times no. of performers. Applies to all 6% or "3x" figures in F4-H5 (but not to H3).

## D. WGA Pay TV to Pay TV

### Contents of Cell F4 (WGA Portion Only)

*WGA* dom: fixed $/yr. for >10 exhib days or 1 yr. Foreign svc 2% GR.

### Notes in Other Cells

**A4**: For made for pay TV product of a type not generally produced for network PT TV: F5 -G5 not F4-G4 for pay TV & HV uses.

### Explanation

The residual for reuse on a domestic pay TV service (e.g., reruns) is a fixed dollar amount per year. The amount depends on the length of the program (half-hour, one hour, etc.) and has increased from time to time. The residual kicks in only after 10 exhibition days or one year.

For reuse on a foreign pay TV service, the residual is 2% of gross. These residuals kick in immediately.

### No Residuals

There are no residuals if the program is broadcast on ten or fewer exhibition days that span no more than one year.

### Pattern Analysis

There is little pattern in F4-G5 reuse.

### Book Cross References

Made for pay TV: p. 28.
Reuse in supplemental markets: p. 41.
Reuse on pay TV: p. 42.
What initial comp covers (exhibition days): p. 54.
Percentage residuals: p. 55.
Unique residual formulas: p. 64.

### Contract References

WGA MBA App. B §§ D.2, 3.a, G.4.

## E. DGA Pay TV and Home Video to Home Video

### Contents of Cells G4-G5 (DGA Portions Only)

**Cell G4:** 2% . . . of GR after 100K units . . . if initial release is on pay TV, must also meet GR brk. . . .

**Cell G5:** see . . . G4.

### Explanation

2% of gross after the earlier of (a) 100,000 units of home video product are sold or (b) a gross break is achieved; but (b) is only applicable if the initial release is on pay TV.

### No Residuals

No residuals if fewer than 100,000 units sold and the gross break (if applicable) is not achieved.

### Pattern Analysis

There is little pattern in F4-G5 reuse.

### Book Cross References

Made for pay TV: p. 28.
Made for home video: p. 29.
Reuse in supplemental markets: p. 41.
Reuse on pay TV: p. 42.
Reuse on home video: p. 42.
What initial comp covers (units): p. 53.
What initial comp covers (gross break): p. 53.
Percentage residuals: p. 55.
Unique residual formulas: p. 64.

### Contract References

DGA BA Paras. 20-100, 400, 700, and SL 7.

## F. SAG-AFTRA Pay TV and Home Video to Home Video

| Reused in:<br>Made for: | Theatrical | Free TV Network Primetime | Free TV Syndication or Non-Primetime | Foreign | Supp. Mkts. Pay TV | Home Video | Domestic Basic Cable | New Media Consumer Pd eRental | EST | New Media Ad Supported |
|---|---|---|---|---|---|---|---|---|---|---|
| Theatrical | | | | | | | | | | |
| Free TV | | | | | | | | | | |
| Pay TV | | | | | | G4 | | | | |
| Home Video | | | | | | G5 | | | | |
| Basic Cable | | | | | | | | | | |
| Deriv. NM | | | | | | | | | | |
| Orig. NM | | | | | | | | | | |
| Exper. NM | | | | | | | | | | |

Also, note unusual SAG-AFTRA proration rule for under four performers.

### Book Cross References

Made for pay TV: p. 28.
Made for home video: p. 29.
Reuse in supplemental markets: p. 41.
Reuse on pay TV: p. 42.
Reuse on home video: p. 42.
What initial comp covers (units): p. 53.
Percentage residuals: p. 55.
Unique residual formulas: p. 64.

### Contract References

SAG TVA Secs. 78(c)(2)a)-c).
AFTRA Netcode Ex. E §§ 2.B, 3.B(1).

### Contents of Cells G4-G5 (SAG-AFTRA Portions Only)

Cell G4: 2% (SAG-AFTRA 3x) of GR after 100K units (... 75K for 30/60 min. pay TV)....

Cell G5: ... see ... G4. *SAG:* G5 break = 100K.

### Notes in Other Cells

Cell H4-H5: SAG-AFTRA: <= 4 performers: 1.5% of GR times no. of performers. Applies to all 6% or "3x" figures in F4-H5 (but not to H3).

### Explanation

6% of gross after 100,000 units of home video product are sold.

[explain proration]

*Exception – for SAG (but not for AFTRA),[*] the unit break is 75,000 units if the product is a 30 or 60 minute pay TV episode (as opposed to, for instance, a pay TV movie). Note that the WGA has a similar provision (see p. 90).*

### No Residuals

No residuals if fewer than 100,000 units sold (75,000 in the case of 30 or 60 minute pay TV product).

### Pattern Analysis

There is little pattern in F4-G5 reuse.

---

[*] Contrast SAG TVA § 78(c)(2)a)(i) with AFTRA Netcode Ex. E § B(1).

## G. WGA Pay TV to Home Video

*Exception: The unit break is 75,000 units if the product is a 30 or 60 minute pay TV episode (as opposed to, for instance, a pay TV movie). Note that SAG has a similar provision (see p. 89).*

### No Residuals

No residuals if fewer than 100,000 units sold (75,000 in the case of 30 or 60 minute pay TV product).

### Pattern Analysis

There is little pattern in F4-G5 reuse.

### Book Cross References

Made for pay TV: p. 28.
Reuse in supplemental markets: p. 41.
Reuse on home video: p. 42.
What initial comp covers (units): p. 53.
Percentage residuals: p. 55.
Unique residual formulas: p. 64.

### Contract References

WGA MBA App. B §§ D.2, 3.b.

### Contents of Cell G4 (WGA Portions Only)

2% . . . of GR after 100K units (. . .: 75K for 30/60 min. pay TV). . ..

### Notes in Other Cells

A4: For made for pay TV product of a type not generally produced for network PT TV: F5-G5 not F4-G4 for pay TV & HV uses.

### Explanation

2% of gross after 100,000 units of home video product are sold.

## H. WGA Home Video to Pay TV and Home Video

### Contents of Cells F5-G5

*WGA*: 2% of aggregate (pay + HV) GR > aggregate GR break.

### Explanation

**WGA**: The producers' gross that a made for home video product achieves in its video sales is added to the producers' gross that the product achieves in its pay TV exhibition (if the product gets any pay TV exhibition). The residual is then 2% of this aggregate producers' gross after a certain level of producers' gross (a "break") is achieved.

### No Residuals

No residuals until the gross break is exceeded.

### Pattern Analysis

There is little pattern in F4-G5 reuse.

### Book Cross References

Made for home video: p. 29.
Reuse in supplemental markets: p. 41.
Reuse on pay TV: p. 42.
Reuse on home video: p. 42.
What initial comp covers (gross break): p. 53.
Percentage residuals: p. 55.
Unique residual formulas: p. 64.

### Contract References

WGA MBA App. B §§ C.2, 3, G.4.

## I. IATSE and AFM Pay TV and Home Video to Pay TV and Home Video

### No Residuals

No residuals for IATSE or AFM.

## J. Pay TV and Home Video to Free TV and Foreign

### Contents of Cells C4-E5

Same as made for free TV (C3-E3). *DGA* - high budget pay television motion picture (product >=80 min and >= $5M budget): 1.2% of gross. *DGA* - other product: 20% discount on residuals until gross break. *IATSE*: $0.

*AFM:* made for pay TV (C4-E4) treated as made for theatrical (C2-E2).

*AFM:* made for HV (A5-K5) treated as theatrical (A2-K2) or free TV (A3-K3) depending on whether created under Theatrical MP Agt. or TV Agt.; except HV to theatrical (B5) always as free TV (B3) and HV to foreign (E5) always as free TV (E3). AGICOA??

### Notes in Other Cells

[tbd]

### Explanation

[tbd]DGA, WGA, SAG-AFTRA, L-SAG and L-AFTRA are the same as if made for free TV, except for the deviations noted here for DGA. See pp. 70, 72 and 78.

### Sideletters

#### Fox

Reuse on Fox is now paid at 100% of network rates. See p. 39.

#### The CW

Reuse on The CW is paid at a reduced percentage of network rates. See p. 39.

### No Residuals

No residuals for IATSE.

### Pattern Analysis

Above the line pattern is maintained except for DGA deviations. AFM treatment is unique.

### Related Cells

Free TV to free TV and foreign: C3-E3.

### Book Cross References

Made for pay TV: p. 28.
Made for home video: p. 29.
Reuse on network primetime: p. 39.
Reuse on other than network primetime: p. 40.
Foreign reuse: p. 41.
Fixed residuals at 100%: p. 59.
Fixed residuals at run by run declining %: p. 61.
Fixed residuals – the residual base: p. 62.
Hybrid residual formulas: p. 63.
Percentage residuals: p. 55.

### Contract References

DGA BA Para. 20-801.

WGA MBA App. B § G.1.

SAG TV Agt. Sec. 78(d)(1).

AFTRA Netcode Ex. E § 4.A.

(Applicability of TVA and Netcode provisions to reuse in foreign (E4-E5) is implicit.)

AFM made for pay TV: AFM Basic Cable Sec. 17.D.2 (& AFM Theatrical Agt. Sec. 15).

AFM made for home video: AFM Theatrical Agt. Sec. 16(b)(i)(17)-(19) (cross-references various provisions in AFM Theatrical Agt. & AFM Television Agt.).

## K. Pay TV and Home Video to Domestic Basic Cable

[Grid table showing Reused in vs. Made for categories, with cells H4 & H5 highlighted in the Domestic Basic Cable column for Pay TV and Home Video rows]

### Contents of Cells H4-H5

2% of gross (2.5% for pre-7/1/84 product) (SAG-AFTRA 3x). IATSE, AFM: $0.

*SAG-AFTRA*: <= 4 performers: 1.5% of GR times no. of performers. Applies to all 6% or "3x" figures in **F4-H5** *(but not to H3)*.

### Explanation

DGA: 2% of gross (2.5% for pre-7/1/84 product).

WGA: same as DGA.
SAG-AFTRA: 3 times this percentage (i.e., 6% or 7.5%).

### No Residuals

No residuals for IATSE or AFM.

### Pattern Analysis

Pattern is maintained, except for unusual SAG-AFTRA proration rule for under four performers.

### Book Cross References

Made for pay TV: p. 28.
Made for home video: p. 29.
Reuse on basic cable: p. 42
[What initial comp covers: p. 52]
Percentage residuals: p. 55.

### Contract References

DGA BA Para. 20-802.
WGA MBA App. B § G.3.
SAG TVA Sec. 78(d)(4).
AFTRA Netcode Ex. E § 4.D.

## L. History of Made for Pay TV and Home Video

| Date | Unions | Event |
|---|---|---|
| 1980 | SAG, AFTRA | Strike establishes residuals and other terms in made for pay TV and home video; 4.5 % of distributors' gross after 10 exhibition days within a year, on each pay-TV system; 4.5% of producer's gross after sale of 100,000 units of videodiscs and cassettes. |
| 1981 | DGA | Residuals established |

| Date | Unions | Event |
|---|---|---|
| 1984 | [DGA, WGA, SAG, AFTRA] | Residuals formula changed to 2% of gross (SAG/AFTRA 3x) from 2.5% [check which reuse pattern] |
| 1985 | WGA | [strike] |
| 2001 | WGA | Increase in residuals for made-for-pay TV |
| 2011 | WGA | Made-for-pay TV half-hour/one-hour fees increase from $3,500 / $6,000 to $4,200 / $7,200 |

94 – *Entertainment Residuals: A Full Color Guide*

# 9. MADE FOR BASIC CABLE

## A. Basic Cable to Domestic Basic Cable

| Run | Percent |
|---|---|
| 2 | 17% |
| 3 | 12% |
| 4 | 11% |
| 5 | 10% |
| 6 | 6% |
| 7 | 4% |

| Run | Percent |
|---|---|
| 8 | 4% |
| 9 | 3.5% |
| 10 | 3.5% |
| 11 | 3% |
| 12 | 2.5% |
| after | 1.5% |

### Contents of Cell H6

"Sanchez" = run by run declining 17%-1.5% of RB/AM/TAM). *WGA alt:* "Hitchcock"= 120% AM difference pmt; H3 when > 12 runs or 5 yrs *AFTRA alt:* Exhibition days yr by yr declining % of scale. IATSE, AFM:$0. 2nd lic: 2% GR (SAG-AFTRA 3X).

### Explanation

The various unions approach this reuse pattern in somewhat different ways.

The **DGA, SAG-AFTRA** and **Legacy-SAG** use the Sanchez formula, described below. The **WGA** offers the producer a choice of the Sanchez or Hitchcock formulas, also described below, or the option to freely bargain for a different formula. **Legacy-AFTRA** offered the producer a choice of Sanchez or an exhibition day formula.

### Sanchez Formula

The Sanchez formula works the same way as the formula for free TV to other than network primetime (D3) (and uses the same RB, AM or TAM), except that the percentages are lower. They're as follows:

For the WGA, SAG-AFTRA, Legacy-SAG and the Legacy-AFTRA Ex. A per run template,[*] payment for runs 2-5 are due in a single payment as soon as payment becomes due for run 2. Thereafter, each run is paid on a run by run basis. This lump-sum approach is not mentioned in the DGA contract nor in the Legacy-AFTRA CW Sanchez template, and so presumably does not apply.

The formula is called "Sanchez" because the 1986 USA Network show *Sanchez of Bel Air* was the first (or perhaps one of the first) shows to use it.

### Hitchcock Formula

This formula is also named after a 1986 USA Network show, *Alfred Hitchcock Presents,* which was a revival of a 1955 show. The thrillmeister had died in 1980, but in an appropriate touch, he too was revived, in the form of colorized clips introducing segments of the show. Like the residuals chart, Hitchcock was better in color, or so the producers thought.

Who knows whether he'd have appreciated that touch (probably), let alone having his name appropriated for a residuals formula (perhaps not). In any case, we submit for your consideration – oops, that's from *The Twilight Zone* – the following explanation:

For high budget dramatic programs (remember, this term includes comedies too), the residual is 120% of the difference between the network

---

[*] This is the Legacy-AFTRA template that reflects Sanchez for other than CW programs. See the discussion of AFTRA Exhibition Day Formulas on p. 95 for more details on the four Legacy-AFTRA basic cable templates.

primetime applicable minimum for the program (i.e., the minimum initial comp that would have been payable had the program been made for network primetime) and the other than network primetime applicable minimum.* For other types of programs, the reuse fee is 84% of the applicable minimum.

The payment covers 12 basic cable runs of the program over a five-year period. The initial run counts as one of the 12 runs (i.e., the residual covers 12 runs, not 12 reruns) and, in fact, the payment is due upon initial exhibition. According to the WGA, the Hitchcock formula is the only case where an initial run triggers a residual payment.

[tbd – mention Canada here; search MBA for references to Canada and Mexico, and add to International chapter]

If a program is reused beyond the initial basic cable cycle and/or the initial Canadian television cycle, then the additional reuse is treated and paid for in the same manner as reuse of a program made for free television (H3, see p. 80).

### AFTRA Exhibition Day Formulas

[tbd]

[discuss templates, CW Supplement][cross-reference dispute]

### License to Different Basic Cable System

[tbd – 2% gross – 2014 onward]

### No Residuals

No residuals for IATSE or AFM.

### Pattern Analysis

Sanchez is in pattern, but the alternative formulas and individually negotiated deals are not.

### Related Cells

Model: D3 free TV to other than network primetime.

### Book Cross References

Made for basic cable: p. 30.
Reuse on basic cable: p. 42.
What initial comp covers (runs): p. 52.
What initial comp covers (exhibition days): p. 54.
Percentage residuals: p. 55.
Fixed residuals at run by run declining %: p. 61.
Fixed residuals – the residual base: p. 62.
Exhibition day formulas: p. 63.

### Contract References

DGA BA Para. 23-104(a).
WGA MBA App. C §§ 2(b)(1)-(3).
SAG-AFTRA Basic Cable Agt. Sec. 3.
L-SAG Basic Cable Agt. Sec. 3.
L-AFTRA Basic Cable templates.

---

* [tbd – Art. references]

## B. Basic Cable to Network Primetime

Cable exhibition is treated as the initial run.

### No Residuals

No residuals for IATSE or AFM.

### Pattern Analysis

DGA and SAG are in pattern *WGA is not*.

### Related Cells

Model: C3 free TV to network primetime.

### Book Cross References

Made for basic cable: p. 30.
Reuse in network primetime: p. 39.
Percentage residuals: p. 55.
Fixed residuals at 100%: p. 59.
Fixed residuals – the residual base: p. 62.

### Contract References

DGA BA Para. 23-104(f).
WGA MBA App. C §§ 2(b)(1), (2).
SAG Basic Cable Sec. 1.
AFTRA Basic Cable templates.

### Contents of Cell C6

*DGA, SAG*: C3. *WGA*: if {>= 10 runs on BC or <= 66 episodes in series} or {Hitchcock}, use H3; else C3. IA, AFM: $0.

### Explanation

**DGA and SAG:** treated as if made for free TV. See p. 70.

**WGA** [tbd]

## 9. Basic Cable Product – 97

### C. Basic Cable to Other than Network Primetime

### WGA

[tbd]

### SAG

[tbd]

➔ In this case, the runs on basic cable are treated as the first *two* runs for purposes of determining where the percentages start. Thus, the first run on free TV begins with the same percentage as run [4 (i.e., 3rd rerun)] does for free TV to non-network. The percentages are as follows:

| Run | Percent |
|---|---|
| 1 | 25% |
| 2 | 25% |
| 3 | 25% |
| 4 | 15% |
| 5 | 15% |

| Run | Percent |
|---|---|
| 6 | 15% |
| 7 | 15% |
| 8 | 10% |
| 9 | 10% |
| after | 5% |

### Contents of Cell D6

*WGA:* H3 or D3 as per C6. *DGA, SAG:* if >= 10 runs or 1 yr on BC: *DGA* (2% of GR) or *SAG* (declining 25% to 5% of TAM, w/large discount based on GR); else D3. D3 starts at 40%. IA, AFM: $0.

### Notes in Other Cells

Cell C6: *WGA:* if {>= 10 runs on BC or <= 66 episodes in series} or {Hitchcock}, use H3; else C3.

### Explanation

[tbd]

### DGA

Re made for free TV to other than network primetime, see p. 72.

➔ Note that the runs on basic cable are not treated as runs for purposes of determining where the percentages start. Thus, the first run on free TV begins with the same percentage as run 2 (i.e., 1st rerun) does for free TV to non-network. The percentages are as follows:

| Run | Percent |
|---|---|
| 1 | 40% |
| 2 | 30% |
| 3 | 25% |
| 4 | 25% |
| 5 | 25% |
| 6 | 15% |

| Run | Percent |
|---|---|
| 7 | 15% |
| 8 | 15% |
| 9 | 15% |
| 10 | 10% |
| 11 | 10% |
| after | 5% |

### AFTRA

[tbd]

### No Residuals

No residuals for IATSE or AFM.

### Pattern Analysis

There is no pattern.

### Related Cells

Partial model: D3 free TV to other than network primetime.

### Book Cross References

Made for basic cable: p. 30.
Reuse in other than network primetime: p. 40
Percentage residuals: p. 55.
Fixed residuals at run by run declining %: p. 61.
Fixed residuals – the residual base: p. 62.

### Contract References

DGA BA Para. 23-104(b)-(e).
WGA MBA App. C §§ 2 (b)(1), (2).
SAG Basic Cable Secs. 5-8.
AFTRA Basic Cable templates.

## D. Basic Cable to Foreign TV

### Contents of Cell E6

Same as made for free TV (E3). IATSE, AFM: $0. [AGICOA?]

### Explanation

Same as made for free TV to foreign. See p. 78.

AFTRA: [tbd]

### No Residuals

No residuals for IATSE and AFM.

### Pattern Analysis

Pattern is maintained.

### Related Cells

Model: D3 free TV to foreign.

### Book Cross References

Made for basic cable: p. 30.
Foreign reuse: p. 41.
Hybrid residual formulas: p. 63.

### Contract References

DGA BA Para. 23-104(f).
WGA MBA App. C §§ 2(b)(1), (2).
SAG BC Sec. 1.
AFTRA Basic Cable templates.

## E. Basic Cable to Supplemental Markets

### Pattern Analysis

Pattern is maintained.

### Related Cells

Model: F3-G3 made for free TV to supplemental markets.

### Book Cross References

Made for basic cable: p. 30.
Reuse in supplemental markets: p. 41.
Reuse on pay TV: p. 42.
Reuse on home video: p. 42.
Percentage residuals: p. 55.

### Contract References

DGA BA Para. 23-104(f).
WGA MBA App. C §§ 2(b)(1), (2).
SAG Basic Cable Sec. 1.
AFTRA Basic Cable templates.
AFM ?

### Contents of Cells F6-G6

Same as made for free TV (F3-G3). IATSE $0.

### Explanation

Same as made for free TV to supplemental markets. See p 81.

### No Residuals

No residuals for IATSE.

## F. History of Made for Basic Cable

| Date | Unions | Event |
|------|--------|-------|
| 1988 | WGA | Residuals established (strike) |
| 1989 | DGA | Residuals established |
| 1997 | AFTRA | Agt. w/Nickelodeon – AFTRA's 1st system-wide basic cable agt. |
| 2001 | WGA | For product where writing services commenced on or after 5/2/02, Sanchez percentages increased to 17%-1.5% from 14.4%, 10.8%, 9%, 9%, 5%, 3%, 3%, 3%, 3%, 2%, 2%, 1%; also, with same effective date, Hitchcock percentages increased from |

| Date | Unions | Event |
|------|--------|-------|
|  |  | 100%/70% to 120%/84% (i.e., 20% increase in amount paid) |
| 2006 | SAG | Sanchez percentages increased to 17%-1.5% from 14.4%-1% |
| 2014 | All ATL | Percentage residual established for license to second cable network. |

# 10. THEATRICAL USE OF TV AND HOME VIDEO PRODUCT

### Contents of Cells B3-B6

*DGA*: U.S./ Canada, 150% theat AM; non-U.S./Canada, 100% of same; both, 150% of same.

*WGA* - made for free TV or basic cable: U.S., greater of theatr AM or 150% of the non network-PT TV AM; non-U.S., same formula but 100% instead of 150%; both, use U.S. formula.

*WGA* - made for pay TV or HV: 100% theat AM.

*SAG, AFTRA*: U.S./Canada, 150% TAM; non-U.S./Canada, same (alt: 50% TAM per ea. non-U.S./Canada zone); both, 200% TAM.

*AFTRA:* BC unclear.

AFM: 50% TV scale.

IA, AFM BC $0.

### Explanation

### DGA

If a television program (i.e., a TV movie or a series episode)[*] is exhibited theatrically outside of the U.S. and Canada, the residual is 100% of the applicable theatrical minimum. This is a one-time payment. Thus, for instance, it doesn't matter if the program is released theatrically in one foreign country or dozens of them; only a single 100% payment will be due.

If a television program is released theatrically in the U.S. or Canada, the residual is 150% of the applicable theatrical minimum. Again, this is a one-time payment.

The latter is also the maximum residual for this reuse pattern. Thus, if a television program is released theatrically in the U.S. and/or Canada and also outside the U.S. and Canada, the total residual due for this reuse pattern is 150% of the applicable theatrical minimum, not 250%.

### WGA – Made for Free TV or Basic Cable

If a program made for free TV or basic cable is exhibited theatrically outside of the U.S., the residual is the greater of (a) 100% of the applicable television minimum[†] and (b) 100% of the applicable theatrical minimum.[‡] This is a one-time payment (one payment for each writer).

If a television program is released theatrically in the U.S. or both in the U.S. and outside the U.S., the residual is the greater of (a) 150% of the applicable television minimum and (b) 100% of the applicable theatrical minimum. This too is a one-time payment.

The latter is also the maximum residual for this reuse pattern. There is no duplication of the above payments. Thus, if the initial theatrical release of the television program takes place outside of the United States and payment is made pursuant to the first paragraph above, then, upon the subsequent theatrical release in the United States, the amount payable will be the difference between the amount provided for in the first paragraph above and the amount provided for in the second paragraph above.

As with the DGA, multiple television programs (such as multiple episodes of a TV series) can be treated and released as a single theatrical movie.

### WGA – Made for Pay TV or Home Video

If a program made for pay TV or home video is exhibited theatrically, the residual is 100% of

---

[*] The same formulas apply if two or more television programs are combined and released as a single theatrical movie. See DGA BA Para. 11-202.

[†] See MBA Arts. 13.B.7.a, b and c.
[‡] See MBA Art. 13.A.1.

the applicable theatrical minimum. This is a one-time payment.

### SAG-AFTRA and L-SAG – Default Rule

If a television program is exhibited theatrically outside of the U.S. and Canada, the residual is 150% of the total applicable minimum.[*] This is a one-time payment (one payment for each actor).

If a television program is released theatrically in the U.S. or Canada, the residual is 150% of the total applicable minimum. Again, this is a one-time payment.

The maximum residual for this reuse pattern is 200% of the total applicable minimum. Thus, if a television program is released theatrically in the U.S. and/or Canada and also outside the U.S. and Canada, the total residual due for this reuse pattern is 200% of the applicable theatrical minimum, not 300%.

### Legacy-SAG – Zone System

As an alternative approach, for a limited theatrical release[†] of a longform television motion picture (a TV movie), the residual is 50% of total applicable minimum for release in each of the following areas:

- Zone 1 – includes the Americas (excluding the U.S. and Canada) and the Caribbean Islands.

- Zone 2 – includes all European countries (including the United Kingdom) except those covered in Zone 4 below.

- Zone 3 – includes the Far East, Australia and New Zealand.

- Zone 4 – includes all other countries not covered in Zones 1, 2 or 3, including the Middle East, Eastern Europe, Africa and the former Soviet Republics (but excluding the U.S. and Canada).

If the producer pays for theatrical release in three or more zones and elects to release the television motion picture for theatrical exhibition in the U.S., the producer must make an additional payment of 50% of total applicable minimum.[‡]

### Legacy-AFTRA

If a program made for network primetime is exhibited theatrically, the residual is calculated using the SAG-AFTRA rules above.

If a program made for pay TV or home video is exhibited theatrically, the residual is "the applicable minimum fee payable under the . . . AFTRA Code had such program been first exhibited in free television."[§] What this means is not entirely clear.

Also unclear is the residual if a program made for basic cable is exhibited theatrically.

### AFM

The residual payable to each musician is 50% of the television scale payments earned by that musician for the product being reused. This applies to free TV, pay TV and home video product. The AFM basic cable agreement omits mention of a residual for this reuse pattern, so there presumably is none.

### No Residuals

No residuals for IATSE or for AFM basic cable product.

### Pattern Analysis

There are similarities but no real pattern.

### Book Cross References

Made for free TV: p. 27.
Made for pay TV: p. 28.
Made for home video: p. 29.
Made for basic cable: p. 30.
Reuse in theatrical: p. 38.
Theatrical reuse residuals: p. 64.

### Contract References

### Re Free TV product (B3)

DGA BA Para. 11-201.

---

[*] TAM is calculated using television wage rates. See TVA sec. 19(c)(4).
[†] The contract does not define the term "limited theatrical release."
[‡] The contract is silent on the question of what happens if the producer pays for only one or two zones and also wishes to theatrically release in the U.S.
[§] AFTRA Netcode Ex. E § 4.C.

WGA MBA Arts. 15.B.13.a-c.
SAG TVA Secs. 19(a)-(c).
AFTRA Netcode Ex. A § 3.
AFM TV Sec. 15(b)(17)(i).

## Re Pay TV & Home Video product (B4-B5)

DGA BA Para. 20-803.
WGA MBA App. B § G.2.
SAG TVA Sec. 78(d)(3).
AFTRA Netcode Ex. E § 4.C.
AFM TV Sec. 15(b)(17)(i).

## Re Basic Cable product (B6)

DGA BA Para. 23-104(f).
WGA MBA App. C §§ 2(b)(1), (2).
SAG Basic Cable Sec. 1.
AFTRA Basic Cable templates.

## History

| Date | Unions | Event |
|---|---|---|
| [tbd] | | |

# 11. NEW MEDIA REUSE OF TRADITIONAL PRODUCT

## A. Theatrical, TV and Home Video to eRental

### Contents of Cells I2-I6

1.2% of gross (SAG 3x, AFTRA TV 3x, IATSE 4.5x, AFM 1%, AFM BC 3.6%)).

Resids only for post-x/x/x product (unless n.d.). x/x/x = DGA n.d. (?); *WGA* 7/1/71; *SAG th.* n.d. (?); *SAG TV* 7/20/52; *AFTRA* n.d. (?); *IATSE* 2/1/73; *AFM* 7/1/71; *AFM BC* n.d. No resids for older product. Date cutoffs apply even to theatrical & non-exhausted free TV.

### Explanation

DGA: 1.2% of gross.
WGA: same as DGA.
SAG-AFTRA: 3 times this percentage (i.e., 3.6%).
IATSE: 4.5 times this percentage (i.e., 5.4%).
AFM: 1% of gross.
AFM basic cable: 3.6% of gross.

### No Residuals

There are residuals only for product (or writing services) older than certain dates. The cutoffs are as follows:

| Union | Date |
|---|---|
| DGA | Unspecified; [(perhaps the only cutoffs are Post-60's (I2) and possibly exhaustion (I3))] |
| WGA | 7/1/71 |
| SAG theatrical | Unspecified; [(perhaps the only cutoff is Post-60's]] |
| SAG TV | 7/20/52 [(perhaps exhaustion also blocks residuals)] |
| AFTRA | Unspecified; [(perhaps the only cutoff is exhaustion)] |
| IATSE | 2/1/73 |
| AFM | 7/1/71 |
| AFM basic cable | Unspecified |

Treatment of exhausted product is unclear.

### Pattern Analysis

Pattern is maintained, except that date cutoffs vary.

### Related Cells

Model: F2-F3 theatrical and free TV to pay TV.

### Book Cross References

Made for theatrical: p. 26.
Post-'60 theatrical motion pictures: p. 27.
Made for free TV: p. 27.
Exhausted free TV product: p. 28.
Made for pay TV: p. 28.
Made for home video: p. 29.
Made for basic cable: p. 30.
Reuse in eRental: p. . 43.
Percentage residuals: p. 55.

### Contract References

DGA BA NM Reuse SL §§ 1, 5.
WGA MBA NM Reuse SL §§ 1.a, 3.a, 5.
SAG CBA/TVA NM Reuse SL §§ 1.A, 4.A.
AFTRA Netcode Ex. A NM Reuse SL §§ 1.A, 5.A.
IATSE NM Reuse SL §§ 1.a, 3.a.
AFM NM Reuse SL §§ 1(a), 3(a).
AFM Basic Cable Ex. B NM Reuse SL § 1A.

## B. Theatrical to Electronic Sell-Through (EST)

### Contents of Cell J2

1.8% to 3.25% of 20% of GR (SAG 3x, IATSE 4.5x, AFM 1% to 1.8%). Break = 50K units. Notes: J3-J6

### Notes in Other Cells

Cells J3-J6: AFM: ratification date. AFM BC date tbd. Other unions: unclear if no resids before dates in I2-I6, or if eff. date of 2008/09 agt. is cutoff, or none

### Explanation

**DGA:** 1.8% of Producer's gross for the first 50,000 units sold, and 3.25% for units sold thereafter.

**WGA:** same as DGA.

**SAG-AFTRA, Legacy-SAG, Legacy-AFTRA:** 3 times these percentages (i.e., 5.4% and 9.75%).

**IATSE:** 4.5 times these percentages (i.e., 8.1% and 14.625%).

**AFM:** 1% of gross, rising to 1.8% at the 50,000 unit break.

Producer's gross equals 20% of worldwide gross receipts received by producer for EST if producer has an affiliated home video company. This is generally the case for the major studios, and generally not the case for non-studios.

These formulas are similar to the formulas for physical home video (see pp. 57, 82), except that the break (the point at which the percentage increases) is at 50,000 units sold, not at achievement of a particular level (such as $1 million) in Producer's gross. Another difference is that the AFM percentage rises at the break, rather than being fixed at 1%.

These formulas are also similar to the formulas for TV and home video to EST (see p. 105), except that there (a) the break is at 100,000 units, (b) the higher DGA and WGA percentage is 3.5% (rather than 3.25%), and (c) and the higher AFM percentage is 1.9% (rather than 1.8%).

### No Residuals

No AFM residuals for product prior to ratification of 2009 AFM agreement.

For other unions, it is unclear if the eRental date cutoffs apply (see p. 103); or if the cutoff is the effective date of the union's 2008/2009 cycle agreement, or some other date or criterion; or if there is no cutoff other than Post-'60.

See related note re TV and home video to EST (p. 105).

### Pattern Analysis

Pattern is maintained, except that date cutoff language varies.

### Related Cells

Model: G2 theatrical to home video, but percentages here are higher.

### Book Cross References

Made for theatrical: p. 26.
Post-'60 theatrical motion pictures: p. 27.
Reuse in EST: p. 43.
Percentage residuals: p. 55.

### Contract References

DGA BA NM Reuse SL §§ 2, 5.
WGA MBA NM Reuse SL §§ 1.b, 3.a, 5.
SAG-AFTRA & L-SAG CBA/TVA NM Reuse SL §§ 1.B, 4.A.
L-AFTRA Netcode Ex. A NM Reuse SL §§ 1.B, 5.A.
IATSE NM Reuse SL §§ 1.b, 3.a.
AFM NM Reuse SL §§ 1(b), 3(a).
AFM Basic Cable Ex. B NM Reuse SL § 1B.

## C. TV and Home Video to Electronic Sell-Through (EST)

### Contents of Cells J3-J6

1.8%-3.5% of 20% of gross (SAG-AFTRA 3x, IATSE 4.5x, AFM (1%-1.9% (vs. J2); BC 5.4%-10.5%)). Break = 100K units.

WGA - per arbitration: No residuals for pre-2/13/08 TV product. AFM: ratification. AFM BC date tbd. Other unions: unclear if no resids before dates in I2-I6, or if eff. date of 2008/09 agt. is cutoff, or none

### Notes in Other Cells

H3: No . . . residuals on exhausted TV product (i.e., if network rerun residuals not still payable (generally, pre-7/1/71 product)).

### Explanation

DGA: 1.8% of Producer's gross for the first 100,000 units sold, and 3.5% for units sold thereafter.

WGA: same as DGA.

SAG-AFTRA, L-SAG, L-AFTRA: 3 times these percentages (i.e., 5.4% and 10.5%).

IATSE: 4.5 times these percentages (i.e., 8.1% and 15.75%).

AFM: 1% of gross, rising to 1.9% at the 100,000 unit break.

Producer's gross equals 20% of worldwide gross receipts received by producer for EST if producer has an affiliated home video company. This is generally the case for the major studios, and generally not the case for non-studios.

These formulas are similar to the formulas for physical home video (see pp. 57, 82), except that the break (the point at which the percentage increases) is at 50,000 units sold, not at achievement of a particular level (such as $1 million) in Producer's gross. Another difference is that the AFM percentage rises at the break, rather than being fixed at 1%.

These formulas are also similar to the formulas for TV and home video to EST (see p. 104), except that there (a) the break is at 50,000 units, (b) the higher DGA and WGA percentage is 3.25% (rather than 3.5%), and (c) the higher AFM percentage is 1.8% (rather than 1.9%).

### No Residuals

No WGA residuals for pre-2/13/08 TV product, per an arbitration decision.[*] No AFM residuals for product prior to ratification of 2009 AFM agreement. Cutoff date for AFM basic cable product tbd.

For other unions, it is unclear if the eRental date cutoffs apply (see p. 103); or if the cutoff is the effective date of the union's 2008/2009 cycle agreement, or some other date or criterion such as exhaustion; or if there is no cutoff. Treatment of exhausted product is unclear.

See related note for theatrical to EST (p. 104).

### Pattern Analysis

Pattern is maintained, except that date cutoff language varies.

### Related Cells

Model: G3 free TV to home video, but percentages here are higher.

### Book Cross References

Made for free TV: p. 27.
Exhausted free TV product: p. 28.
Made for pay TV: p. 28.
Made for home video: p. 29.
Made for basic cable: p. 30.
Reuse in EST: p. 43.
Percentage residuals: p. 55.

---

[*] [cite]

## Contract References

DGA BA NM Reuse SL §§ 2, 5.
WGA MBA NM Reuse SL §§ 1.b, 3.a, 5.
SAG-AFTRA & L-SAG CBA/TVA NM Reuse SL §§ 1.B, 4.A.
L-AFTRA Netcode Ex. A NM Reuse SL §§ 1.B, 5.A.
IATSE NM Reuse SL §§ 1.b, 3.a.
AFM NM Reuse SL §§ 1(b), 3(a).
AFM Basic Cable Ex. B NM Reuse SL § 1B.

## D. Theatrical to Ad-Supported

| Reused in: | Theatrical | Free TV Network Primetime | Free TV Syndication or Non-Primetime | Foreign | Supp. Mkts. Pay TV | Supp. Mkts. Home Video | Domestic Basic Cable | New Media Consumer Pd eRental | New Media Consumer Pd EST | New Media Ad Supported |
|---|---|---|---|---|---|---|---|---|---|---|
| Theatrical | | C2 to E2 | | | | | | | | K2 |
| Free TV | | | | | | | | | | |
| Pay TV | | | | | | | | | | |
| Home Video | | | | | | | | | | |
| Basic Cable | | | | | | | | | | |
| Deriv. NM | | | | | | | | | | |
| Orig. NM | | | | | | | | | | |
| Exper. NM | | | | | | | | | | |

### Contents of Cell K2

1.2% of gross (SAG-AFTRA 3x, IATSE 4.5x, AFM 1%) for post-7/1/71 product. No resids for older product. See also AVOD note below.

### Notes in Other Cells

**K3-K6:** *WGA, SAG-AFTRA: No residuals for AVOD use of pre-2014 product.*

### Explanation

**DGA:** 1.2% of gross.
**WGA:** same as DGA.
**SAG-AFTRA, L-SAG:** 3 times this percentage (i.e., 3.6%).
**IATSE:** 4.5 times this percentage (i.e., 5.4%).
**AFM:** 1% of gross.

### No Residuals

No residuals for pre-7/1/71 product. Also, the WGA and SAG-AFTRA agreements commencing in 2014 provide that there are no residuals for use of pre-mid-2014 product on a cable, satellite or telco system's AVOD service. *The DGA agreement is silent on this.*

### Pattern Analysis

Pattern is maintained, except perhaps with respect to pre-mid-2014 AVOD product.

### Related Cells

Model: **C2-E2** theatrical to free TV and foreign.

### Book Cross References

Made for theatrical: p. 26.
Post-'60 theatrical motion pictures: p. 27.
Reuse on ad-supported platforms: p. 45.
Percentage residuals: p. 55.

### Contract References

DGA BA NM Reuse SL §§ 3.B, 5.
WGA MBA NM Reuse SL §§ 2.a, 3.a.
SAG-AFTRA & L-SAG CBA/TVA NM Reuse SL §§ 2.D, 4.A.
IATSE NM Reuse SL §§ 2, 3.a.
AFM NM Reuse SL §§ 2, 3(a).

## E. TV and Home Video to Ad-Supported

| Reused in:<br>Made for: | Theatrical | Free TV Network Primetime | Free TV Syndication or Non-Primetime | Foreign | Supp. Mkts. Pay TV | Supp. Mkts. Home Video | Domestic Basic Cable | New Media Consumer Pd eRental | New Media Consumer Pd EST | New Media Ad Supported |
|---|---|---|---|---|---|---|---|---|---|---|
| Theatrical | | | | | | | | | | |
| Free TV | | | | | | | | | | **K3 to K6** |
| Pay TV | | | | | | | | | | |
| Home Video | | | | | | | | | | |
| Basic Cable | | | | | | | | | | |
| Deriv. NM | | | | | | | | | | **K7** |
| Orig. NM | | | | | | | | | | |
| Exper. NM | | | | | | | | | | |

### Contents of Cells K3-K6

Current product: Free win. of 7 days or 24 days (1st 7 eps. of a new series and any one-time programs) or 17 days (kids shows) (but always 7 days for K3), then two 26 wk. windows ea. @ 4% (rising in contract year 2 to 4.5% then 5% in contract year 3) of RB/AM/TAM, then (1 year after end of free win) 2% GR (SAG-AFTRA, AFM BC 3x). RB/AM is non network-PT. AFM BC: RB = scale wages earned.

Note: former WGA imputed gross formula was deleted in 2014.

WGA, SAG-AFTRA: *No residuals for AVOD use of pre-2014 product.*

Product prior to 2008/09 Agt. (but see H3 note): 2% of gross (SAG-AFTRA, AFM BC 3x).

Foreign streaming: use E3-E6.

IATSE, AFM non-BC: no residuals.

### Notes in Other Cells

K1: foreign streaming of TV/HV product uses E3-E6.

H3: No . . . residuals on exhausted TV product (i.e., if network rerun residuals not still payable (generally, pre-7/1/71 product)).

### Explanation

#### Summary

This formula is intricate, but the overall structure is easy to summarize: for current product, there is first a several-day "streaming window" (i.e., free window) during which no residuals are payable, followed by two 26-week windows during which a small fixed residual is payable, and then, one year after the end of the free window, by a percentage residual.

Now let's look at the details.

#### Streaming Window

For product produced starting in mid-2014, the streaming window is generally 7 consecutive days, but it is 24 consecutive days for the first seven episodes of a new television series or for any one-time program, and it is 17 consecutive days for children's programming.[*]

For product produced prior to mid-2014, the streaming window was 24 days in the first season of a television series or for any one-time program, and was 17 days in subsequent seasons.

During the streaming window(s), the producer can make the episode or one-time program available without having to pay residuals.

The streaming window may be divided between the period immediately prior to and immediately following the initial exhibition of the episode or one-time program on television in any ratio determined by the producer. However, beginning mid-2014, there's another alternative for each episode of a series in its first year: the free streaming window may commence up to thirty (30) days before the initial exhibition on television of the episode.

[tbd rerun streaming window]

#### First 26 Week Period

If the producer wants to stream the episode or program after the streaming window, but within one year of the expiration of the streaming window, then the producer must make a fixed residual payment. (The amount of the residual payment is discussed below). The residual payment covers a 26 consecutive week period beginning on the first day that the episode or pro-

---
[*] The term "children's programming" is not defined in the agreements.

gram is available for streaming following the expiration of the streaming window.

Note that the 26 week period does not have to be contiguous with the streaming window. So, for instance, the producer could make the program available during the streaming window, then take it off the Internet for ten weeks, then once again make it available. The 26 week period would not start until the program is made available for streaming, i.e., 10 weeks after the streaming window ends.

### Second 26 Week Period

If the producer wants to stream the episode or program for all or any part of the 26 consecutive week period immediately following the 26 consecutive week period described in the preceding subsection, but within one year of the expiration of the streaming window, then the producer must make another fixed residual payment.

The amount of the payment is calculated in the same fashion as the payment for the first 26-week period.

### Residual Amount for 26 Week Period

We've referred to the residual that's due for each 26 week period but haven't yet explained what that amount is. Here it is:

DGA: A small percentage (see table below) of the residual base. The residual base is the other than network primetime residual base – i.e., the applicable figure found in BA Sec. 11-101(b)(2) – even if the product was made for network primetime. Thus, the figures in Sec. 11-101(b)(1) are not used.

WGA: A small percentage (see table below) of the applicable minimum. As with the DGA, the other than network primetime applicable minimum (MBA Art. 13.B.7.a-c) is used, even if the product was made for network primetime.

*However, for 30 or 60 min. network primetime teleplays written on or after May 2, 2010\* but prior to May 2, 2014,† the residual for each 26 week window was 2% of "accountable receipts."*

That 30/60 minute formula sounds like a gross-based formula, but it's not, because accountable receipts are defined in the 2008 MBA to be a fixed number: $20,000 (30 min.) or $40,000 (60 min.). That means that the residual amount is actually a fixed amount, $400 or $800 (for 2010-2011).

Thus, the apparent gross formula is not a gross formula at all. The WGA highlighted this departure from pattern as a significant accomplishment in the resolution of the 2007-2008 strike, in order to say that it had achieved something in its negotiations that the DGA had not.

Ironically, the gross figures are slightly lower than the 3.5% fixed residual that would otherwise have been effective, which calculates out to $449.99 and $817.95.‡

The 2011 MBA provided for 2% annual bumps to the $20,000 / $40,000 figures for the next three years. That's the same rate at which the applicable minimum increased. Thus, the pseudo-gross formula continued to track the fixed residual formula used by the other unions. However, in the 2014 MBA, the pseudo-gross formula disappeared. Instead, the residual is a small percentage of applicable minimum, in pattern with the DGA and SAG-AFTRA.

SAG-AFTRA: A small percentage (see table below) of the total applicable minimum.

AFM Basic Cable: A small percentage (see table below) of the residual base. [verify 2014 and beyond] The residual base is equal to scale wages earned by the musicians. This appears to mean the aggregate scale wages earned. This aggregate amount is then allocated pro rata to each musician in accordance with the scale wages he or she earned.§

### The "Small Percentage"

The "small percentage" referred to above has increased over time. Here's a table:

---

\* This is the date that the third year of the 2008 MBA began.
† This is the date that the 2014 MBA took effect.

‡ 3.5% times the AM ($12,857 or $23,370, respectively). See MBA Art. 13.B.7.c (2008).
§ See p. 129.

| Date | Percentage |
|---|---|
| Initially – i.e., first day of 2008/2009 contract (mid-2008 for DGA, WGA and AFTRA or mid-2009 for SAG) | 3% |
| Two years thereafter (mid-2010 or mid-2011) | 3.5% |
| Mid-2014 | 4% |
| Mid-2015 | 4.5% |
| Mid-2016 | 5% |

It's not always obvious what the effective dates apply to, however, except in the case of SAG-AFTRA, where the language states that they refer to commencement of principal photography. For instance, for SAG-AFTRA the 4% rate applies to television product whose principal photography commences on or after mid-2014 (specifically, July 1, 2014). [tbd check old MOAs]

In the case of the other unions, though, it's not clear how to interpret the effective date provisions, because the language simply says things like "four percent (4%) effective May 2, 2014" (the WGA language).

Does that mean that the 4% rate applies for (a) any streaming that occurs on or after that date, (b) streaming during a 26-week period that commences on or after that date, (c) product whose principal photography commences on or after that date, (d) product whose teleplay was ordered on or after that date, (e) product whose teleplay was commenced on or after that date, or (f) product whose teleplay was completed on or after that date?

Option (a) seems the most straightforward linguistic interpretation, but it's out of pattern with SAG-AFTRA and also awkwardly implies that the older 3.5% rate applies to the portion of the 26-week period that precedes the date cutoff (i.e., if the May 2, 2014 date falls in the middle of the 26-week period). Option (b) is a less straightforward interpretation but easier to apply – but it's still out of pattern. Options (c)-(f) are in pattern, but are not what the language expressly says.

In any event, note that this is a fixed residual, not a percentage of gross. Thus, the SAG-AFTRA small percentage (4% or whatever) is the same as the DGA and WGA small percentage. As with, for instance, syndication residuals (D3), there is no 3x multiplier.

## Prorated 26 Week Period

Sometimes the producer does not get the benefit of a full 26 week window because the producer commences streaming "late." In such cases, the residual is prorated in weekly units to cover the shorter use period.

For example, suppose that the producer streams a program during the streaming window and then does not stream the program again until 39 weeks after the expiration of the streaming window.

Since only 13 weeks remain within the one year period prior to the percentage residual kicking in, the producer will only get the benefit of one-half of a 26 week period (i.e., 13/26). Therefore, the residual due for this period will be one-half of what would have been due for an entire 26 week period.

## One Year After the Streaming Window

Beginning one year after the expiration of the streaming window (or, in some cases, a year after initial exhibition on television), a percentage residual applies, as follows:

DGA: 2% of gross.
WGA: same as DGA.
SAG-AFTRA: 3 times this percentage (i.e., 6%).
AFM Basic Cable: 3 times this percentage (i.e., 6%).

The one-year period usually runs from the end of the streaming window. However, if the episode or program has not been streamed during the one-year period following initial exhibition on television, or if it has been streamed only during the streaming window, then the one-year period is deemed to begin on the date of initial exhibition on television.

## Special Rule Regarding Excerpts (Clips)

During the streaming window, or during either of the 26 consecutive week (or shorter) periods, the producer may allow excerpts (of those episodes or programs that are being streamed) to be used on ad-supported new media platforms without making any additional excerpt fee payment.*

### Older Product

Product produced (or in the case of the WGA, written) prior to the effective date of a union's 2008/2009 agreement is not subject to the above formulas at all. Rather, the residual for such product (other than exhausted free TV product) is as follows:

DGA: 2% of gross.
WGA: same as DGA.
SAG-AFTRA: 3 times this percentage (i.e., 6%).
AFM Basic Cable: 3 times this percentage (i.e., 6%).

### Motivation for the Formulas

Why are the formulas for this reuse pattern so complex? The answer has to do with the way in which ad-supported Internet rights are licensed. Those rights usually are licensed by the producer to the network as part of the telecast rights.

In current practice (2015), only the five most recent episodes of the current season are made available on ad-supported streaming services such as Hulu, commencing the day after television broadcast. That means that the usual residual is presumably just a payment for a single 26-week window.

### Foreign Ad-Supported Services

Ad-supported new media services outside the U.S. are not covered by the above formulas. Rather, such reuse is treated the same way as foreign free TV and basic cable exhibition, and is subject to the formulas in E3-E6. The logic is that foreign streaming rights are generally licensed as part of the license of foreign television rights.

### No Residuals

No residuals for IATSE, for AFM free TV, pay TV or home video product, and for exhausted TV product. Also, the WGA and SAG-AFTRA agreements commencing in 2014 provide that there are no residuals for use of pre-mid-2014 product on a cable, satellite or telco system's AVOD service. *The DGA agreement is silent on this.*

### Pattern Analysis

Pattern is maintained, except perhaps with respect to pre-mid-2014 AVOD product and except for the defunct WGA provision relating to 2% of "accountable receipts."

### Related Cells

K7 derivative new media to ad-supported uses a similar pattern (with some deviation), i.e., a free window (but 13 weeks, not 17/24 days), followed by two 26 week windows each payable at 3.5% of a residual base (but a different base than is used in K3-K6) and thereafter a 2% gross residual.

I7-J7 derivative and original new media to consumer paid has a 26 week free window, but the formula thereafter is a gross residual. There is no fixed residual component, in contrast to K3-K6 and K7.

### Book Cross References

Made for free TV: p. 27.
Exhausted free TV product: p. 28.
Made for pay TV: p. 28.
Made for home video: p. 29.
Made for basic cable: p. 30.
Reuse on ad-supported platforms: p. 45.
Percentage residuals: p. 55.
Fixed residuals at 100%: p. 59.
Fixed residuals – the residual base: p. 62.
Hybrid residual formulas: p. 63.

### Contract References

DGA BA NM Reuse SL §§ 3. A, 5.
WGA MBA NM Reuse SL §§ 2.b, 3.a.
SAG-AFTRA & L-SAG CBA/TVA NM Reuse SL §§ 2.A, B, 4.A.
L-AFTRA Netcode Ex. A NM Reuse SL §§ 2.A, B, 5.A.
AFM NM Reuse SL §§ 2.
AFM Basic Cable Ex. B NM Reuse SL §§ 2.A.

---

* This is an exception to the normal rule, which is that whenever a producer wants to use excerpts of a program for any purpose other than promotion of the program, recap of prior episodes, or the like, the producer has to pay excerpt fees, also known as clip fees. See p. 145.

## F. History of New Media Reuse and of Made-For New Media

This grid combines history related to this chapter and the next, since they're intertwined. For detailed information on 2007-2009 history, see my book HOLLYWOOD ON STRIKE!

| Date | Unions | NM Reuse Patterns | Event |
|---|---|---|---|
| 2001 | WGA, SAG | Traditional to [tbd] | [tbd] |
| 2002 | DGA | Traditional to [tbd] | [tbd] |
| 2005 | | | [modifications] |
| 2008 | DGA | All | Current made-for NM & NM reuse formulas established |
| 2008 | WGA, AFTRA (FOB), AFTRA (Ex. A) | All | Pattern adopted with minor deviations: (a) WGA imputed gross in TV and home video to ad-supported (K3-K6) and (b) apparently inadvertent linguistic variations in budget test portion of definition of experimental new media (B9-K9) |
| 2009 | SAG | All | Pattern adopted |
| 2009 | AFM | All except derivative NM based on BC | Pattern adopted |
| 2010/11 | All | TV & HV to ad-supported NM (K3-K6) | Per 2008/2009 agreements, fixed residual in 26-week window automatically increased from 3% to 3.5% |
| 2010 | AFM | Derivative NM based on basic cable (row 7) | Draft SL prepared. Remained unsigned as of end of [2014] |
| 2011 | WGA | Network PT free TV to ad-supported (K3) | 2% annual bumps (paralleling the 2011-2014 wage bumps) to 2010-level $20K/$40K imputed gross |
| 2013/14 | DGA, SAG-AFRA. WGA | High-budget SVOD (I10) | Reuse formulas established |
| 2013/14 | DGA, SAG-AFRA. WGA | TV & HV to ad-supported NM (K3-K6) | Change in duration of streaming window; addition of AVOD; [tbd] |

# 12. MADE FOR NEW MEDIA

Derivative and original new media productions are treated somewhat similarly for residuals purposes. Where there are differences, derivative product is more likely to be subject to residuals than original.

## A. Derivative and Original New Media to Consumer Paid

### Contents of Cells I7-J8

26 wk. free win. then 1.2% of GR (SAG-AFTRA, AFM BC-Deriv. 3x; IATSE 4.5x, other AFM 1%).

No resids if {for Orig. NM, budget <= $25K/min.}; or {for Orig. NM or Deriv. NM except AFM BC-Deriv} if {*IA:* < 2 IA crew} or {*IA, other AFM:* 1st release is consumer paid}.

### Explanation

First, there is a 26 week free window, starting on the day the program is first available for exhibition on any consumer paid new media platform. (Contrast this with the 13 week free window in derivative new media to ad-supported, K7, and the 17/24 day free window in TV and home video to ad-supported, K2-K6.)

Thereafter, the residuals formulas are:

DGA: 1.2% of gross.

WGA: same as DGA.

SAG-AFTRA: 3 times this percentage (i.e., 3.6%).

IATSE: 4.5 times this percentage (i.e., 5.4%).

AFM residual for derivative new media based on basic cable: 3 times this percentage (i.e., 3.6%).

AFM residual for derivative new media based on free TV and for original new media: 1%.

### No Residuals

There are no residuals if any of the following apply:

● If the program is original new media and the budget is less than or equal to $25,000 per minute, then there are no residuals for any union. (Contrast this with the definition of experimental new media, which has a budget test that includes a cutoff of $15,000 per minute. See p. 36.)

● If there are fewer than two crew members employed under the IATSE Basic Agreement, then there are no IATSE residuals. This applies to derivative or original new media.

● If the first release is to a consumer paid platform (rather than first to an ad-supported platform or concurrently to both types of platforms), then there are no IATSE residuals. This applies to derivative or original new media.

● If the first release is to a consumer paid platform (rather than an ad-supported platform or concurrently to both types of platforms), then there are no AFM residuals. This applies to original new media and to derivative based on a free TV program, but does not apply to derivative new media based on a basic cable program.

### Pattern Analysis

Pattern is maintained as to window, percentages and budget threshold. *The below the line no-residuals tests are unusual.*

### Book Cross References

Derivative new media: p. 31.
Original new media: p. 35.
Reuse in eRental: p. 43.
Reuse in EST: p. 43.
What initial comp covers: p. 52.
Percentage residuals: p. 55.

## Contract References

### Re Derivative New Media Product

DGA BA Made for NM SL §§ E.1.a, d (& NM Reuse SL § 5).

WGA MBA Made for NM SL §§ 2.b.(4)(a), (d).

SAG CBA/TVA Made for NM SL §§ B.3(a), (d) (& NM Reuse SL § 4.A).

AFTRA Netcode Ex. A NM Reuse SL §§ 4.A(4), 5.A.

IATSE BA Made for NM SL §§ F(1)(c), (d).

AFM Made for NM SL §§ F(1)(b)-(d).

AFM Basic Cable Ex. B Made for NM SL §§ A(1), (4).

### Re Original New Media Product

DGA BA Made for NM SL §§ E.2.a, b (& NM Reuse SL § 5).

WGA MBA Made for NM SL §§ 3.b.(4)(a), (b).

SAG CBA/TVA Made for NM SL §§ D.3(a), (b) (& NM Reuse SL § 4.A).

AFTRA Netcode Ex. A NM Reuse SL § 4.B(2).

IATSE BA Made for NM SL §§ F(1)(a), (b)(ii), (c), (d).

AFM Made for NM SL § F(1).

## B. Derivative New Media to Ad-Supported

### Contents of Cell K7

13 wk free win, then two 26-wk wins. @ {{3.5% (was 3%) of {DGA, WGA: RB/AM (C7-C8)},{AFM BC-Deriv: 1st TV replay fee}}; {*SAG-AFTRA: $20-$25 ea actor*}} ea win, & (1 yr after free win ends) 2% GR (SAG-AFTRA, AFM BC-Deriv 3x). IA, AFM Free TV Deriv: $0.

### Notes in Other Cells

**C7-D8**: WGA C7-D8 & K7 residuals are aggregate, not per writer.

### Explanation

This formula is intricate, but the overall structure is similar to the formulas for TV and home video to ad-supported platforms (K3-K6, see p. 108). The initial free window is much longer here though – 13 weeks.

So, the formula in summary is: there is first a 13 week free window* during which no residuals are payable, followed by two 26-week windows during which a small fixed residual is payable, and then, one year after the end of the free window, by a percentage residual.

Now let's look at the details.

### Free Window

The initial free window is 13 weeks, starting on the day the program is first available for exhibition on any ad-supported new media platform..

---

* The contract does not refer to this free window as the "streaming window," in contrast to the terminology used in K3-K6.

---

No residual is payable for reuse on ad-supported platforms during this period.

### First 26 Week Period

If the producer wants to stream the program after the free window, but within one year of the expiration of the free window, then the producer must make a residual payment. (The amount of the residual payment is discussed below). The residual payment covers a 26 consecutive week period beginning on the first day that the program is available for streaming following the expiration of the free window.

Note that the 26 week period does not have to be contiguous with the free window. So, for instance, the producer could make the program available during the free window, then take it off the Internet for ten weeks, then once again make it available. The 26 week period would not start until the program is made available for streaming, i.e., 10 weeks after the free window ends.

### Second 26 Week Period

If the producer wants to stream the episode or program for all or any part of the 26 consecutive week period immediately following the 26 consecutive week period described in the preceding subsection, but within one year of the expiration of the streaming window, then the producer must make another residual payment.

The amount of the payment is calculated in the same fashion as the payment for the first 26-week period.

### Residual Amount for 26 Week Period

We've referred to the residual that's due for each 26 week period but haven't yet explained what that amount is. Here it is:

**DGA**: 3.5% of the residual base. The residual base is the other-than-network-primetime residual base, i.e., the applicable figure found in BA Sec. 11-101(b)(2).†

---

† To be precise, this is the residual base if the underlying TV series (on which the derivative new media program is based) is a scripted network primetime series. If the TV

Note that the applicable figure varies depending on the length of the derivative new media program (not the length of the underlying program). For instance, if the derivative new media program is 3 minutes long, then the "7 minutes and under" figure is used as the residual base. It's not relevant that the underlying TV series (on which the derivative new media program is based) is a one-hour or half-hour program.

**WGA**: 3.5% of the applicable minimum. The other-than-network-primetime applicable minimum (MBA Art. 13.B.7.c) is used, even if the product was made for network primetime.*

As with the DGA, the applicable figure varies depending on the length of the derivative new media program, not the length of the underlying program. For derivative new media programs up to and including ten minutes in length, the Art. 13.B.7.c amount may need to be prorated in five minute increments.†

The Art. 13.B.7.c amount (prorated if necessary) is an aggregate amount and is used even if the Story by and Teleplay by credits on the derivative new media program are different from each other, e.g., Story by Bill, Teleplay by Jane, rather than a single writer (Written by Chad). The payment is allocated among the writers. The contract does not say how the allocation is to be performed, but presumably it is done as if it were a percentage residual (e.g., 25% to Bill and 75% to Jane in this example).‡

The contract says that "In no event shall any payment be less than $20.00,"§ but it is not explicit as to whether this means before or after the allocation is performed.**

**SAG-AFTRA**: *$20 to each actor if the derivative new media production is 10 minutes or less in length; $25 if longer.*

**AFM Derivative New Media Based on Basic Cable**: 3.5% of the residual base. The residual base is equal to scale wages earned by the musicians. This appears to mean the aggregate scale wages earned. This aggregate amount is then allocated pro rata to the musicians in accordance with the scale wages each one earned.††

The 3.5% figure used in the above formulas represents an increase from its previous level, 3%. Here's a historical table:

| Date | Percentage |
|---|---|
| Initially – i.e., first day of 2008/2009 contract (mid-2008 or mid-2009, depending on union) | 3% |
| Two years thereafter (mid-2010 or mid-2011) | 3.5% |
| xxx | |

## Prorated 26 Week Period

Sometimes the producer does not get the benefit of a full 26 week window because the producer commences streaming "late." In such cases, the residual is prorated in weekly units to cover the shorter use period, in the same fashion as described on p. 110.

## One Year After the Streaming Window

Beginning one year after the expiration of the streaming window (or, in some cases, a year after initial exhibition on television), the residual formula is as follows:

**DGA**: 2% of gross.
**WGA**: same as DGA.
**SAG-AFTRA**: 3 times this percentage (i.e., 6%).
**AFM Basic Cable**: 3 times this percentage (i.e., 6%).

---

series is non-network, or non-primetime, or non-scripted, then other residual bases apply. See the contract for details, BA Made for NM SL E.1.b.(i).

* To be precise, this is the applicable minimum that is used for scripted non-serials. See MBA Made for NM SL 2.b.(4)(b)(i) for the appropriate figures for other program types.
† See BA Made for NM SL E.1.b.(i)(F).
‡ This contrasts with the way fixed residuals work in television. If the credits on a TV episode are Story by Bill, Teleplay by Jane, then Bill's residual would be calculated with reference to a Story by table such as Art. 13.B.7.a and Jane's with reference to a Teleplay by table such as Art. 13.B.7.b. There would be no 75%-25% calculation and the bargain rate table (such as Art. 13.B.7.c) would not be used. Refer to p. 129 for additional discussion of allocation.
§ See BA Made for NM SL E.1.b.(i).

** In any event, proration of the 26 week period could presumably result in smaller checks.
†† See p. 129.

## No Residuals

No residuals for IATSE, or for AFM derivative new media based on a free TV series.

## Pattern Analysis

*The SAG-AFTRA specified dollar residual is out of pattern.*

## Related Cells

Similar: K3-K6 TV and home video to ad-supported reuse is also structured as a free window (but a much shorter one), followed by two 26-week windows with a fixed residual of 3.5% of RB/AM (and of TAM, for SAG-AFTRA, in contrast to the fixed $20/$25 fee here) and then by a 2% gross residual.

## Book Cross References

Derivative new media: p. 31.
Reuse on ad-supported platforms: p. 45.
What initial comp covers: p. 52.
Percentage residuals: p. 55.
Fixed residuals at 100%: p. 59.
Fixed residuals – the residual base: p. 62.
Hybrid residual formulas: p. 63.

## Contract References

DGA BA Made for NM SL §§ E.1.a-c (& NM Reuse SL § 5).

WGA MBA Made for NM SL §§ 2.b.(4)(a)-(c).

SAG CBA/TVA Made for NM SL §§ B.3(a)-(c) (& NM Reuse SL § 4.A).

AFTRA Netcode Ex. A NM Reuse SL §§ 4.A(1)-(3), 5.A.

IATSE BA Made for NM SL §§ F(1)(a), (b)(i).

AFM Made for NM SL §§ F(1)(a), (b)(i).

AFM Basic Cable Ex. B Made for NM SL §§ A(1)-(3).

*118 – Entertainment Residuals: A Full Color Guide*

## C. Original New Media to Ad-Supported

### Book Cross References

Original new media: p. 35.
Reuse on ad-supported platforms: p. 45.
What initial comp covers (entire market): p. 52.
No residuals: p. 54.

### Contract References

DGA BA Made for NM SL § E.2.a.
WGA MBA Made for NM SL § 3.b.(4)(a).
SAG CBA/TVA Made for NM SL § D.3(a).
AFTRA Netcode Ex. A NM Reuse SL § 4.B(1).
IATSE BA Made for NM SL §§ F(1)(a), (b)(i).
AFM Made for NM SL § F(1).

### Contents of Cell K8

No residuals.

## D. Derivative and Original New Media to Free TV

[Grid table showing Reused in (columns): Theatrical, Free TV Network Primetime, Free TV Syndication or Non-Primetime, Foreign, Supp. Mkts. (Pay TV, Home Video), Domestic Basic Cable, New Media Consumer Pd (eRental, EST), New Media Ad Supported; Made for (rows): Theatrical, Free TV, Pay TV, Home Video, Basic Cable, Deriv. NM, Orig. NM, Exper. NM. Highlighted cells: C3 to D3, C7 to D8.]

### Contents of Cells C7-D8

C7-D8 is like C3-D3 (except AFM BC-Deriv).

*DGA* RB: D3 RB.

*WGA* AM: D3 bargain rate (high budget for Deriv. NM, low for Orig. NM), prorated for NM<=15 min. WGA C7-D8 & K7 residuals are aggregate, not per writer.

*SAG-AFTRA* RB: for Deriv NM: C3 resid ceiling for source program, prorated; for Orig NM: C3 resid ceiling (if NM < half hr use prorated half hr ceiling; else closest <= NM length).

. . .

AFM BC-Deriv: 100% (for C7) or 75%-5% (for C8) of AFTRA program fee.

*DGA, WGA,* AFM BC-Deriv: PT runs of NM<=15 mins treated as non-PT.

IA, AFM Orig, AFM Free TV Deriv: $0.

### Explanation

[tbd] 2010 network primetime freeze

### No Residuals

No residuals for IATSE, AFM derivative new media based on a free TV series, or AFM original new media.

### Pattern Analysis

The overall concept – that network primetime residuals are calculated as 100% of something and other than network primetime are calculated as a declining percentage of something – is maintained, *but there are numerous differences among the unions in the way in the calculations are made.*

### Related Cells

Partial model: C3-D3 free TV to free TV.

### Book Cross References

Derivative new media: p. 31.
Original new media: p. 35.
Reuse on network primetime: p. 39.
Reuse on other than network primetime: p. 40.
[Percentage residuals: p. 55.

### Contract References

#### Re Derivative New Media Product

DGA BA Made for NM SL E.1.e.(1).

WGA MBA Made for NM SL 2. b.(4)(e)(I).

SAG CBA/TVA Made for NM SL B.3(e)(i).

AFTRA Netcode Ex. A NM Reuse SL 4.A(5)(a)(i).

AFM Basic Cable Ex. B Made for NM SL § A(5)(a) (also AFTRA Netcode 2(A)(2)(a)(i), 73).

#### Re Original New Media Product

DGA BA Made for NM SL § E.2.c(1).
WGA MBA Made for NM SL § 3.b.(4)(c)(i).
SAG CBA/TVA Made for NM SL § D.3(c)(i).
AFTRA Netcode Ex. A NM Reuse SL§ 4.B(3)(a).

*120 – Entertainment Residuals: A Full Color Guide*

## E. Derivative and Original New Media to Foreign TV

media, and for **AFM** derivative new media based on free TV.

As for **other unions** (and **AFM** derivative new media based on basic cable): the relevant contract clauses make no provision for residuals. Thus, it appears that there may not be any, although the union position may be that there are such residuals.

A similar analysis applies to derivative and original new media to theatrical (**B7-B8**). See p. 123.

### Contents of Cells E7-E8

. . . E7-E8 = B7-B8. . . .

### Notes in Other Cells

**B7-B8:** Not explicitly specified.

### Explanation/No Residuals

Contract structure makes it clear that there are no residuals for **IATSE**, for **AFM** original new

### Book Cross References

Derivative new media: p. 31.
Original new media: p. 35.
Foreign reuse: p. 41.
No residuals: p. 54.

### Contract References

Not explicitly specified. See contract provisions listed on p. 119.

## F. Derivative and Original New Media to Supplemental Markets

### Book Cross References

Derivative new media: p. 31.
Original new media: p. 35.
Reuse in supplemental markets: p. 41.
Reuse on pay TV: p. 42.
Reuse on home video: p. 42.
Percentage residuals: p. 55.

### Contract References

#### Re Derivative New Media Product

DGA BA Made for NM SL § E.1.e.(2).
WGA MBA Made for NM SL § 2.b.(4)(e)(ii).
SAG CBA/TVA Made for NM SL § B.3(e)(ii).
AFTRA Netcode Ex. A NM Reuse SL § 4.A(5)(a)(ii).
IATSE BA Made for NM SL § F(2).
AFM Made for NM SL § F(2).
AFM Basic Cable Made for NM SL Ex. B § A(5)(b) (& Netcode Ex. D § 3(A)(1)).

#### Re Original New Media Product

DGA BA Made for NM SL § E.2.c(2).
WGA MBA Made for NM SL § 3.b.(4)(c)(i).
SAG CBA/TVA Made for NM SL § D.3(c)(ii).
AFTRA Netcode Ex. A NM Reuse SL § 4.B(3)(b).
IATSE BA Made for NM SL § F(2).
AFM Made for NM SL § F(2).

### Contents of Cells F7-G8

Same as if made for free TV (F3-G3); except *AFM BC-Derivative NM*: pay TV 3.6% of gross; HV 3.6% (of 20%) of gross.

### Explanation

Same as if made for free TV, except that **AFM** derivative NM based on basic cable pays at 3.6%, not 1%. See pp. 81 and 82.

### Pattern Analysis

Pattern is maintained.

### Related Cells

Model: F3-G3 free TV to supplemental markets.

## G. Derivative and Original New Media to Domestic Basic Cable

| Reused in:<br>Made for: | Theatrical | Free TV Network Primetime | Free TV Syndication or Non-Primetime | Foreign | Supp.Mkts.<br>Pay TV / Home Video | Domestic Basic Cable | New Media Consumer Pd<br>eRental / EST | New Media Ad Supported |
|---|---|---|---|---|---|---|---|---|
| Theatrical | | | | | | | | |
| Free TV | | | | | | **H3** | | |
| Pay TV | | | | | | | | |
| Home Video | | | | | | | | |
| Basic Cable | | | | | | | | |
| Deriv. NM | | | | | | **H7 & H8** | | |
| Orig. NM | | | | | | | | |
| Exper. NM | | | | | | | | |

### Contents of Cells H7–H8

Same as if made for free TV (H3); except *AFM BC-Derivative NM: 3.6% of gross.* IATSE, AFM Orig, AFM Free TV Deriv: $0.

### Explanation

Same as if made for free TV, except that **AFM** derivative new media based on a basic cable program pays at 3.6%, not 1%. See p. 80.

### No Residuals

No residuals for IATSE, AFM derivative new media based on a free TV series, or AFM original new media.

### Pattern Analysis

Pattern is maintained.

### Related Cells

Model: **H3** free TV to basic cable.

### Book Cross References

Derivative new media: p. 31.
Original new media: p. 35.
Reuse on basic cable: p. 42.
Percentage residuals: p. 55.

### Contract References

#### Re Derivative New Media Product

DGA BA Made for NM SL § E.1.e.(2).

WGA MBA Made for NM SL § 2.b.(4)(e)(ii).

SAG CBA/TVA Made for NM SL § B.3(e)(ii).

AFTRA Netcode Ex. A NM Reuse SL § 4.A(5)(a)(ii).

AFM Basic Cable Made for NM SL Ex. B § A(5)(b) (& Netcode Ex. D § 3(A)(1)).

#### Re Original New Media Product

DGA BA Made for NM SL § E.2.c(2).

WGA MBA Made for NM SL § 3.b.(4)(c)(i).

SAG CBA/TVA Made for NM SL§ D.3(c)(ii).

AFTRA Netcode Ex. A NM Reuse SL § 4.B(3)(b).

## H. Derivative and Original New Media to Theatrical

### Contents of Cells B7-B8

Not explicitly specified. Also, . . . barg history varies among unions. IA, AFM Orig, AFM Free TV Deriv: $0.

### Explanation/No Residuals

Contractual structure makes it apparent that there are no residuals for IATSE, for AFM original new media, and for AFM derivative new media based on free TV.

As for other unions (and AFM derivative new media based on basic cable): the relevant contract clauses make no provision for residuals. Thus, it appears that there may not be any, although the union position may be that there are such residuals.

A similar analysis applies to derivative and original new media to foreign (E7-E8, see p. 120), but with one difference: with regard to theatrical reuse (B7-B8), the WGA and SAG raised the issue of residuals in their 2010/2011 negotiations. They did not achieve any changes in the contract on this issue, but by raising the issue arguably acknowledged a current lack of residuals.

### Book Cross References

Derivative new media: p. 31.
Original new media: p. 35.
Reuse in theatrical: p. 38.
No residuals: p. 54.

### Contract References

None. See contract provisions listed on p. 119.

## I. Experimental New Media

### Contents of Cells B9-K9

Optional coverage. **Defn**: (a) budget ≤ $15K/min. & $300K/episode & $500K/order and (b) no DGA prior e/ee; no prof'l wtr; no covered performer; < 4 experienced crew; or < 2 active AFM musicians.

### Explanation/No Residuals

An experimental new media production is a production which is intended for initial release on the Internet or mobile devices, and which is not derivative new media, and (a) whose **budget falls below certain thresholds** and (b) whose **use of experienced personnel falls below certain thresholds**.

The difference between original and experimental new media is significant: original new media productions are subject to residuals in most cases, but experimental new media productions are not subject to residuals in any scenario.

In order to be considered experimental new media, a production must meet **both** the budget test and the personnel test with respect to a particular union; otherwise, it is considered original new media by that union.

### Budget Test

The budget test is as follows:

- **Per Minute:** The production budget must be less than or equal to $15,000 per minute; and

- **Per Episode:** The production budget must be less than or equal to $300,000 per episode; and

- **Per Order:** The production budget must be less than or equal to $500,000 per series order (which typically means a single "cycle," i.e., season of the new media series).

→ The per minute budget threshold ($15,000) should not be confused with the $25,000 per minute threshold that original new media must meet in order to trigger residuals for consumer paid new media (I8-J8).

What if a production meets some but not all of the budget tests; for example, suppose the budget is $14,000 per minute but $310,000 per episode and $490,000 per series order. Can this be experimental new media?

No. A production must meet all three of the budget tests (that is, must fall at or below all three thresholds) in order to be considered experimental new media. This conclusion is definitive in the DGA, SAG-AFTRA and Legacy-SAG, AFTRA front of book, IATSE and AFM agreements, although the language requires close analysis.[*]

→ In contrast, the language in the WGA and Legacy-AFTRA primetime agreements[†] is subtly different from the corresponding language in the other union agreements, and implies that a production which only meets one or two of the budget tests would still be considered experimental new media under those two agreements. However, negotiators on both the union and management sides have told me that this result, and the differing language, were unintentional. Thus, a production's budget must fall at or below all three thresholds in order to be considered experimental new media.

In any case, the above budget levels were actually considered quite high. At least initially, few short form new media projects exceeded those thresholds. Would that mean that most (non-derivative) new media is classified as experimental new media? Not necessarily.

---

[*] Refer to the DGA, SAG, AFTRA Front of Book, IATSE and AFM definitions cited in the Contract References on p. 126.
[†] Refer to the WGA and AFTRA Ex. A definitions cited in the Contract References.

There's another test that new media must meet in order to be considered experimental

## Personnel Test

As noted above, a production must also meet a *personnel test* in order to be considered experimental new media. This test varies by union and is as follows (note that each of the tests is phrased as a negative):

- **DGA:** The production must **not** utilize an employee in any DGA-covered category who has previously been employed under a DGA collective bargaining agreement.* DGA covered categories under the BA are director, unit production manager, first assistant director, second assistant director,† and associate director (formerly technical coordinator).‡ If the production does utilize any such employee, then it is not experimental new media (for DGA purposes), regardless of budget levels.

- **WGA:** The script must **not** have been written by or acquired from a "professional writer."§ This is a defined term in the MBA and means, roughly, someone who has had a certain number of weeks' employment as a motion picture, television or radio writer (for dramatic programs), or has received certain theatrical, television, radio or professionally produced stage play credits, or has published a novel.** If the script was written by or acquired from a professional writer, then the production is not experimental new media (for WGA purposes), regardless of budget levels.

- **SAG-AFTRA and Legacy-SAG:** The production must **not** utilize a "covered performer."†† If the production does utilize a covered performer, then it is not experimental new media (for SAG-AFTRA or Legacy-SAG purposes), regardless of budget levels.

The term "covered performer" is defined as an individual who has been employed pursuant to the terms of a collective bargaining agreement covering his or her employment as a performer and who meets any of the following criteria:‡‡

(1) has at least two television (including free television, pay television, basic cable or direct-to-video) or theatrical credits;

(2) has at least two credits in a professional stage play presented on Broadway, off Broadway (as that term is understood in the live theater industry), under the LORT, COST or CORST contracts§§ or as part of an Actors Equity national tour;

(3) has been employed as a performer on an audio book;

(4) has been employed as a principal performer, announcer, singer or dancer in a national television or radio commercial, interactive game or non-broadcast/industrial production; or

(5) has been employed as a principal performer pursuant to the terms of a SAG-AFTRA, Legacy-SAG or Legacy-AFTRA contract and is employed as a principal performer on the new media production.***

- **Legacy-AFTRA Ex. A:** The production must not utilize a covered performer.††† If the production does utilize a covered performer, then it is not experimental new media (for Legacy-AFTRA purposes), regardless of budget levels.

The definition of "covered performer" is slightly different from the SAG-AFTRA definition; the criteria are any of the following:

(1) same as SAG-AFTRA (1);

(2) has had thirteen weeks of employment as a performer in radio (including satellite radio) in a major market;

---

\* See DGA BA Made for NM SL § B.
† Including key second assistant directors, second second assistant directors and additional second assistant directors.
‡ See DGA BA Para. 1-300.
§ See WGA MBA Made for NM SL § 1.
\*\* See MBA Art. 1.C.1.b. Note that it's possible to be a member of the WGA but not be a "professional writer," because WGA membership criteria are different from the definition of "professional writer." According to the WGA, this situation is fairly rare.
†† See SAG CBA/TVA Made for NM SL § C.

‡‡ I've numbered the following clauses for convenience, but they are unnumbered in the contract itself.
§§ These are various Actors Equity contracts. Actors Equity is the union that represents stage actors.
\*\*\* The last paragraph of the definition ("has been employed as a principal performer pursuant . . .") was added by paragraph 8.A of the SAG 2011 MOA.
††† See AFTRA Netcode Ex. A Made for NM SL § C.

(3) same as SAG-AFTRA (2);

(4) same as SAG-AFTRA (3);

(5) has been employed as a royalty artist on a sound recording which has been commercially released by a major label or a bona fide independent label;*

(6) same as SAG-AFTRA (4); or

(7) same as SAG-AFTRA (5).†

- **AFTRA Front of Book:** The production must **not** utilize a covered performer.‡ That term is not defined, however. If the production does utilize a covered performer, then it is not experimental new media (for AFTRA purposes), regardless of budget levels.

- **IATSE:** The production must **not** utilize four or more experienced crew members in IATSE job classifications.§ Experienced crew members\*\* are those who are listed in the IATSE Industry Experience Roster, the IATSE New Media Roster or, for job classifications without a roster, those who have 30 or more days of work experience within the last three years under certain IATSE agreements covering that job classification. For further details, see the IATSE BA Made for New Media Sideletter.

- **AFM:** The production must **not** utilize two or more recording musicians within the U.S. or Canada who have worked under a major AFM agreement†† within the last three (3) years.‡‡

Because these personnel tests differ from union to union, it's possible for a new media production to be experimental new media in the eyes of one union and original or derivative new media in the eyes of another.

### Pattern Analysis

Budget test language inadvertently varies, but no difference in intent is apparently intended.

### Book Cross References

Experimental new media: p. 36.
What initial comp covers (entire market): p. 52.
No residuals: p. 54.

### Contract References

DGA BA Made for NM SL § B.

WGA MBA Made for NM SL § 1.

SAG CBA/TVA Made for NM SL § C.

AFTRA Netcode Ex. A Made for NM SL § C.

IATSE BA Made for NM SL § B.

AFM Made for NM SL § B.

AFM Basic Cable Ex. B Made for NM SL – none.

---

\* "Bona fide independent label" is not defined.
† [Item (7) is actually an assumption I'm making. There does not appear to be a AFTRA Netcode Exhibit A 2011 MOA, so this provision would be implicit.]
‡ See AFTRA Netcode Front of Book Made for NM SL § C.
§ See IATSE BA Made for NM SL ¶ B.
\*\* The term "experienced crew members" does not appear in the IATSE contract. That is, there is no summary term in the contract; instead, there is a long paragraph of detail with no clarifying summary.
†† Specifically, the Basic Theatrical Motion Picture Agreement, the Basic Television Motion Picture Agreement, the TV Videotape Agreement, the Sound Recording Labor Agreement or the Television or Radio Canadian Broadcasting System Agreements.
‡‡ See AFM Made for NM SL ¶ B.

## J. High Budget SVOD to Subscription Consumer Paid New Media Platform

[chart goes here – highlight I10]

### Contents of Cell I10

On the original subscription platform (or related or affiliated foreign platforms): 1 free **year** and, thereafter, a **year by year** declining 30%-1.5% of network PT RB/AM/TAM; or 65% of foregoing if < 15m subs in U.S. & Canada.

### Explanation

[see WGA 2014 MOA pp. 25-26]

### No Residuals

The high budget SVOD provisions became effective with the beginning of the 2014 contract cycle, mid-2014 for the above the line unions. Prior to that date, some shows (such as Netflix's *House of Cards*) were produced under individually negotiated terms.

### Pattern Analysis

Pattern is maintained.

### Related Cells

None.

### Book Cross References

Made for high budget SVOD: p. 36.
Reuse on subscription consumer pay NM: p. 43.
What initial comp covers (time period): p. 53.
Fixed residuals at yr. by yr. declining %: p. 61.
Fixed residuals – the residual base: p. 62.

### Contract References

2014 MOA's [tbd]

## K. High Budget SVOD to Other Consumer Paid

[tbd]
I10-J10

## L. High Budget SVOD to Ad-Supported

[tbd]
K10

## M. High Budget SVOD to Traditional

High budget SVOD product is considered a flavor or variant of either original new media (usually) or of derivative new media (in the unlikely instance where the SVOD product is based on an underlying program (p. 31)). When high budget SVOD product is reused in traditional media, the same rules apply as for reuse of any other original or derivative new media in traditional media. Accordingly, please see pp. 119-123.

## N. History of Made-For New Media

See p. 112.

# 13. RESIDUALS CALCULATION

The preceding chapters of this book explain how to calculate the basic amount of a particular residual for current product. However, there are other factors that can alter the amount the producer has to pay or the amount that a particular director, writer, actor or musician receives. This chapter discusses those factors.

## A. Date

As the previous paragraph notes, the residuals formulas discussed in this book are for current product. Older product may be subject to different formulas, because many of the formulas have changed over time. This book includes some of the older formulas in the history grids but is not a comprehensive reference.

In addition, determining the date of a product for residuals purposes is sometimes tricky. In general, the applicable date is the date of commencement of principal photography of the movie or episode. However, in the case of the WGA, the applicable date for some reuse patterns is instead the date that writing services were contracted for or were commenced, or the date that credits were determined. Consult the history grids and, as always, the MBA.

As we noted early in the book (see p. 10), you should use caution when looking at date restrictions in any of the union's collective bargaining agreements. For instance, suppose a union's 2014 agreement says "For motion pictures whose principal photography commenced on or after July 1, 1971, a residual of 1.2% of producers gross is payable." This seems clear enough: the effective date of this formula is July 1, 1971.

But what if instead the 2014 agreement says: "For motion pictures whose principal photography commenced on or after July 1, 2014, a residual of 1.2% of producers gross is payable." What does this tell you about product whose product commenced prior to that date?

Answer: nothing whatsoever. If you look at the 2011 agreement for that union, you might find virtually identical language: "For motion pictures whose principal photography commenced on or after July 1, 2011, a residual of 1.2% of producers gross is payable." That formula might have been put in place years ago, but they needlessly keep updating the date restriction, lending a false sense of newness to the formula and confusing the reader as to the effective date.

Or, indeed, in the 2011 agreement you might find a different formula, with a different date restriction. Or, perhaps, you'll find no formula at all, which may mean that no residual is payable for older product – or that it will require an arbitration to determine what to do about older product.

## B. Budget

Lower budget content may or may not be subject to residuals. Below is a list of some key data points by made-for medium. In addition, unions may be willing to make other accommodations for low-budget product on a one-off basis.

- **Theatrical.** DGA, WGA, SAG-AFTRA, Legacy-SAG and IATSE (as well as the Teamsters, not relevant here) all have low-budget agreements. Consult the agreements to determine whether and how residuals are payable. AFM? [tbd]

- **Free TV.** The applicable minimums or residuals bases may be lower. Consult the agreements.

- **Pay TV.** [tbd]

- **Basic Cable.** Terms and conditions for low-budget basic cable product are negotiable with the DGA and WGA. Others? [tbd]

- **New Media.** There are no residuals for original new media exhibited on consumer-paid platforms (eRental and EST) if the budget is below $25,000 per minute (see p. 113). There are no residuals for experimental new media (see p. 124).

- **SVOD.** Lower budget SVOD product (i.e., below the budget thresholds for high budget SVOD) is treated as original or derivative new media (depending on which is applicable) or as experimental new media if it qualifies neither as original new media nor as derivative new media.

## C. Waivers

It is always important to determine whether a project was produced under a waiver or other special arrangement that may affect the residuals calculation.

This is particularly true for productions shot outside the U.S., and for anything other than a feature film or live-action scripted network primetime TV product of standard length (half hour, one hour or TV movie). Another area to watch out for is product made for then newly devised media, such as shows (like *House of Cards*) made for Netflix prior to the standardization of residuals terms for high budget SVOD.

The takeaway: non-standard shows have non-standard economics, which can lead producer to request, and the unions (in their discretion) to grant, modified deals to accommodate the differences.

## D. Signatory Status

As previously discussed (see p. 9), residuals are only payable if the producer is signatory to the applicable union. Thus, for instance, if a producer is signatory to SAG-AFTRA but not the WGA or DGA, then residuals will only be payable to actors, not the director or writer(s). Accordingly, the total residuals payable will be less than if the producer were signatory to all three unions.

## E. Allocation Among Members

Residuals are paid by producers or distributors, but to whom are they paid, and in what proportions? The answer varies from union to union.

There are two key principles: (a) fixed residuals are virtually always calculated and paid per-person (or per-team or per-credit, in the case of writing teams); and (b) percentage residuals are allocated among the qualifying members of the given union. Residuals other than fixed residuals that are a specified dollar amount are either per-person or allocated, depending on the reuse pattern.

(As for what happens after a person dies, see p. 156.)

### DGA

In most cases, residuals are paid entirely to the director. However, in some reuse patterns, percentage residuals are shared with the assistant directors, UPM, and pension plan.

[Tbd]

Unit Production Managers, Assistant Directors, Associate Directors and Stage Managers are also eligible for residual payments on videocassette/DVD and Pay TV reuse of Features and programs which are made for Free and Basic Cable television. Directors and crew members share all residuals for reuse of programs made for Pay Television. The DGA Basic Pension Plan gets a large share of residuals generated by theatrical films.

HV residuals, but not pay TV residuals? Interesting. The DGA has pension (and BTL) taken out for both HV and pay TV.

Director gets 1/2 of pay TV. Pension gets 1/3, which means pension is at the rate of 50% of the members' residual, vs. a typical 7.5% or so.

Director gets 2/3 of HV. Pension gets 20%, which means pension is at the rate of 25% of the members' residual.

Remaining DGA residuals are all to director

### WGA

As noted earlier, credited writers, and only credited writers, receive residuals. How are residuals allocated among the various credited writers?

- **Fixed residuals** are payable to each credited writer or writers per the formulas given in this book. That is, the formulas are per credit (with two exceptions noted below).

For instance, when a free TV episode is reused in network primetime (C3), the residual is 100% of the residual base. If one writer wrote the story and another the teleplay, then the residual for the first writer will be 100% of the residual base for writing a story and the residual for the second writer will be 100% of the residual base for writing a teleplay.

In contrast, if a single writer wrote both the story and teleplay, the residual would be 100% of the residual base for story and teleplay.

➜ Exception: Unusually, the WGA residuals formulas for reuse of derivative and original new media on free TV (C7-D8) and for derivative new media on ad-supported platforms (K7) are fixed residuals that are not per-credit. Instead, the total amount of the formula is allocated among the credited writers. The MBA doesn't specify the allocation, but presumably the rules for percentage residuals apply (see next bullet point).

● Percentage residuals are allocated based on credit, as follows:

♦ 100% to the writer(s) who receive "Written by" credit; or (if no "Written by" credit):

♦ 25% to the writer(s) who receive "Story by" (or "Screen Story by" or "Television Story by") credit and

♦ 75% to those who receive "Screenplay by" or "Teleplay by." If there is a screenplay or teleplay credit but no story credit, then the screenplay/teleplay writer(s) get 100%.

♦ Miscellaneous credits like "Adaptation by" or "Narration Written by" are good for 10%, which comes out of the "Written by" or screenplay or teleplay share.

♦ "Created by" (a television credit) results in a separate, additional flow of residuals – separated rights residuals (see p. 142).

♦ "Developed by" is a television credit similar to "Created by," but it does not result in residuals.

♦ Source material credits, such as "Based on the Book/Article by," are not WGA writing credits and do not generate residuals.

♦ "Based on a Screenplay/Teleplay by" credit [tbd].

If two or more writers share a credit, they split the allocated portion of the residual equally. So, "Written by A and B" means that A and B each receive 50% of the residual.

However, the WGA will allow members of a writing team to agree to a different split as between themselves. So, "Written by A & B" means that A and B each receive 50% of the residual unless they've agreed on a different split.

When teams of writers share a credit with other writers or teams, each team is considered as a single person for calculating the allocation. Thus, "Written by A and B & C" means that A will get 50% of the residual, and B and C will get 25% each, rather than A, B and C each receiving a third of the residual.

As a more complicated example, the perhaps unlikely credit "Story by A and B & C, Screenplay by D and E" means that A will get one-half of 25% (i.e., 12.5%) of the residual, B and C will each get one-half of one-half of 25% (i.e., 6.25%) of the residual, and D and E will each get one-half of 75% of the residual (i.e., 37.5%).

A writer who has two credits on a project will receive portions of the residual attributable to each. For instance, if the credit is "Story by A and B, Screenplay by B and C and D," then B's share is one-half of 25% (i.e., 12.5%) of the residual plus one-third of 75% of the residual (i.e., 25%), for a total of 37.5%.

● Specified dollar-amount residual: The pay TV to pay TV residual (F4) is an aggregate flat dollar amount that is allocated among the credited writers. The MBA doesn't specify the allocation, but presumably the above rules apply.

[References: Arts. 51.C.5 (reuse in supplemental markets)][shared story minimum]

### SAG-AFTRA and Legacy-SAG

Principal performers (including performers, [body doubles, looping], professional singers, stunt performers, stunt coordinators, pilots, dancers employed under Schedule J and puppeteers) receive residuals **if their performance remains in the final product**. Background performers (extras) do not receive residuals (unless they've been upgraded to principal).

- **Fixed residuals** are payable to each performer per the formulas given in this book. That is, the formulas are per performer.

- **Percentage residuals** are allocated among the eligible performers using a formula that takes account of their relative wages and days of work, with caps so that high-paid stars do not completely swamp the allocation.*

Here's how the formula works. Each performer earns time units and salary units, as follows:

Time units: The performer is credited with units for the time worked on a production as follows:

Each day = 1/5 unit
Each week = 1 unit
Maximum = 5 time units per performer

[tbd guaranteed days in excess of days actually worked]

Salary units: The salary of each performer is converted to units as follows:

Day performer: each multiple of daily scale compensation = 1/5 unit

All other performers: each multiple of weekly scale compensation = 1 unit

Maximum = 10 salary units per performer

The performer's time units and salary units are added together. Thus, the minimum number of units a performer will receive is 2/5, and the maximum is 15.

The units of all performers are added together to determine the total number of units the project generated. There is no limit to this number: an (unlikely) project with 100 principal performers could generate 1500 units (15 x 100).

Each performer receives a pro rata share of the residual – that is, his or her share is proportionate to the number of units he or she is credited with, divided by the total number of units the project generated.

For instance, if a movie has 20 day players (2/5 units each) and four stars (15 units each), then the total number of units is 68 (20 x 2/5 plus 4 x 15). Each day player will receive less than 1% of the residual (2/5 divided by 68 is approximately 0.006), while each star will receive about 22% of the residual (15 divided by 68).

Now let's add 10 actors who each work a week at scale compensation. They each are credited with one time unit and one salary unit, or 2 units. The total number of units generated by the project is now 88 (68 plus 10 x 2). Each day player receives about 0.4% of the residual (rather than 0.6% as before). Each star receives about 17% of the residual, and each of the weekly players receives about 2% of the residual.

A final example: a movie with one star who works several weeks (15 units) and one day player who works one day (2/5 units). The star will receive over 97% of the residual and the day player will receive less than 3%. The ratio between what the star receives and what the day player gets is 37.5.† This is the maximum disparity possible between any two performers on a single project.

- **SAG-AFTRA specified dollar-amount residuals** are stated on a per-person basis. As mentioned earlier, the only example of this formula in the SAG agreements is derivative new media to ad-supported (K7).

### Legacy-AFTRA

[tbd]

### IATSE

The residual is paid entirely to the P&H plans. There is no allocation among workers, because the residual is not credited to each worker separately. Instead, the pension and health plans are each big pots of money, and a worker's ultimate share depends on various factors that don't relate to residuals (income, number of years of employment, etc.).

### AFM

Residuals are allocated among participating musicians based on their wages.

---

* See SAG-AFTRA CBA Section 5.2B and SAG-AFTRA TVA Sec. 18.2.

† I.e., 15 divided by 2/5.

## Participating Musicians

"Participating musicians" means:

● Any musician (including leaders, conductors and contractors) employed to record music utilized in the product.

● Any sideline musician (musician photographed playing an instrument on camera) whose performance is utilized in the product.

● Any music preparation musician (including orchestrators, copyists and librarians) provided that there was at least one original AFM scoring session or sideline session for the specific product they worked on.

● Any musician entitled to receive a "new-use" payment for the inclusion of a pre-existing song as part of the music score for the product if the product was produced after January 1, 1991. The song must have been recorded in the U.S. or Canada under the auspices of the AFM.

## Allocation

For theatrical product reused on free TV and supplemental markets (C2-G2), the residual is allocated to the participating musicians in the same proportion as their session wages (i.e., initial compensation).* For instance, if the total session fees for a project were $100,000 and Jeff musician received $25,000 of that amount, then he would receive 25% of the residual.

The same rule applies to product made for free television when released in supplemental markets (F3-G3).†

However, a slightly different rule applies to product made for basic cable when reused on new media platforms (I6-K6). There, proration is according to *scale wages* earned.‡ Presumably, that means the proration here ignores any overscale amounts in the musicians' session wages.

---

* See AFM Basic Theatrical Motion Picture Agreement Secs. 15(b)(i)(5), 16(b)(i)(4).
† See AFM Basic Television Motion Picture Agreement Sec. 14(b)(i)(4).
‡ See AFM Basic Cable Ex. B NM Reuse § SL 1.A, 2.A(2), (5), 2.B.

When other product is reused on new media platforms (I2-J5, I7-J8, K2), proration is referred to but not defined.§

There are other reuse patterns where proration is necessary, but is not discussed contractually at all, such as foreign reuse of free TV product (E3) or use of basic-cable-based derivative new media on ad-supported new media (K7).

### F. Proration

The next issue we consider is proration. If a portion of the work on a film is done under a particular union's jurisdiction and a portion is not, the employer may be permitted to pay a partial residual with respect to that union. This is called proration, because the partial residual is usually calculated as a proportionate share of the full residual, with the proportion based on the ratio of the amount of work done under the union jurisdiction to the amount of work done in total. Proration is used in other instances as well. The union by union rules are as follows:

[EP Prorating Percentage Payments sheet]

#### DGA

[tbd]

#### WGA

[tbd]

Canadian Sideletter – WGC jurisdiction, but WGA member gets U.S. residuals. The WGC production fee and royalty payments go toward satisfying this requirement.**

#### SAG

[tbd][lt 4 perfs or intl]

Int'l: as for Global Rule One, they prorate based on the time units and salary units based on the Day Out of Dates forms. Art. 5.C, p. 9.

Ultra Low Budget Agt., mixed cast xxx

---

§ See AFM NM Reuse SL §§ 1.a, 1.b, 2 and AFM Made for NM SL §§ F(1)(c), (d).
** See http://www.wga.org/subpage_writersresources.aspx?id=194.

### AFTRA

[tbd]

### IATSE

[BA vs. otherwise, p. 44] [\wk\ent labors\resids\unused\EmployerNotificationForm (re MPIPHP proration).pdf]

### AFM

[See p. 44 of 2002 Theatrical Agt., p. 145 of AMPTP and AFM Basic TH MP Agreement of 2010_04-14-2010 to 02-23-2013.pdf]

## G. Allocation Across Markets and Products

See discussions in the several sections starting on p. 58.

## H. Crediting / Offset / Application of Excess

If a union member is receiving a participation in gross or net, or if the union member's initial compensation exceeds a particular amount (such as twice the union minimum), some of the union agreements permit the producer to credit the participation or overscale portion of the compensation against residuals, or to credit the residuals against the participation. The union agreement may condition the producer's right (if any) to do so, by requiring that the personal services agreement (the individual contract between the union member and the producer) explicitly authorize this.

For that reason, producers may wish to include a provision in their agreements with writers, director or actors with terminology that authorizes "crediting," "offset," "application of excess" or the like. Conversely, talent representatives will tend to oppose such language, or seek contrary language expressly prohibiting such.

The specific rules for crediting vary by union and are as follows;

### DGA

[tbd]11-304, 11-305, 4-110, 18-109

### WGA

[15.A.3.g, B.3, 64 (p. 225)], Art. 64.E.2; App. B, Sec. E

### SAG

[CBA Secs. 5.F, [tbd] and TV Agt. Secs. 18(d), (f), 19(g), 78(c)(1)d), (2)d)]

### AFTRA

[tbd]

### IATSE

Not applicable, since the entire residual is paid to the pension and/or health plans.

### AFM

[tbd]

## I. Buyouts

Sometimes producers would like to make a lump sum additional payment to talent upfront as a substitute altogether for paying residuals: in other words, a buyout. This is allowed by some foreign entertainment unions (see p. 157) but seldom if ever in the U.S. (and probably never by the above the line unions).

One instance where a buyout was almost implemented involved the AFM and the film *The Age of Adaline,* which was to be scored in Los Angeles in November 2014.* The union agreed to a 25% boost in upfront compensation in lieu of residuals, then later canceled the deal when it discovered the film was to be distributed by Lionsgate, a firm the AFM has targeted as the largest non-signatory to its collective bargaining agreement. The buyout concept is controversial, with most members of the AFM's LA local reportedly opposed, while younger musicians support it as a means to reverse the dramatic outflow of film scoring work to London and Eastern Europe where wages are lower and/or residuals can be bought out or avoided.

---

* See Jon Burlingame, *Runaway Recordings Generate Discord Among L.A. Musicians,* VARIETY (1/6/15), *available at* http://variety.com/2015/music/news/runaway-recordings-generate-discord-among-l-a-musicians-1201393025/.

## J. Pension and Health

### Introduction

An important part of union and guild member's benefits are Pension and Health plans (P&H), also known as Health and Retirement (H&R), Pension, Health and Welfare (PH&W) or the like. There are at least two plans per union, one pension and one health. Some unions have more than one of each.

The plans are funded in part by employer contributions at an aggregate rate that is currently (2015) around 17%. The rate varies from union to union and contract to contract (for instance, the rate in a union's commercials agreement may be different than in its TV/theatrical agreement). The rates have been increasing in recent years due primarily to the escalation in health care costs and the recession of 2008-2009, which caused a precipitous decline in the value of pension plan assets (some of the lost ground has since been regained).

A portion of the percentage goes to the pension plan(s) and a portion to the health plan(s). The allocation varies depending on the union and sometimes on the reuse pattern. There may also be a lower rate for pilots and new series.

The contributions are calculated based on some portions of the member's earnings. For instance, if a member received $100,000 for writing or working on a film, the employer would also pay $17,000 to the P&H plan (for a union contract with a 17% rate).

However, some portions of a member's compensation are not subject to P&H. That, of course, leads to the question of whether residuals are subject to P&H.

The answer varies depending on the union, the reuse pattern, and other matters, such as numerical ceilings. And, it's important to note that there are not two but three possible answers to the question:

- **Yes:** The residual is subject to P&H. That means that the employer has to pay P&H on top of the residual. This is the most advantageous scenario for the employee (and the P&H plans), and the least for the employer. As an example, if the residual is $1,000, the employee will receive a check for that amount and the employer will also pay $170 to the applicable P&H plans (i.e., the WGA plans if the employee is a writer, the DGA plans if a director, etc.). The total outlay by the employer would be $1,170.

- **No:** The residual is not subject to P&H. This of course is the least advantageous for the employee and plans and the most advantageous for the employer. The employer's total outlay is $1,000.

- **Included:** The residual is subject to P&H, but the P&H contribution is included as part of the residual and therefore reduces what the member receives. For instance, suppose the residual is $1,000 but P&H is included. If the P&H rate is 17%, then the employee will receive a residual check for $854.70 and the P&H plans will receive $145.30(i.e., 17% of $854.70), which together add up to $1,000. The employer's total outlay is $1,000.

The union by union rules are as follows:

### DGA

[tbd]

19-102 re theatrical to free TV and foreign

See Signatory Guide in P&H folder

### WGA

Some residuals are subject to P&H – in which case, the P&H is always additional – and some are not. The rules are set forth in MBA Arts. 17.B.1 & 17.C.1:

- **Theatrical Product:** Residuals are not subject to P&H.

- **Television Product:** Residuals up to a ceiling are subject to P&H. The ceiling is the greater of (a) 250% of the Applicable Minimum* or (b) the writer's initial compensation. However, in the case of TV movies of at least 120 minutes and closed-end series of at least 120 minutes, the ceiling is the lesser of (1) the ceiling in the preceding sentence and (2) specific per-project dollar limits.†

---

* See MBA Art. 13.B.7.a-c.
† See MBA Arts. 17.B.1.e & 17.C.1 for details.

- **Reuse in Supplemental Markets:** Residuals are not subject to P&H.

- **Reuse of Pay TV or Home Video Product on Pay TV or Home Video:** Residuals are subject to P&H. Presumably the television product ceilings apply (see above).

- **Home Video Product:** The MBA has no P&H exclusions relating to residuals for home video product, suggesting that such residuals are subject to P&H. It's unclear if the television product ceilings apply.

- **Reuse of Traditional Media Product on New Media Platforms:** Here again, the MBA is silent, so such residuals are presumably subject to P&H. It's unclear if ceilings apply.

- **New Media Product (Original, Derivative and High Budget SVOD):** Again the MBA contains no exclusion, meaning that such residuals are probably subject to P&H, except when new media product is reused in supplemental markets. It's unclear if ceilings apply.

- **Separated Rights Payments:** No P&H. (See p. 141 for discussion of separated rights.)

- **Script Publication Fee:** No P&H. (See p. 143 for discussion of the script publication fee.)

- **Clip Fees:** No P&H. (See p. 145 for discussion of clip fees.)

### SAG-AFTRA and Legacy-SAG

[tbd]

CBA 5.A, theatrical to free and foreign TV residuals include P&H (dbl check . . . inconsistent with http://www.sagph.org/html/ertreport03.htm)

818-973-4472

CBA 5.2A, theatrical to supplemental markets includes P&H; possible reduced rates for cassettes

Theatrical residual payments are not subject to IAC or IACF contributions. P&H on theatrical to supplemental markets are payable at a lower rate than P&H on other residuals.

IACF table:

| Reused in: / Made for: | Theatrical | Free TV Network Primetime | Free TV Syndication or Non-Primetime | Foreign | Supp. Mkts. Pay TV | Supp. Mkts. Home Video | Domestic Basic Cable | New Media Consumer Pd eRental | New Media Consumer Pd EST | New Media Ad Supported |
|---|---|---|---|---|---|---|---|---|---|---|
| Theatrical | NA | | | | | | | | | |
| Free TV | | Y | Y | Y | Y | | | | | |
| Pay TV | | Y | Y | Y | Y | | | | | |
| Home Video | | Y | Y | Y | Y | | | | | |
| Basic Cable | | Y | Y | Y | Y | | | | | |
| Deriv. NM | | | | | | | | | | |
| Orig. NM | NA | | | NA | | | | | | NA |
| Exper. NM | | | | NA | | | | | | |

### Legacy-AFTRA

[tbd]

### IATSE

The entire residual is paid to the pension and health plans.

### AFM

[tbd]

## K. Commissionability

Agents generally commission talent compensation at 10%, lawyers do so at 5% (sometimes 7.5% if there's no agent on the deal) and managers at 10% or, still sometimes 15%.

The commissions are typically payable on initial compensation (although in some cases initial compensation has be at least scale plus 10% in order to be commissionable), deferments and percentage compensation. But what about residuals?

In other words, do these representatives commission residuals?

No law prevents this, but union and guild regulations do, in some cases – but even then, only with respect to agents. That's because the unions and guilds regulate agents – via a contract called a franchise agreement – but not lawyers and managers. Some of the latter follow the lead of agents and take commission only on residuals that agents commission; others may commission all residuals, or none. It's not clear what the general practice is, if any.

As to agents, the various unions and guilds have different rules. They are as follows:

## DGA

Agents are not permitted to commission residuals. The only exception to this is if the agent negotiates overscale residuals – i.e., residuals that exceed the DGA formulas – which is extremely rare. However, if the agent does obtain overscale residuals, he or she can commission the residual, so long as the commission does not reduce the residual below the DGA formulas.* Xxx website says commission can only be on overscale portion

## WGA

Same rule as the DGA.†

## SAG-AFTRA

As of this writing, SAG-AFTRA members are permitted to sign with agents who are signatory to the legacy SAG franchise agreement or the legacy AFTRA franchise agreement, or both. [verify – can members

The SAG franchise agreement applies if (a) the agent has signed it and (b) the work is covered by the legacy SAG collective bargaining agreement.

The AFTRA franchise agreement applies if (a) the agent has signed it and (b) the work is covered by the legacy AFTRA collective bargaining agreement.

This parallelism is illusory, however, because most agencies are signatories to the AFTRA franchise agreement but not the SAG one. That's because the SAG agreement, negotiated between SAG and the talent agent associations (Association of Talent Agents, or ATA, and National Association of Talent Representatives, or NATR), expired in 2002 and has not been renewed.

http://www.sagaftra.org/what-commissionable

http://www.sagaftra.org/files/sag/documents/16g_commissionchart_2013.pdf xxx

## SAG

Agents who are not signatory to the SAG franchise agreement can freely commission residuals, and many do.

Agents who are signatory to the franchise agreement are subject to commissionability rules that vary according to reuse pattern and even in some cases, according to the region that the SAG-AFTRA member lives in. The regional differences are a result of a region-by-region vote taken many years ago (long before the 2002 non-renewal of the agreement).

The rules are shown via abbreviations in the following chart.‡ Where the rules differ by region, the abbreviation in front of the slash refers to Los Angeles, Chicago, Detroit, Atlanta, Washington D.C. and Hawaii, and the abbreviation after the slash refers to New York and all other areas.

| Reused in: Made for: | Theatrical | Free TV Network Primetime | Free TV Syndication or Non-Primetime | Foreign | Supp. Mkts. Pay TV | Domestic Home Video | Basic Cable | New Media Consumer Pd eRental | EST | New Media Ad Supported |
|---|---|---|---|---|---|---|---|---|---|---|
| Theatrical | NA | 1 | | ? | 1 | | 1 | ? | | ? |
| Free TV | 1/Y | 2/4 | 1/3 | 1 | 1/Y | | | ? | | |
| Pay TV | ? | ? | ? | ? | ? | ? | | ? | | ? |
| Home Video | ? | | | | ? | | | | | |
| Basic Cable | 1/3 | 1/3 | 1/3 | 1 | 1/Y | | 1/3 | | | |
| Deriv. NM | NA | ? | ? | NA | ? | ? | ? | ? | | NA |
| Orig. NM | | | | | | | | | | |
| Exper. NM | NA | | | | | | | | | |

The codes used in the chart are as follows:

| Code | Meaning |
|---|---|
| 1 | Residual is commissionable only if the agent negotiates overscale residuals (extremely rare). The commission cannot reduce the residual below scale. |
| 2 | Residual is commissionable only if the *initial compensation* was overscale. The commission cannot reduce the residual below scale. A 10% commission on the residual would require that the initial compensation was at least scale + 10%. |

---

* See Agreement between Association of Talent Agents and Directors Guild of America, Inc. of January 1, 1977 (as restated January 1, 2004), Para. 7.
† See WGA Artists' Manager Basic Agreement of 1976, Rider W, Sec. 3(a) (pp. 18-19).

‡ See SAG Working Rule 16(g), Sec. XI.C (pp. 19-20) and "Agreed Interpretation" (pp. 74-75).

| Code | Meaning |
|---|---|
| 3 | If residual is at scale, commission is payable only for 2nd and 3rd runs (i.e., 1st and 2nd reruns). If agent negotiates overscale residual (extremely rare), commission is payable on every rerun, but the commission cannot reduce the *aggregate residual for all runs* below scale (i.e., below the aggregate implied by the residuals formula). |
| 4 | If the *initial compensation* was at scale (which necessarily means that the residual is also, at scale, due to the particular residual formula that applies), commission is payable only for 2nd and 3rd runs. If initial compensation was overscale, commission is payable on every rerun, but the commission cannot reduce the *aggregate residual for all runs* below scale. |
| Y | Residual is commissionable, with no limitations on reducing compensation below scale (referred to as "invading scale"). |
| NA | Not applicable, because there is no residual. |
| ? | Unknown. |

### AFTRA

In general, residuals cannot be commissioned unless they are overscale (very rare), and the commission must not reduce them below scale.*

However, there's an exception: for free TV product reused on domestic free television (C3-D3), the first two re-runs can be commissioned if the runs occur within three years from the first air date of the programs, the initial compensation was at least scale plus 10%, and the performer's residual check is more than $100.

But see http://www.sagaftra.org/files/sag/documents/12c_commissionchart_for_agents_2013.pdf. xxx

### AFM

[tbd]

## L. Dues

Union and guild dues are usually calculated in part as a percentage of the member's compensation. They're paid by the union member, of course, not the producer. Are dues charged on residuals?

### DGA

Yes, at a rate that can aggregate to 2.5%. More precisely, one component of DGA percentage dues is charged at 1.5% on gross earnings, including residuals, but only on gross annual earnings of $10,000 to $300,000. In addition, a second component of DGA percentage dues is charged at 1% on total residuals.

### WGA

Yes, at the rate of 1.5%. With respect to residuals collected on behalf of non-members or the beneficiaries of deceased members, the Guild charges a 5% administrative fee instead.

### SAG-AFTRA

Yes. Normal SAG-AFTRA dues apply. These are $198 plus 1.575% of earnings (up to $500,000 in earnings).

### AFM

Membership dues are not charged [xxx verify], but administrative expenses for the Film Musicians Secondary Market Fund (the organization that collects and disburses musicians' residuals) are deducted. These vary from year to year, but generally range from 5.5% to 6%.

## M. Taxes

Residuals raise a host of tax issues.

### Talent Issues

- **Characterization.** Residuals are ordinary income, not capital gains or "royalties." They are generally taxed as employee income (W2 wages), not as independent contractor income (1099). Taxes are withheld.

- **FICA.**

- [AFM treatment differs] xxx self-employment tax

- **Loan-Outs.** The existence of a loan-out corporation doesn't change the amount of residual, but subsequently paying that money from the loan-out to the talent raises difficult tax issues

---

* See AFTRA Working Rule 12-C, Sec. XIII.A, .B & .I (pp. 18-19).

under I.R.C. (Internal Revenue Code) § 409A if not structured properly.[*]

- **LA Business Tax.** For Los Angeles residents, treatment of residuals for purposes of the Los Angeles City Business Tax and the Creative Artist Exemption depends on how the talent was originally paid (employee vs. independent contractor), whether the person is retired or not, where the work was done and others factors.[†]

- **Absence from California.** If a California resident is absent from California (whether elsewhere in the U.S. or out of the country) for at least 18 months consecutively, there is an argument that she can avoid California tax on the residuals attributable to the work done outside California.[‡]

- **Taxing Jurisdiction – U.S. States.** If a resident of one state (say, California) works in another state (say, Massachusetts) on a production, the residuals she later receives may be subject to taxation by that latter state, just as the relevant portion of her initial compensation was – even though the residuals are paid years later, perhaps by a California studio.[§] Whether in practice these taxes are actually paid is a different question.[**]

- **Taxing Jurisdiction – Foreign Countries.** A similar issue arises internationally. If an American works in a foreign country on a production, the residuals she later receives may be subject to taxation by that country, just as the foreign-attributable portion of her initial compensation was – even though the residuals are paid years later and possibly by a U.S. company. Canada[††] and the UK[‡‡] are known to take this position. The payor may be required to withhold taxes from the residuals.[§§] Note, too, that Canada has

---

[*] See Bradford S. Cohen & Robin C. Gilden, *The Taxation of Deferred Compensation in Standard Service Agreements*, LOS ANGELES LAWYER 19 (May 2010), *available at* http://www.lacba.org/Files/LAL/Vol33No3/2703.pdf; Schuyler M. Moore, TAXATION OF THE ENTERTAINMENT INDUSTRY ¶ 1106 (2012).

[†] See Entertainment Creative Talent FAQ items 2 & 20, http://finance.lacity.org/content/entertainmentcreativetalentfaq.htm.

[‡] See Alan J. Epstein, *"Star Wars" – How To Win the Tax Battle When Your Talent Clients Work Abroad* at 21, The 2013 Entertainment Industry Conference, Cal. CPA Education Foundation (June 12, 2013), *available at* http://documents.jdsupra.com/369fc7d7-25d9-4e06-b54b-12dcb0881826.pdf.

[§] See Navjeet K. Bal (Massachusetts Comm'r of Revenue), *A Report on the Massachusetts Film Industry Tax Incentives* at 21 (July 2009), *available at* http://www.mass.gov/dor/docs/dor/news/2009filmincentivereport.pdf ("Although there are no legal decisions on this point, residual income on movies filmed in Massachusetts and received by non-resident actors or producers may be taxable in the Commonwealth as income derived from a trade or business carried on in the state (subject to offset by credit for income taxes paid to other jurisdictions).").

[**] See *id.* ("In practice, such income appears to have been rarely reported by non-residents, especially non-residents who have no other taxable business interests in the Commonwealth and who are not otherwise required to file tax returns in Massachusetts."); Bruce Mohl, *Hollywood Stars Not Paying Taxes?*, COMMONWEALTH (Spring 2011; April 12, 2011), *available at* http://www.commonwealthmagazine.org/News-and-Features/Inquiries/2011/Spring/Hollywood-stars-not-paying-taxes.aspx.

But cf. the more optimistic gloss of the state's Film Office: "Big stars must also pay Massachusetts taxes on any residual income they receive in the future for work they performed here. So the state will be collecting income taxes from them for years to come." http://www.mafilm.org/2009/07/06/dor-movie-spending-in-ma-is-676-million/.

[††] See Canada Revenue Authority (CRA) Form NR603, *Remittance of Non-Resident Tax on Income from When Completed Film or Video Acting Services*, *available at* http://www.cchwebsites.com/content/pdf/tax_forms/ca/en/nr603.pdf; CRA, Form NR4, *Statement of Amounts Paid or Credited to Non-Residents of Canada*, *available at* http://www.rbcds.com/TaxReporting/_assets-custom/pdf/NR4.pdf; CRA, *Taxation of Non-Resident Actors Providing Film or Video Acting Services in Canada*, http://www.cra-arc.gc.ca/tx/nnrsdnts/flm/ctrs/wthhld-eng.html; CRA, *Non-Resident Actors*, http://www.cra-arc.gc.ca/tx/nnrsdnts/flm/ctrs/menu-eng.html; CRA, *Actors – Election to File a Return*, http://www.cra-arc.gc.ca/tx/nnrsdnts/flm/ctrs/lctn-eng.html; CRA, *General Guide for Non-Residents - 2013 - Electing Under Section 216.1*, http://www.cra-arc.gc.ca/E/pub/tg/5013-g/5013-g-01b-13e.html; Alan J. Epstein, *"Star Wars" – How To Win the Tax Battle When Your Talent Clients Work Abroad* at 26, The 2013 Entertainment Industry Conference, Cal. CPA Education Foundation (June 12, 2013), *available at* http://documents.jdsupra.com/369fc7d7-25d9-4e06-b54b-12dcb0881826.pdf; Mark Jadd, Norman Bacal & Kay Leung, *Performing in Canada: Taxation of Non-Resident Artists, Athletes, and Other Service Providers*, 56 CANADIAN TAX JOURNAL 589, 607-08, 629-30 (2008), *available at* http://www.ctf.ca/ctfweb/Documents/PDF/2008ctj/08ctj3-jadd.pdf.

[‡‡] See Clay & Assoc., *Changes [A]ffecting Talent Working in the UK* (Summer 2010), http://www.clayassociates.co.uk/news/default.html.

[§§] See *id.* (re UK); CRA, *Information on Withholding Tax on Residuals and Contingent Compensation*, http://www.cra-arc.gc.ca/tx/nnrsdnts/flm/ctrs/wthhldng-eng.html.

different rules for actors than for directors and others.

- **Transfer.** Transfers of residuals "raise assignment of income and I.R.C. § 409A issues (and) they may not constitute 'property' and thus may not qualify for certain tax-free transfers. I.R.C. §351, 721."*

## Producer Issues

- **Payor/Payee Issues.** See above.

- **Depreciation.** Subject to certain limitations, the producer can include residuals (and participations) in the depreciable basis of a film under the so-called "income forecast" method for federal tax purposes[†] but not for California tax purposes.[‡]

- **Tax Incentive Programs.** Production tax incentive programs raise at least two issues related to residuals: Are residuals counted as production expenses for determination of whether the project is over or under a budget threshold or limit? Do residual expenses count as qualified production spending within the jurisdiction for purposes of credits, rebates and refunds? The answers may vary depending on the incentive program at issue and other factors.

## N. Coogan Accounts

According to one source, Coogan or other blocked account[§] deductions are not always made from residuals payments even though they should be if such an account has been established for a minor.** Conversely, according to the source, if Coogan deductions are being made from residuals, the talent should promptly notify all employers when he or she turns 18, so that deductions cease.

## O. Charitable Donation

Several of the guilds have associated charitable foundations, some of which expressly invite members to donate their right to receive residuals.[††]

## P. Unemployment Benefits

In California, residuals payments (and commercials holding fees) are considered wages for unemployment purposes.[‡‡] This means that if a person (such as an actor between jobs) who is receiving unemployment benefits also receives a residuals or holding payment during that time, whether directly or through a loan-out corporation,[§§] his or her unemployment benefits will be reduced.

---

* See Bradford S. Cohen, Elizabeth R. Glasgow & Eric S. Jones, *Income, Estate, and Gift Taxation of Entertainment Assets*, LOS ANGELES LAWYER 12, 18 n.. 2, 19 n. 27 (May 2012), available at http://www.lacba.org/Files/LAL/Vol35No3/2921.pdf.
† See Internal Revenue Code § 167(g)(7); *Transamerica Corp. v. U.S.*, 670 F.Supp 1454. (N.D. Cal. 1986), rev'd, 999 F.2d 1362. (9th Cir. 1993); KPMG, FILM FINANCING AND TELEVISION PROGRAMMING: A TAXATION GUIDE 6th ed. at 630-31 (January 2012), available at http://www.kpmg.com/Global/en/IssuesAndInsights/ArticlesPublications/film-financing/Documents/taxation-guide.pdf.
‡ See Cal. Rev. & Tax. C. §§ 17250.5(a)(4) (personal taxes), 24349(f)(5) (corporate taxes).
§ Coogan accounts, named for former child actor Jackie Coogan (whose earnings were taken and spent by his parents), are required by California law to be set up by the parents of a minor who renders "render artistic or creative services," such as acting. 15% of the child's earnings must be deposited in the account and cannot be withdrawn except by the child once he or she reaches age 18. New York, Louisiana and New Mexico have similar laws.
** See http://www.bizparentz.org/residualpayments.html.
†† See http://www.sagfoundation.org/plannedgiving/residuals and http://www.sagfoundation.org/plannedgiving/residuals/benefits; https://www.wgfoundation.org/donate-writing-foundation/leave-a-legacy/; http://www.wgaefoundation.org/content/giving-wgae-foundation.
‡‡ See Employment Development Dept., *Instructions to Claimants for Reporting Residual Payments and Holding Fees, DE 4005*, Rev. 2 (3/2011), available at http://www.edd.ca.gov/pdf_pub_ctr/de4005.pdf.
§§ See SAG, *Loan-Out Corporations and Unemployment Insurance Benefits in California* (4/20/2010), available at http://www.sagaftra.org/files/sag/documents/Loan-OutCorporationsandUnemploymentInsuranceBenefitsInCalifornia.pdf.

## Q. Payroll Company Fees

Independent producers, advertisers (for commercial residuals) and some studio productions use payroll companies to calculate and issue residuals checks. In such cases, the payroll company may charge a fee to the producer. This is an additional cost the producer must bear, and does not change the amount of the residual received by the talent.

## R. Contingent Compensation

Residuals are considered a distribution expense for purposes of net profit (defined proceeds) definitions. [cite tbd]

# 14. SEPARATED RIGHTS AND SIMILAR REUSE PROVISIONS

This chapter discusses reuse payments that are triggered when aspects of a movie or television *script* are reused, rather than reuse of the completed film or television program itself. Examples of this include remakes, sequels, spinoffs, and the like.

[see Residuals Survival Guide]

## A. Introduction

There are a number of provisions of the WGA MBA that provide for payments of the sort alluded to.

With one exception (noted below), these payments are not generally referred to as residuals, but they're discussed here because they are nonetheless reuse payments.

Several of these payments center on a complex concept called separated rights, so we start with a brief explanation of key aspects of that concept, then discuss reuse payments under separated rights and other provisions.

Finally, there is a discussion of an analogous DGA reuse provision.[*]

## B. What Are Separated Rights?

When writers sell "literary material" (screenplays, teleplays and the like – i.e., generally speaking, a script or treatment), or perform writing services, the virtually universal practice in the industry is that the writer's personal services agreement (a) designates the material as a work for hire and (b) makes the material the subject of a "backup assignment" of all rights.

As a result, the studio or producer usually acquires all rights in the material. In a non-union situation, what the writer receives in return is only what she or her agent or lawyer can negotiate: upfront compensation, credit, a profit participation, perhaps a deferment, and, occasionally, various other rights.

Residuals are never part of the package; nor, generally, are any other reuse fees, other than, in some cases, a backend – typically, a net profit (or defined proceeds) participation that usually amounts to nothing.

In a WGA-covered deal, there are residuals, of course, but there's also something more: if a writer meets certain qualifying tests, certain rights are reserved to the writer, notwithstanding the work for hire and assignment language in the contract.

These rights, and the contractual structure that establishes them (primarily MBA Art. 16), are referred to as separated rights, because the rights are separated out and reserved to the writer.

These provisions have their origins in the nature of early motion picture and television writers, as briefly addressed below.

The qualifying tests, and the reserved rights, are different for made for theatrical and made for television.

### Made for Theatrical

The qualifying tests are an initial qualification and a final qualification.

The initial qualification, in essence, is that the story (a defined term in the MBA, roughly meaning a detailed description of plot and principal characters) must be original, meaning that it is not based on a story that has been previously published or produced, or acquired outside of WGA jurisdiction.[†]

In addition, the material must be written under employment or else purchased from a "professional writer," which is a defined term in the MBA.[‡] It means, roughly, someone who has had

---

[*] Sources for this chapter include Grace Reiner, *Separation of Rights for Screen and Television Writers*, 24 Los Angeles Lawyer 28-33 (Apr. 2001); and Writers Guild of America, west, *Understanding Separated Rights* (WGAw, 2000 & Supp. 2007).

[†] See Art.16.A.2.
[‡] See Art. 1.B.1.b.

a certain number of weeks' employment as a motion picture, television or radio writer (for dramatic programs), or has received certain theatrical, television. radio or professionally produced stage play credits, or has published a novel.

There are many additional nuances, but this summary will suffice.

The final qualification, in essence, is that the writer receives Story by, Written by or Screen Story by credit on the movie.*

If both of the qualifying tests are met, the writer receives separated rights. These rights include provisions for reuse payments related to publication and dramatic stage rights and sequels and spinoffs. These are discussed below.

There are other important separated rights, such as a right to reacquire the script if it doesn't get produced, that don't relate to the subject of this book and are therefore not covered here.

The reservation of publication rights in particular reflects the fact that a number of prominent early screenwriters were novelists, who wanted to be able to further develop and publish material they created.

### Made for Free TV

Television separated rights are very different in two respects. First, the qualification test is a single stage and, second, *all rights* are reserved to the writer, except for limited-duration television rights.

[test, relevant rights, Art. 1.C.1.b]

### Made for Pay TV and Home Video

Separated rights in pay TV and home video product work the same way as in free TV, with one exception, noted below.

### Made for Basic Cable

[tbd]

### Made for Derivative New Media

[tbd]

---

*See Art.16.A.3.

### Made for Original New Media

[tbd]

### Made for High Budget SVOD

### Non-Primetime Scripted Programming

See p. 145.

### Made for Interactive Media (Videogames)

See p. 145.

## C. Publication Rights Payments

## D. Dramatic Stage Rights Payments

## E. Theatrical Sequel and Spinoff Payments

Series Sequel Payments

Incl. in pay TV and HV (Per App. G, Sec. H)

Basic cable?

Incl in original NM and there's something in derivative

## F. Spinoffs

Art. 13.B.7.r(3)

## G. Series Sequel Payments

## H. Residuals on Series Sequel Payments (Separated Rights Residuals)

Aka Separated Rights Residuals

Per App. G, Sec. H, none on made for pay TV or made for HV

Basic cable?

## I. Adapters Royalty

## J. Remakes

Art. 13.A.17

## K. Foreign Remakes

[Art. 13.B.7.o and SL; see 2011 MOU p. 19]

## L. Other Reuse of Literary Material

Arts. 13.B.7.r(3), 15.B.14

## M. Merchandising

## N. Character Payments

## O. Script Publication Fee

The producer is required to pay the writer a one-time $10,000 fee for the right to publish the screenplay on physical home video device (e.g., DVD/Blu-ray) and on new media platforms.* It's due whether or not the writer qualifies for separated rights.

In addition, the fee is payable regardless of whether the producer actually wants to or does publish the screenplay in this fashion, and even regardless of whether a DVD/Blu-ray is ever released or new media release ever occurs.

Indeed, it appears that the fee is payable even if the movie never gets a theatrical release. In essence, it's a mandatory bonus payment.

The fee is to be paid through the WGA Residuals Department and is due within thirty days after final determination of writing credit on the movie (but not before). It cannot be prepaid, offset or credited against any other compensation.

---

* See MBA Art. 16.A.10.

## P. DGA Series Bonus

BA 10-103(d)

## Q. History

| Date | WGA Event |
|---|---|
| 1951 | **Theatrical**: collective bargaining establishes that studios will allow screenwriters to individually negotiate to retain book publishing, radio and dramatic stage rights, and that if Co. does acquire those rights, separate consideration will be payable for those rights when purchasing original material from a writer who is also employed to perform additional services on the material acquired |
| 1953 | **Television**: MBA establishes that (a) writer is eligible for separated rights when s/he writes an original story and teleplay, (b) Co. has specified number of years to produce script for TV (thereafter, Co. and writer share right); (c) Co. has specified number of years to produce a series based on script (thereafter, right reverts to writer); (d) Co. must pay series sequel payments and residuals thereon; (e) all other rights in material (incl. publication, merchandising, theatrical motion picture and all other rights not yet devised) are reserved to writer; and (f) writers reserve or retain most derivative rights in the script |
| 1960 | **Theatrical**: Mel Nimmer (GC of WGA at the time, later became the nation's preeminent copyright expert) obtained the following in form that was virtually unchanged as of 2001 article cited below: (a) test for initial qualification, (b) test for final qualification, (c) various substantive rights (not clear from article which rights were included |
| 1970 | **Theatrical**: Reacquisition right established (eff. date) |
| 1977 | **Theatrical**: Reacquisition right modified (eff. date) |
| 1981 | **Theatrical**: Reacquisition right modified (eff. date) |
| 1988 | **Theatrical**: Reacquisition right modified (eff. date) to current form as of 2011 |
| late '90s | **Interactive Media (Videogames)**: Separated rights established |
| Late '90s | **Television**: MBA establishes that interactive rights are reserved to writer |

| Date | WGA Event |
|---|---|
| 2001 | **Theatrical**: Script publication fee ($5,000) established; right to reacquire rewrites established |
| 2008 | **Derivative and Original New Media**: Separated rights established |
| 2011 | **General**: Upset price and script publication fee frozen; various other figures increase at same rate as minimums (2%/year) |
| 2014 | **Theatrical**: Script publication fee increased to $10,000 |

# 15. OTHER ENTERTAINMENT RESIDUALS AND REUSE PAYMENTS

## A. Non-Primetime Scripted Programming

[tbd, incl. separated rights]

## B. Excerpts (Clip Fees)

When an excerpt, or clip, from a project is re-used in another project, fees are payable. See row 15.B of the chart on p. 179 for references to the applicable contract provisions. Note also the requirement for consent, unique to SAG-AFTRA and Legacy-SAG, found at CBA Art. 22 and TV Agreement Art. 36 (and implicit in Legacy-AFTRA Netcode Exs. A & E).

Refer to the New Media Reuse sideletters for provisions on the use of clips of traditional product on new media platforms. There are detailed definitions of promotional use, which is not subject to residuals. See also p. 110 for the special rule regarding excerpts applicable to use of TV and home video product on ad-supported platforms (K2-K6).

## C. "Unscripted" Programming

Terms and conditions, including residuals where applicable, for "unscripted" – i.e., thinly-scripted – programming such as game shows, comedy-variety shows (such as *Saturday Night Live* and *The Tonight Show*) and the like are beyond the scope of this book. Refer to the following contracts and provisions for details:

- **DGA.** Freelance Live and Tape Television Agt. (FLTTA), New Media Reuse Sideletter (regarding reuse of such product in new media) and Made for New Media Sideletter (regarding such product made for new media, such as a game show made for new media).

- **WGA.** MBA App. A and the New Media Sideletters.

- **SAG-AFTRA and Legacy-AFTRA.** Netcode front of book and the New Media Sideletters to the front of book (not the Exhibit A New Media Sideletters).

- **Legacy-SAG.** not applicable; Legacy-SAG did not cover such shows.

- **IATSE.** [no residuals for such product.]

- **AFM.** [tbd].

## D. Interactive Media (Videogames)

[tbd, incl. separated rights]

### History

| Date | Unions | Event |
|------|--------|-------|
| 1980s | AFTRA | Late 1980s, contract established |

| Date | Unions | Event |
|------|--------|-------|
| 1995 | WGA | Residuals established |
| 2009 | SAG | Contract renewal defeated |
| 2011 | AFTRA | Cloud gaming streaming fee |

## E. Animation

[tbd]

## WGA

The WGA covers only Fox primetime animation. [tbd]

## SAG-AFTRA

## Legacy-SAG

## Legacy-AFTRA

## IATSE

There are no IATSE residuals for animated product.

## AFM

## F. Industrials

[tbd]

## G. Music from Other Sources

Motion pictures and television programs use various types of music that generates AFM residual or reuse payments if the music was recorded under an AFM contract. It also generates SAG-AFTRA residuals or reuse payments if there are singers who recorded under a SAG-AFTRA or AFTRA contract. Some of this is covered in the book. Below is a chart – "product" means theatrical, free TV, pay TV, basic cable, home video, new media or interactive product.

| Source of the music/song that is reused | AFM Residuals | SAG-AFTRA Residuals |
|---|---|---|
| Music/song that is recorded specifically for the product in which it is used; what residuals are payable when the motion picture or television program is reused? | See Chapters 5-12 | |
| Music/song that was previously recorded for a different product, when the music/song is reused *with* the accompanying footage (example: a living-room scene in a movie includes a shot of a TV set that is playing a clip from a TV show, and the clip includes music); what fee is payable for use of the clip? | See AFM Theatrical Agreement Art. 8A or AFM TV Agreement Art. 8A (see also Section 15.B above) | |
| Music/song that was previously recorded for a different product, when the music/song is reused *without* the accompanying footage (examples include movie sequels that include music recorded for an earlier installment of the franchise); what fee is payable for use of the music/song? | See AFM Theatrical Agreement Art. 8A or AFM TV Agreement Art. 8A (see also Section 15.B above) | |
| Music/song that was recorded for a sound recording or album (example: a movie or TV episode uses a preexisting recording of a song from a new or established group); what fee is payable for use of the music? | See AFM Theatrical Agreement Art. 8B or AFM TV Agreement Art. 8B; and AFM Sound Recording Labor Agreement Art. [tbd] (previously known as the Phonograph Record Labor Agreement) | |

| Source of the music/song that is reused | AFM Residuals | SAG-AFTRA Residuals |
|---|---|---|
| Music/song (aka "jingles") that was recorded for a commercial (example: hard to think of one, since it's rare that a movie or TV show will include a commercial jungle); what fee is payable for use of the music? | See AFM Theatrical Agreement Art. 8B or AFM TV Agreement Art. 8B; and AFM Commercial Announcements Agreement Art. [tbd] | |
| Music that was recorded for a stage play under an AFM agreement | [tbd] | |
| Music that was not recorded under an AFM agreement; what fee is payable for use of the music? | No residuals. | |

Issues related to trailers, pilot episodes, use of music from another episode of the same television series, and the like, are addressed in Art. 8 of the AFM Theatrical Agreement and AFM TV Agreement, and in Art. [tbd] of the [SAG-AFTRA agreement].

## H. Soundtrack Albums

When music recorded for a motion picture or television show is also released as a sound recording – such as release as part of a soundtrack album – reuse payments are due. For details, see AFM Theatrical Agreement Arts. 8, 8C and 8D, and the same Articles in the AFM TV Agreement, and Art. [tbd] of the [SAG-AFTRA agreement].

## I. Foreign Levies

Foreign levies are beyond the scope of this book, but here's a brief description of what they are.

There are agreements between the DGA, WGA and SAG/SAG-AFTRA and collection societies in various countries. These pertain to distribution of foreign levies (also known as foreign royalties or neighboring rights royalties), which are taxes imposed by some foreign governments on cable TV subscriptions, DVD rentals, blank DVDs and the like. The guilds receive and distribute a portion of these monies to writers, directors and actors (including guild members and non-members), while the studios receive the remainder.

➔ It's important to understand that foreign levies are completely different from foreign residuals (col E). There's no connection between the two whatsoever. Indeed, you'll find no mention of foreign levies in the collective bargaining agreements, because collection of such levies was not collectively bargained.

## J. Live Stage

[tbd][Also stage designers, lighting and sound, and directors]

## K. Copyright Royalty Tribunal Monies

BA Art. 21, MBA Art. 59

## L. AGICOA Monies

# 16. COMMERCIALS

Most of this book focuses on entertainment residuals – that is, residuals that relate to programming. However, this chapter discusses commercial residuals – i.e., residuals that relate to advertisements.

SAG-AFTRA and the AFM have jurisdiction over commercials work by their members, and their commercials contracts provide for residuals. The residuals systems are very different from the formulas discussed in the rest of this book. This chapter briefly discusses the commercials residuals system for those two unions

The DGA and IATSE also have commercials contracts, but there are no residuals. The WGA does not have jurisdiction over commercials work.

## A. SAG-AFTRA

[tbd]

https://www.artpayroll.com/GenericTabPage.php?TO=1&MENU=TPG&START=1&GOTO=TalentPaymentGuide/radiosess.php

See SAG_Commercial__Industrial__FAQ.doc in \wk\guild\commercials

Holding fee—same amount as a session fee, paid every 13 weeks

Class A Network or Program – the big money, when the commercial is shown at the same time, same station, all across the networks (ABC, CBS, Fox, NBC). Paid for each use, getting smaller and smaller the more the commercial is run.

Wildspot (by unit, based on population) – local buys, paid lump sum for 13-week cycle

Dealer A - 6 month cycle which might be outside the 13 weeks

Cable – (by unit = 350,000 subs, based on sub counts) min: $592.20, max (2,000 unit): $2,836.00 *This is what most commercials pay now. Paid in 13-week cycles.

Internet Use

New Media

For these two, 8 week cycle (133% of $592.20) or 1 year buy (350% of $592.20)

Theatrical/Industrials

1 time payment

30 days or less – 100% of scale ($592.20). else 160% of scale

21 mo. MPU

Foreign

Outside U.S., Canada and Mexico

100% session fee per country for MPU

Radio

Industrial/Educational

Checks are sent directly from the ad agency to the actor, rather than being sent to the union for forwarding (as is the case with entertainment residuals).

There is P&H on commercial residuals.

Payment is due 15 business days from the first air date

GRP

## B. AFM

Music used in commercials is referred to as "jingles." Use or reuse of a spot for 13 weeks in television or radio triggers a reuse fee equal to 75% of the session fees. Use or reuse of a spot for 8 weeks in radio only triggers a reuse fee equal to 80% of 13 week cycle payment. Use and reuse fees are paid under scale in effect at the time of the original session.

Jingles made for initial use on the Internet: there is an Initial Use payment for first 6-month period of use; one dub fee (equivalent) for second 6-month period of use; and one dub fee (equivalent) for each subsequent 52-week period of use. [tbd]

https://www.artpayroll.com/GenericTabPage.php?TO=3&MENU=TPG&START=1&GOTO=TalentPaymentGuide/jinglesess.php

## C. History

| Date | Unions | Event |
| --- | --- | --- |
| 1952-1953 | SAG | Commercials strike |
| [1953] | AFM | Residuals established |
| 1978 | SAG, AFTRA | Commercials strike |
| 1988 | SAG, AFTRA | Cable commercials residuals established |
| 2000 | SAG, AFTRA | Commercials strike |

# 17. ECONOMICS

Residuals are economically significant. Here's some available macro- and micro-economic data.

## A. Total Entertainment Residuals

This table shows the latest available data – and, where data is unavailable, my estimates in italics – for entertainment residuals collected.

| Union (and source/note) (2013) | Residuals |
|---|---|
| *DGA (est.)* | *$485* |
| WGA West | $374 |
| *WGA East (est.)* | *$125* |
| SAG-AFTRA | *$800* |
| IATSE (MPIPP, IAP, MPIHP) | $337 |
| AFM (FMSMF) | $87 |
| Total | $2,208 |

[need to update AFM figures to weighted average]

Note the following:

● The DGA figure is my rough estimate since the union doesn't publicly report. It's derived by backing out the reported WGA West reuse payments that are specific to writers (essentially, those described in Chapter 14 – the line items for TV Creator Royalties and Script Publication Fee) and adding the resulting figure to the WGA East figure. Implicitly, this relies on the fact that the DGA residuals formulas are similar or identical to the WGA's. It also assumes that most of the economically significant movies and TV programs are produced under the jurisdiction of both unions, which seems a fair assumption.

● The WGA West publicly reports the amount of residuals collected in a calendar year in the annual reports that it posts on its website.

● The WGA East does not publicly report. The rough estimate above (1/3 of the WGA West figure) is based on the facts that the WGA East is less than half the size of the WGA West and that significantly fewer entertainment programs are produced under WGA East jurisdiction.

● SAG-AFTRA does not publicly report. However, in January 2014, a union source advised me that total member annual earnings were approximately $4 billion; that approximately 50% of this was TV/theatrical; and that residuals were approximately 40% of earnings. $4b x 50% x 40% = $800K. As a reality check, compare with the last reported residuals figures from SAG (which did report, from 2001-2010): $238 million theatrical and $228 million television. Adding in 75% of the TV figure as an estimate to account for AFTRA (which did not report) yields a $640 million figure for 2010. Now grow the figures by the same amount that the WGA figures increased from 2010 to 2013: essentially zero increase for theatrical residuals and a 33% increase for television, yielding about an estimated $775 million for 2013, effectively the same as the $800 million rough estimate.

● The IATSE figures are those reported by the applicable pension (Motion Picture Industry Pension Plan and Individual Account Plan) and health (Motion Picture Industry Health Plan) plans on their IRS / Department of Labor Form 5500s, which are publicly available.*

● The AFM figures are publicly reported by the FMSMF, but on an April 1-March 31 fiscal year. The figure shown is the latest available (2013-2014). The FMSMF is the Film Musicians Secondary Market Fund, which is the organization that collects and pays AFM film and television musicians' residuals.

## B. Comparisons

[do charts, graphs, and resized version of residuals chart representing relative importance]

### By Made-For Medium

[from WGAW and SAG data]

---

* Visit https://www.efast.dol.gov/portal/app/disseminate and search for EIN 951810805, Plan No. 001 (for the Pension Plan) or EIN 956042583, Plan No. 501 (for the Health Plan). The relevant figures are the line items for Supplemental Markets Income and Post '60s Income, which in the Year 2013 reports (filed in 2014) are found on pp. 87 and 162, respectively.

### By Reuse Market

[from WGA data]

### By Reuse Pattern

[from WGA data]

## C. WGA West Data in Detail

[raw; and in relation to initial comp]

[trends – do 2 WGAW snapshots in residuals chart form]

## D. SAG Data in Detail

[raw; and in relation to initial comp]

## E. Commercials Data

[SAG and AFM – raw; and in relation to session fees]

## F. Aggregated SAG Data

## G. IATSE/MPIPHP Data

## H. AFM/FMSMF Data

Breakdowns from FMSMF paper

## I. Historicals

Incl AFM from FMSMF white paper p. 9

Aggregate $1B SAG residuals 1952-87, http://www.sagaftra.org/guild-headquarters 1988-92 $1B, 2004 over $1B/yr

## J. Pattern Bargaining Multiplier Effect

2. The formulas for reuse of theatrical in any medium work like this: DGA percentage varies (see below), WGA=DGA, SAG=3xDGA, IA=4.5xDGA, and AFM generally = 1% (see below). So this translates to a total of 9.5xDGA, plus AFM.

For release on TV (free, foreign, pay or basic), eRental, and ad-supported nm, the DGA percentage is 1.2% and AFM is 1%, so total is 9.5 x 1.2% + 1% = 12.4%.

For home video, the DGA is 1.5%, escalating to 1.8% at a gross break. AFM is 1%. Total is thus 15.25% to 18.1%. These are calculated on producers gross, but that term as you know generally equates to 20% of worldwide wholesale gross.

For EST, DGA is 1.8%, escalating to 3.25% at 50K units. AFM is 1%, escalating to 1.8% at the same break. Total is thus 18.1% to 32.675%. As with physical HV, this is usually calculated against a 20% base.

| Reused in:<br>Made for: | Theatrical | Free TV Network Primetime | Free TV Syndication or Non-Primetime | Foreign | Supp.Mkts. Pay TV | Home Video | Domestic Basic Cable | New Media Consumer Pd eRental | EST | New Media Ad Supported |
|---|---|---|---|---|---|---|---|---|---|---|
| Theatrical | | 12.4% (18.6% if outright sale, rare) | | 12.4% | 3.1%to 3.6% * | 12.4% | 12.4% | 3.6%to 6.6%† | 12.4% |
| Free TV | | | | 6% after brk | | 10% | 12.4% (or 15% for BC) | 3.6% to 7% ‡ | 10% (16% for BC) after 1 yr. or for library product |
| Pay TV | | | | | >brk 10% | 10% | | | |
| Home Video | | | | | | | | | |
| Basic Cable | | | | | see above | | | | |
| Deriv. NM | | | | | see above | 10% ‡‡ | 12.4% ** | 10% ‡‡ |
| Orig. NM | | | | | ** | †† | | | |
| Exper. NM | | | | | | | | | |

| | Note |
|---|---|
| * | HV 15.25% to 18.1% x 20% = 3.05% to 3.62% |
| † | 18.1% to 32.675% x 20% = 3.62% to 6.535% |

| | Note |
|---|---|
| ‡ | 18.1% to 35.15% (add 3x1.8 − 1, 3x3.5 − 1.9, for BC = 22.5%-43.75%) 3.62% to 7.03% (4.5%-8.75%) [tbd] |
| ** | re BC Deriv add 2.6 |
| †† | re BC Deriv add 2.6 or 20% thereof |
| ‡‡ | BC Deriv add 3.6 |

Home Video – Studio Gross and DGA Residual

| Market | Cell | Gross | Residual (low / hi) |
|---|---|---|---|
| High Def EST (e.g., iTunes) | J2 | $17.50 | $0.063 / $0.11375 |
| Blu-ray sellthr (Best Buy, Amazon) | G2 | $15 | $0.045 / $0.054 |
| DVD sellthrough (Best Buy, Amazon) | G2 | $12 | $0.036 / $0.0432 |
| VOD (i.e., PPV) (HBO PPV) | I2 | $3.50 | $0.042 |
| SVOD (Netflix online) | I2 | $1.50 | $0.018 |
| Store rental (Blockbuster) | G2 | $1.45 | $0.00435 / $0.00522 |
| Kiosk rental (Redbox) | G2 | $1.25 | $0.00375 / $0.0045 |

## K. Theatrical Trends in Home Video

Back in the mid-1940's, a third of the country went to the cinema every week. Today, Americans see only about five movies per year in theaters. The rest are watched at home, but how they're watched affects the residual. Today's most popular channels, such as pay-per-view and kiosk rental, generally generate smaller residuals than DVD/Blu-ray purchase. And that latter, referred to as "sell-through," isn't high to begin with (recall the "four cents per DVD" discussion on p. 57).

To see this requires knowing how much the studio makes via different channels. A 2013 article* provided those figures, to which we can then apply the corresponding residuals formula. The result is this table.

## L. Trends in Network Primetime Reruns

In the past, most network primetime program episodes were rerun at least once in network primetime, yielding a large fixed residual (C3). [tbd]

The residual base will increase 2% in each year of the agreement, rather than 3%. Syndication and foreign reruns (D3-E3), and ad-supported new media reruns (K3), will increase at the same rate as wages.

## M. Residuals Vs. Total Compensation

SAG-AFTRA chart

SAG, 43%, http://judiciary.house.gov/_files/hearings/pdf/Almeida%2011162011.pdf, 2008

SAG-AFTRA 58% of income for middle-income actors, Development of a Joint Strategic Plan on Intellectual Property Enforcement, in \wk\ent...\residuals\unused http://www.dga.org/Initiatives/~/media/Files/Internet%20Theft/DGAIATSESAGAFTRAIPEC%20submission%20re%20joint%20strategic%20plan81012.pdf

SAG-AFTRA 40%

WGAW from chart

---

* Source for studio gross: chart, *What Studios Pocket Per Transaction,* VARIETY (print edition only), Sept. 6, 2013 (based on data credited from Time Warner and Nomura Research). Chart accompanied the print version of article *Studios Find Their Best Hope for Offsetting a DVD Decline* by Susanne Ault.

DGA, 19% incls above & BTL

http://www.dga.org/Initiatives/~/media/Files/Internet%20Theft/DGA%20%20Submission%20to%20the%20Rep%20of%20Ireland%20Copyright%20Review%20Committee71311.pdf

DGA Submission to the Rep of Ireland Copyright Review Committee71311.pdf in \wk\ent...\residuals\unused

IATSE 0

AFM unk

DGA Pension Plan 70% funded by residuals – see above DGA sources and RE: Request for Comments on Department of Commerce Green Paper, Copyright Policy, Creativity, and Innovation in the Digital Economy. Docket No 130927852-3852-01, in unused folder, http://www.ntia.doc.gov/files/ntia/directors_guild_of_america_post-meeting_comments.pdf

MPI HP – 65%, some of above (Almeida), also http://www.cecc.gov/sites/chinacommission.house.gov/files/documents/hearings/2010/CECC%20Hearing%20Testimony%20-%20Thea%20Lee%20-%209.22.10.pdf

### N. Writer's Case Study

Screenwriter John August has published[*] some information the residuals he received for writing the movie *Go*. His comments and charts reflect that he received $70,000 up front for writing the script and over $300,000 in residuals. In other words, residuals were about 80% of his total compensation on the movie. That's a very high ratio: in aggregate, residuals are about a third of a screenwriter's income or a quarter of a television writer's income.[†]

Here are his 2011 comments, followed by a pair of graphs that he prepared.[‡]

"*Go* was a movie I wrote in '96, the movie came out in 1999. All in, I was paid about $70,000 for *Go*, that was them buying the rights to the script, and me rewriting the script and production and everything else, I was paid about $70,000.

"The movie was moderately successful, it made about $17 million in box office. The budget was $5.5 million, so nobody was really losing money, but with advertising, they had probably... they weren't really making money theatrically on the movie.

"My first residual check for *Go* came in November 1999, it was for $36,000. . . . The checks keep coming on a movie, and so my most recent check for go was in August 2011. It was for $1,863. A lot less, but still money."

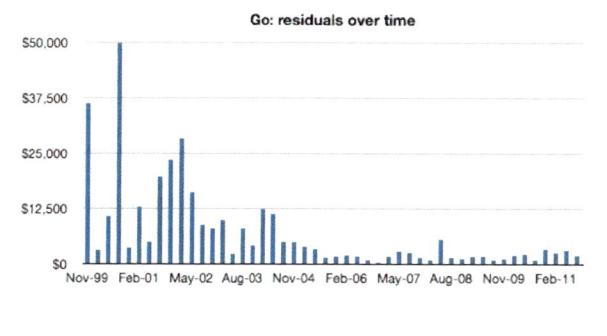

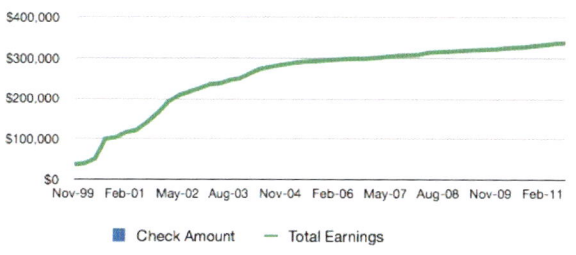

---

[*] See http://johnaugust.com/2011/how-residuals-work and http://johnaugust.com/2011/scriptnotes-ep-14-how-residuals-work-transcript.
[†] See the earnings and residuals figures in the WGA West Annual Financial Report, e.g., the 2014 report, *available at* http://www.wga.org/subpage_whoweare.aspx?id=230.
[‡] The comments and charts are © John August and reprinted by permission.

# 18. PAYMENT MECHANICS

This chapter touches briefly on mechanical issues related to payment of residuals. [BA Art. 22, Exs. A-1, A-2, B-1, B-2]

Epic fails, http://deadline.com/2014/06/fox-error-residuals-checks-voided-741629/; also Doe

## A. Due Dates

The union contracts usually specify when residuals payments are due. The studios and producers generally receive some data, such as foreign exploitation, more slowly than other data. Recognizing this, the union contracts typically provide for longer payment timeframes for such reuse patterns.

The specific timeframes can generally be found in the contract within a few subsections of the residuals formula itself.

Here's a table summarizing the rules for the WGA:*

| Made for: \ Reused in: | Theatrical | Free TV Network Primetime | Free TV Syndication or Non-Primetime | Foreign | Supp. Mkts. Pay TV | Supp. Mkts. Home Video | Domestic Basic Cable | New Media Consumer Pd eRental | New Media Consumer Pd EST | New Media Ad Supported |
|---|---|---|---|---|---|---|---|---|---|---|
| Theatrical | | Q60 | Q60 | | Q60 | Q60 | Q60 | | Q60 | Q60 |
| Free TV | | T30 | T4 | T6 | | | Q60 | Q60 | | Q60 |
| Pay TV | | | | | | | | | | |
| Home Video | | T30 | T4 | T6 | | | Q60 | | | Q60 |
| Basic Cable | | T30 | T4 | T6 | Q60 | | T4* | | | |
| Deriv. NM | | | | | | | | Q60 | | Q60 |
| Orig. NM | | | | | | | | | | |
| Exper. NM | | | | | | | | | | |
| HB SVOD | | | | | | | | | | |

http://www.sagaftra.org/when-are-residuals-due

Here's a quick guide: Made-for-Television then released to:

Network Prime Time - 30 days after air date

Non-Prime Time Network - 30 days after air date

Syndication - 4 months after air date

Foreign Free TV - No later than 30 days after producer obtains knowledge of the first foreign telecast and never later than six months after that first telecast

Basic Cable – Quarterly when the producer receives revenue

Supplemental Markets – 4 months after initial exhibition, then quarterly when the producer receives revenue

Made-for-Theatrical then released to:

Network Prime Time - 30 days after initial broadcast, then quarterly when the producer receives revenue

Free TV, Non-Network - 4 months after initial broadcast, then quarterly when the producer receives revenue

Supplemental Markets - 4 months after initial exhibition, then quarterly when the producer receives revenue

## B. Prepayment

[tbd]

[distinguish from buyout]

---

* See http://wga.org/uploadedfiles/writers_resources/residuals/residuals_due_dates.pdf and MBA.

## C. Payment Obligations

[acquisition by a signatory, assumption agreements, QDs, transfer statute, personal guarantees, security deposits (incl. WGA Art. 47, etc.]

[see Kohanski excerpt for Payment chapter.doc]

[SAG CBA: Qualified Residual Payor, Qualified Distributor or Qualified Buyer]

## D. Residuals Deposits

[tbd]

## E. Workflow

[checks to agents, etc; no EDI; workload; small check policies]

[incl Aaxis]

The WGA West handles residuals processing for the WGA East, as the West coast union has twice as many members as its east coast counterpart and is more Hollywood-centric.

FMSMF

Commercials

## F. Payment Statistics

[stats re quantity of checks (slides 4, 6), AFM stats]

Per its latest annual report and per a white paper (p. 20), the FMSMF spent about $4.5m in 2008-2009 and wrote about 24,600 checks (one check per recipient) in the same period (June 2008 distribution).

Film Musicians Secondary Markets Fund, Financial Statements: March 31, 2010 and 2009

AFM per white paper, Dreith, Dennis, FMSMF White Paper (Film Musicians Secondary Markets Fund: May 13, 2009)]

That's $183 per check. However, it's a fully burdened figure - it includes the salaries of the head of the organization, IT staff, paralegal, etc.

To compare apples to apples, we need to approximate a non-fully-burdened figure.

Fully-burdened salaries are $3m

Rent is $500K

Other G&A is $800K

If we deduct rent, other G&A and an arbitrary 2/3 of salaries from the $4.5m, we get $1.2m, for a per-check cost of $49.

First, it's expensive and time-consuming to monitor usage in diverse media then report, process and mail physical checks to a member's guild, which then processes the checks and remails them to the member – or to the agent, who may then take a commission where permitted and then mails a check again, this time to the guild member. The WGA alone received as many as 5,000 checks a day in 2002. In 2010, SAG processed 2 million residuals checks a year and received $2 million in residuals payments a day.[*] The volume coupled with the convoluted process result in a 48-day lag time in delivering residuals checks.[†]

In addition, residuals checks are too often for absurdly small amounts. Some actors get checks for $2 – or even for a penny. See p. 174 for an example. Zero cent checks are possible too, and negative amount statements are said to be as well.

[SAG-AFTRA 3.8m checks 2014]

## G. Small Check Rules

Many residuals are quite small. This is especially true for actors, where checks as low as one

---

[*] http://www.variety.com/article/VR1118029219 (12/18/10).
[†] *Id.*

cent are not unheard of. (See p. 174 for an example.)

To alleviate the costs associated with producing, tracking and mailing a blizzard of small checks, the WGA has an optional program that allows members to elect not to receive residuals payment until the amount due has aggregated to at least $100. The DGA and SAG-AFTRA do not have such programs, however. The FMSMF sends only one check per year to each person entitled to AFM residuals.

### H. Beneficiaries

http://www.sagaftra.org/content/estates

AFM BOB

### I. Unlocatable Recipients

http://www.sagaftra.org/search-unclaimed-residuals

### J. Grievance and Arbitration

What happens if a producer or studio fails to pay what it owes? This can happen for a variety of reasons: error, cash flow shortages, bankruptcy, malfeasance, or a good faith dispute as the interpretation of a contract clause or its application to a particular project.

When a member doesn't receive an expected check, he or she is likely to call the union and complain. Sometimes the member or a friend will have learned that the movie or TV series is playing overseas or in syndication, yet he or she has received no corresponding check.

In these circumstances, the union Residuals Dept. will generally investigate. Not infrequently, the member is in error: perhaps a payment is not yet due for the usage that the member observed, or perhaps no residuals are contractually triggered by the usage.

[tbd SAG-AFTRA says it does] Note that the unions do not appear to have a proactive system for policing compliance with residuals obligations. Theoretically, they could ingest data feeds regarding exploitation of product – e.g., databases that indicate the date, time, place and medium by which various product was exploited – and then automatically compare this data to the checks that were received.

However, the unions don't actually appear to do this, and the data feeds and custom software to do so wouldn't come cheap. Instead, it's often the members who police compliance. It's unknown – and perhaps unknowable – what amount of residuals go unpaid each year.

[tbd]

[1956 SAG Telemount – Billboard article and case, Northrup pp. 85-86]

Residuals disputes are subject to arbitration under the above the line union agreements. [IATSE, AFM?]

The WGA has an expedited arbitration process available when the company is not financially responsible, or it is likely that the company's assets will be depleted or transferred.[*]

[tbd WGA West collection figures]

### K. Tri-Guild Audits

The collective bargaining agreements provide for tri-Guild Audits (DGA, SAG-AFTRA, WGA) of residuals payments and tri-Guild arbitrations, so long as the company is not a Qualified Distributor, Qualified Buyer and/or a Qualified Residuals Payor,[†]

Also, the New Media Reuse Sideletters provide that the unions will have periodic access to unredacted license, distribution and other agreements pertaining to new media exploitation.

[Unpublished Sideletter Regarding Renewal of Gross Receipts Residuals Payments Monitoring Fund in 2011 WGA MOA]

---

[*] See MBA Art. 11.G.
[†] See DGA BA Sideletter 17; WGA MBA Sideletter to Art. 11.H; SAG CBA Sideletter 18; SAG TV Agt. Sideletter E.

# 19. INTERNATIONAL AND LINGUISTIC ISSUES

This chapter discusses international issues related to U.S. union residuals, and also briefly describes the residuals systems used by several foreign countries' entertainment unions.

## A. International Issues for U.S. Persons

International issues affect U.S. entertainment unions in several ways.

### Foreign Reuse

Product reused on foreign free TV, foreign basic cable or foreign ad-supported services is subject to the formulas in cells E2-E9. TV and home video to theatrical is addressed in B3-B6, but the formulas differ somewhat for foreign use. The formulas for most or all other reuse patterns are worldwide.

To summarize, here's a chart:

| Reuse Type | Market Name (if different) | Col. |
|---|---|---|
| Theatrical | | B |
| Free TV | Foreign | E |
| Pay TV | | F |
| Home video | | G |
| Basic cable | Foreign | E |
| eRental | | I |
| EST | | J |
| Ad-supported services (theatrical product) | | K |
| Ad-supported service (TV and home video product) | Foreign | E |

Foreign reuse does raise practical concerns regarding allocation and payment. See pp. 58 and 155. [add note re HV distributors arb decn]

In addition, some countries for political or economic reasons may inhibit or prohibit repatriation of revenue to the U.S. That is, the studio may not be able to get its money out of the foreign country. This problem – referred to as blocked funds or frozen funds – is not common today, but in any case, the union agreements provide that blocked funds are not counted in producers gross until the funds are freely convertible to U.S. dollars and are remitted to the U.S.*

### Foreign Remakes

See p. 143.

### English Dubbing of Foreign-Language Product

Xxx SAG agts. – 4 agts.

### Non-English Production in the U.S.

Xxx MBA 2011 pdf p. 157 (p. 143)

### Foreign Levies

See p. 147.

### Production in the U.S. for Foreign Markets

[tbd]

### Foreign Producers in the U.S.

The DGA, WGA and SAG-AFTRA (but not IATSE) generally require that members working in the U.S. must work only for companies that have signed the appropriate union agreement. The rules, and the agreements (including the residuals formulas), apply regardless of whether the producer is a foreign company or not.

[check AFM]

### Foreign Productions

If a production is produced overseas, [tbd]

Regarding proration, see p. 132.

### International Tax Issues Re Residuals

See the discussion under Taxes beginning on p. 137.

---

* See, e.g., MBA Art. 15.A.3.c.

## B. Canada

Writers – see producer_handbook (WGC)

ACTRA commercials – see \wk\Guilds and Unions\ACTRA & DGC & WGC\client-alert-7-9-13.pdf

Incl. Quebec

### Writers

### Directors

### Actors

## C. United Kingdom

### Writers

### Directors

Directors UK since June 2008, not Directors Guild of Great Britain

### Actors

## D. Australia

### Writers

### Directors

The Australian Directors Guild is a small professional organization, not a union, and has been unable to obtain provision for residuals or retransmission monies.[*]

### Actors

---

[*] See ADG, *Submission to the National Cultural Policy* (Oct. 2011), http://creativeaustralia.arts.gov.au/assets/Australian_Directors_Guild.pdf.

## E. New Zealand

### Writers

The NZ Writers Guild had achieved residuals in the past, including a provision for as high as 7.5% of gross on international sales,[†] but political winds changed and there are now no standard contracts and seldom any residuals[‡] (other than a creator's per-episode fee for the creator of a television series.[§]

### Directors

NZ directors may get residuals when their work is screened in Australia. xxx

### Actors

New Zealand has the world's only well-developed yet non-unionized English-speaking film and television industry.[**] Thus, NZ Actors Equity has been unable to collectively bargain on behalf of actors. However, NZAE and a producer's association, SPADA, negotiated a recommended contract form for actors on motion pictures, television series, television movies and other productions. Also negotiated was an (apparently optional) Back End Agreement (also referred to as a Backend Agreement), pursuant to which "Key Performers" share equally in a pool equal to 5% of "Producer's Net Income," with those and various other terms defined.[††]

In commercials, session fees buy 12 months use in a wide range of media. A second 12 month "rollover" costs 100% of the session fee and a third 12 month rollover is available at a fee to be negotiated.[‡‡]

---

[†] See *A History of the New Zealand Writers Guild* at 5, http://www.nzwritersguild.org.nz/assets/pdfs/history.pdf.
[‡] See http://www.nzwritersguild.org.nz/resources/faqs/the-answers/.
[§] See http://www.nzwritersguild.org.nz/assets/pdfs/writingrates.pdf (recommended rates and negotiating points).
[**] See my book THE NEW ZEALAND HOBBIT CRISIS for discussion of a failed attempt to unionize actors on *The Hobbit*, and the aftermath.
[††] See http://www.actorsequity.org.nz/index.php?option=com_docman&task=cat_view&gid=49&Itemid=93.
[‡‡] See http://www.actorsequity.org.nz/index.php?option=com_docman&task=cat_view&gid=46&Itemid=93.

## F. Other Countries

Note federations, see Biblio

# 20. RECENT HISTORY

Back on p. 15 we gave a history of residuals in a nutshell. This chapter provides more detail on the recent history. The material in this chapter is also reflected in the body of the book.

## A. 2007-2009 Negotiating Cycle

This cycle saw the introduction of a comprehensive set of formulas for product made for or reused in new media. See Chapters 11-12. The deal was reached in January 2008 by the DGA and AMPTP while the WGA strike (which began in November 2007) was ongoing. Later in 2008, the WGA (with minor changes) and then AFTRA accepted the template set by the DGA deal. SAG worked without a contract until finally accepting the DGA template in June 2009.

## B. 2010-2011 Negotiating Cycle

The notable change in this cycle was the network primetime residuals freeze, a reflection of economic challenges to the network television business. See p. [tbd]. Also notable: SAG and AFTRA negotiated first and set the pattern.

## C. 2013-2014 Negotiating Cycle

[tbd change voice]

The new three-year studio deal reached by the Directors Guild reflects both an improved economy and secular changes within the television industry.

### Wage Increases and Network Primetime Residuals

The agreement's wage increases – essentially, 3% per year[*] – contrast with 2% annual increases in the last contract negotiations (in 2010), although those increases were coupled with a 1.5% increase in pension and health contributions, making those increases effectively 2.5%. Still, this year's increase represents a slight loosening of the studios' cost control mantra.

However, what one hand gives, another takes away, at least partially. Television residuals for reruns on traditional platforms (C3-E3) usually increase at the same rate as wages, but that's not entirely true this time, nor was it in the last round. Under the deal, the DGA residual base for reruns in network primetime (C3) will increase 2% in each year of the agreement, rather than 3%. Syndication and foreign reruns (D3-E3), and ad-supported new media reruns (K3), will increase at the same rate as wages. In contrast, in the last round of negotiations, a three-year *freeze* on network primetime residuals was agreed to (see p. [tbd]). The residual bases didn't increase at all.

So, network primetime residuals are now increasing at a slower rate than wages. That may be less of a blow than it seems, since network primetime reruns themselves are disappearing as reruns shift to ad-supported new media platforms (K3) such as Hulu.

### Ad-Supported New Media Residuals

Those new media reruns are governed by one of the more complex formulas in the entire residuals system. In brief, here's how it works (see p. 108 for a detailed explanation). First, there is a free streaming window during which no residuals are due. Under the existing (2008) deal, that window is 24 days for a new series or 17 days for a series in its second or subsequent season. The free window has been sharply criticized by the guilds, since most viewership of network reruns occurs within a few days, meaning that the free window insulates most reruns from paying residuals.

Under the new deal, the free window has been reduced to seven days for programs after the first seven episodes of a new series. Effectively, that treats viewership within the first seven days as being part of the episode's initial airing (and hence residual-free). That's congruent with the television industry's position in the DVR realm that ratings should be based on Live+7 viewing as appointment television fades and is replaced by on demand viewing of broadcast product.

---

[*] 2.5% in the first year, but with a 0.5% increase in pension plan contributions, amounting to a combined 3% increase; and 3% increases in the second and third years.

After the free streaming window, residual rates are currently 3.5% of the residual base for each 26-week period during the one year period following the free streaming window. That's been the figure since mid-2010 / mid-2011 (the exact date depends on the union; initially, the figure was 3%).

That 3.5% figure will increase to 4% of the residual base in the first year of the new agreement, 4.5% in the second year of the agreement, and 5% in the third year of the agreement for programs exhibited. (These increases are in addition to the 3% annual increase in the residual base itself.)

The new agreement's rates represent a significant increase, on a relative basis. However, these numbers are still much lower than the network primetime reruns they replace, which are paid at 100% of the residual base. Although the primetime residual base is now a bit lower than the residual base used for ad-supported new media, primetime residuals are still about ten to twenty times higher than ad-supported new media residuals. See p. 152 for an explanation.

After the one year period, residuals will be paid at the rate of 2% of employer's gross, i.e., 2% of the license fee. This is unchanged from the current formula.

## SVOD Product

Now let's look at product made for subscription video on demand (SVOD) – programs like Netflix's *House of Cards* and Amazon's *Betas*. It was anticipated that there would be adjustment to the new media terms for such programs, and there was. Indeed, I had been previously told that *House of Cards* had been made pursuant to modified guild deals.

The new deal eliminates or reduces the need to craft one-off deals for such shows. Instead, it establishes, for the first time, minimum wages, terms and conditions for high budget original and derivative dramatic new media productions made for subscription video on demand (SVOD) that exceed certain minimum budget thresholds. Below the minimum budget thresholds, rates and conditions will remain freely negotiable. Those thresholds have not yet been disclosed by the DGA and AMPTP.

Under the new deal, for SVOD services with more than 15 million subscribers (such as Netflix),[*] original and derivative dramatic new media productions above a second budget level (also not yet disclosed) will receive network primetime rates and conditions. Productions below that second budget level will receive basic cable rates and conditions.

For SVOD services with fewer than 15 million subscribers (which may include Amazon Prime),[†] original and derivative dramatic new media productions will receive basic cable terms and conditions.

Residuals for high budget original and derivative dramatic new media productions made for SVOD will be paid as a percentage of the applicable network prime time residual base starting in the second year of exhibition.

## Motion Pictures

Residuals for motion pictures are calculated based on gross receipts or license fees (row 2) and are unchanged in the new agreement.

## Made-For Basic Cable Product

The new agreement also includes amended residual provisions to encourage sale of library product for second sales in basic cable. These apply when a basic cable show is sold to a second basic cable network (i.e., when the program is rerun on a second basic cable network).

## Intermediate Digital Channels

The new agreement also includes amended residual provisions to encourage sale of library product to intermediate digital broadcast channels (like channel 4.1, 4.2, etc.).

## Script Publication Fee

The WGA achieved a provision doubling the script publication fee (see p. 143).

---

[*] Re Netflix subscriber base, see http://www.bloomberg.com/news/2013-10-21/netflix-poised-to-pass-hbo-in-paid-u-s-subscribers.html.
[†] Re Amazon Prime subscriber base, see http://www.businessinsider.com/amazon-prime-10-million-members-morningstar-2013-3.

## 21. POLICY ISSUES

Entertainment residuals are problematic and controversial. This chapter looks at the issues, the arguments, and some proposals for reform.

Sections A and F represent my own opinions, whereas Section B is intended as a balanced presentation, and Sections C and D (by Schuyler Moore) and Section E (by the AMPTP) express the opinions and/or proposals of their respective authors at the time they were published, though not necessarily at present.

Read on, and consider your vote.

### A. Strikes, Technology and Residuals

The history of Hollywood labor has been marked by waves of turmoil, followed by periods of quiet.[*] The unions that are now known as AFTRA, SAG, DGA and WGA were born in struggle during the 1930s, while the nation was still gripped by the Depression. The coming of war didn't calm things, and the struggle for recognition by management continued into at least the mid-1940s.[†] Next came the blacklists and Red scares, then a strike in 1952[‡] and two in 1960.[§]

Then, silence. For two decades, management and labor enjoyed the fruits of a newly booming industry – television – without significant labor interruptions. Why? Strike fatigue – the memory of the previous wrenching and costly 1960 strikes – is no doubt one reason, but another is more subtle.

#### Absorbing New Technology

To understand the second factor, look at the 1952 and two 1960 strikes. All three focused on residuals paid for television broadcasts, a new medium introduced commercially in the late 1940s.

From the late 1940s through 1960 or so is about a dozen years, and that's how long it took labor and management to adjust residuals structures to the economics of the new medium. No new media were introduced in the 1950s, 1960s and most of the 1970s.[**] That is probably one reason that labor peace prevailed throughout the 1960s and 1970s.

#### Storm Clouds

By the late 1970s, though, cable TV (particularly pay services such as HBO) and home video (i.e., videocassettes) were beginning to make their presence felt. These were fundamentally new media, with new forms of costs and revenues – new business models. In another development during that time period, foreign television sales – the sale of U.S. television programming to foreign networks – grew in importance.

Thus, once again, management and labor struggled to adjust and to apportion compensation. Five strikes ensued in the 1980s, three of them lengthy.[††] Capping the decade was the 1988 writers strike, which lasted more than five months.

#### The 1990s

Then – again – silence. The 1990s were a period of labor peace in Hollywood. Unions remained frustrated by the heavily pro-studio formula used to calculate home video residuals, but they weren't willing to strike over the issue, particularly in light of the devastating economic effects of the 1988 strike. The burgeoning growth of a fourth national network, Fox, led to a push to

---

[*] This Section was first published in slightly different form in my book HOLLYWOOD ON STRIKE!.
[†] Company management "recognizes" a union when it commences bargaining with the union and acknowledges that the union is the sole representative of the employees.
[‡] Actors strike, 2-1/2 months.
[§] SAG (6 weeks), WGA (21 weeks), regarding residuals for reuse of movies on television.
[**] Color television, commercially introduced in the mid-1960s, was an enhancement to an existing medium, rather than a new medium.
[††] 1980 (SAG/AFTRA, 3 months, regarding pay TV and home video), 1981 (WGA, 3 months), 1985 (WGA, 2 weeks), 1987 (DGA, 3 hours and 5 minutes), 1988 (WGA, 22 weeks).

end the discounted level of residuals on that network. Although the discount persisted longer than might have seemed reasonable, this wasn't a strikeworthy issue, and the residuals were eventually bargained up to full network levels.

Although there were no strikes in the 1990s, there were plenty of changes in technology and business models. One driver of these changes was the elimination of federal rules prohibiting studios and networks from owning each other, the so-called Financial Interest and Syndication, or Fin-Syn, rules. This triggered a wave of corporate mergers and the birth of two new broadcast networks, UPN (owned by Paramount) and the WB (owned by Warner Bros.), which later merged to form the CW.

As these new networks generated programming and swallowed up local TV stations as affiliates, the off-network syndication market – that is, the business of rerunning network shows on unaffiliated stations across the country – began to collapse, because there were fewer and fewer unaffiliated stations. Basic cable took up the slack, becoming a huge market for reruns. Meanwhile, pay TV services started producing original movies and, later, original series.[*]

Technology also drove change. Videogames became a growing threat to the television business, but also a source of income for studios (which received revenue from licensing movies to videogame producers) and for actors and writers. The home video business skyrocketed with the introduction of DVD. And the Internet evolved from a government experiment to a consumer necessity.

## The 2000s

All of this laid the groundwork for renewed turmoil. The '00 decade started with the six month SAG-AFTRA commercials strike in 2000, then moved on to tense negotiations in 2001 involving the studios, Writers Guild and Screen Actors Guild. The entertainment industry waited on tenterhooks, but – although the WGA didn't reach a deal until five days after contract expiration – there were no Hollywood strikes in 2001.

---

[*] More recently, basic cable networks have also started to run original programming.

The next round of Writers Guild negotiations, in 2004, were also difficult. Indeed, the writers worked without a contract for about five months and the possibility a strike seemed real. None materialized however.

Meanwhile, SAG agreed to a one-year extension of its contract, and then negotiated a customary three year deal in 2005 without incident. Both unions had wanted an increase in the home video residuals formula, but both settled for deals with no increase.

That decision stung activist members of both guilds, and the storm clouds began to gather. In late 2005, both unions elected new leadership teams that promised to take a much harder approach to bargaining with the studios. The flashpoints were bound to be not just home video, but also digital media, which was advancing inexorably.

With the new elected leadership in place, and new executive directors installed in 2005 and 2006, it was clear that one or both of the guilds might strike the next time the contracts were up. Studios began stockpiling scripts as early as December 2006 in anticipation of a possible writers strike the following fall.

For its part, the WGA decided to delay negotiations until mid-2007 – just a few months before contract expiration – a form of brinksmanship that stoked industry concern. The studios charged that the WGA had promised to hold early talks in January, then reneged. Fear and mistrust were in the air, and by the time the negotiation process began, the stage was set for a meltdown.

## The 2007-2009 Strike and Stalemate

That meltdown came in late 2007, when the WGA began a strike that ultimately lasted 100 days. As the national economy worsened, leaving most people in the country happy to simply have a job, Hollywood writers picketed for better compensation formulas in new media – an area that even now generates scant revenue for studios or writers. Meanwhile, by pounding the pavement rather than their keyboards, writers were forgoing millions of dollars in aggregate that they could have been earning for motion picture and television work.

The fourteen-week strike ended a month after the DGA reached an agreement on new media, with the Writers Guild adopting most aspects of the directors' new media deal. It seemed possible that the actors would do so as well, but it didn't work out that way. Instead, AFTRA accepted the Directors Guild template, but SAG did not.

Nor, however, did SAG strike. Instead, a stalemate ensued, resulting in a work stoppage in motion pictures that persisted for about a year, with the actors incurring tens of millions of dollars in lost earnings. SAG suffered institutionally too, as new television work fled to AFTRA.

Finally, in mid-2009, two years after the Writers Guild negotiations began, SAG ratified a contract – one that was no better than what it could have achieved a year earlier, and in some ways worse. To almost no one's surprise, the new media terms mirrored those of the Directors Guild, Writers Guild and AFTRA.

## B. Residuals Pro and Con

Let's zero in on the arguments people make for and against residuals.

### Pro

Advocates of residuals offer a number of arguments, including:

- **Technological Displacement:** Residuals compensate people for, in effect, competing against themselves by creating recorded product that deprives them of work they might otherwise have had,

This was the key original arguments for residuals – see Section 1.0 – but it may seem less compelling today, now that the default assumption is that people will get their audiovisual entertainment in recorded form (movies, TV shows, webisodes) rather than live (live TV or as live stage plays).

On the other hand, entertainment companies and their executives are also at risk for technological displacement – or disintermediation – as Hollywood monopolies on distribution fall to the likes of Apple / iTunes, Amazon and Google / YouTube. So perhaps a degree of sympathy – even empathy – would be appropriate.

- **Fairness:** Residuals allow the people who created a product to participate in its success. That's a matter of simple fairness.

- **Who's Overpaid?** Studios like to cry poverty when it's time to talk about residuals – but if they really mean it, why don't they try cutting back on multi-million dollar executive pay packages?

- **A Right of Authorship:** "Residuals exist because we don't . . . maintain copyright over the material we write," says screenwriter Craig Mazin.* "They are designed to compensate us for the reuse of our authorship," he adds, comparing residuals to book authors' and playwrights' royalties.

- **Prevention of Windfalls:** Eliminating residuals would allow studios to reap unjustified windfall when a movie or show succeeds, or when a new technology like television, home video or the Internet brings fresh value to existing studio libraries.

- **Incentivization:** By allowing people to participate in the upside, residuals incentivize people to work harder, which benefits producers, studios and networks as well as the union members.

- **Non-Uniqueness:** Residuals are not as strange a concept as critics contend – or pretend. There are parallels: book authors get royalties; artists in some countries (but not the U.S.) receive a fee under a concept called "droit d'suite" whenever their artworks are resold; stars get profit participations; and even executives and software developers receive stock options.

- **Benefit of the Bargain:** Residuals are agreed-upon deal terms. Their economic value was part

---

* See johnaugust.com/2011/how-residuals-work.

of the bargain that labor and management made.

- **Settled Expectations:** Tens of thousands of people made their career and other economic decisions based in part on the knowledge that residuals are part of the economic package. The entertainment industry is built on an assumption that these payments will be there. So are the pension and health plans that depend on residuals for funding (see Section 13.J) and the unions themselves, which depend on the dues money generated from residuals (see Section 13.L).

- **Economic Importance:** Residuals are a significant share of one's income for middle-class actors, writers and some directors.

- **Maintenance of a Stable Labor Pool:** By providing income between jobs, residuals allow trained individuals to stay in the entertainment labor force. Without residuals, many would have to change careers, which would reduce the supply of trained labor. That would be to management's detriment: movie stars can afford to live without income between jobs, but you can't make a movie without talented non-star actors as well.

- **Forced Savings.** Residuals are a form of forced savings – compensating the writer, director, actor or musician over time benefits the recipient and thus the industry at large.

- **Strikeworthiness:** As a practical matter, unions will strike if studios attempt to eliminate residuals – as the 2007-2008 writers strike demonstrated. Trying to eliminate them just isn't worth the cost that a strike imposes on management.

- **Health of the Industry:** The entertainment industry is healthy, and studio claims to the contrary are not credible, particularly in light of the movie and TV industry's long history of deceptive accounting practices.

- **Reduction of "Alienation":** Compensating people for reuse of the products they create reduces the degree to which they are merely cogs in an alienating system; it helps reset the balance between capital and labor. More particularly, it gives them an enduring connection to the fruits of their labor.

## Con

Critics of residuals see things in a very different light:

- **Affordability:** The industry is in trouble economically and simply can't afford residuals. They're one of the costs that drive work to less-expensive locales: out of California to other states, which reduces IATSE residuals (since the IATSE residuals system only applies to work done in California and several western states) and out of the U.S. to other countries where residuals are cheaper or non-existent. The result is less work for the very members the unions are supposed to be helping.

- **Changed Circumstances:** Theatrical residuals were agreed to on the assumption that most movies could at least recoup their costs via exhibition in the primary market, i.e., theatrically. That seldom happens today. Likewise, high fixed residuals for network primetime reruns are a relic of a bygone era when network audiences were huge and advertising revenues were too.

- **Illusory Profits:** The WGA campaigned in 2007-2008 for new media residuals with the slogan "If they make money, we make money" – but that's not how it works at all. Union members profit even when the studio doesn't: fixed residuals are payable regardless of whether the project is garnering revenue, and percentage residuals are a percentage of gross, not net, which means they're payable even if the project isn't making a profit – or never does.

- **Fairness:** Residuals are an unfair windfall for the recipient. After all, the studio, not the union member, is the one risking its investment capital. Union members get paid their initial compensation – their upfront wages – regardless of the project's success. Adding residuals to the pot is just an unfair second helping.

- **Irrelevant Incentives:** The economic success of most projects is tied to a small number of people – a visionary director or showrunner, a movie star who attracts a broad audience or, sometimes, the owner or creator of the underlying book, comic book or even toy (such as Transformers) that a successful project is built around. Most of those people are incentivized with high salaries, profit participations and the like. In contrast, residuals matter most to the smaller actors and writers who are not individually responsible for a project's success – and who are, in fact, replaceable.

● **Over-Inclusiveness:** Too many people receive residuals who don't deserve them. Why should a day player – an actor who works a single day on a movie or TV show – receive residuals? And why should a Teamsters truck driver on a movie receive residuals, even if indirectly? (I.e., in that the Teamsters participate in the same P&H plan as IATSE does.)

● **Contract of Adhesion:** Residuals are part of what lawyers term a "contract of adhesion" – a take it or leave it deal. Today's studio heads never were offered a realistic chance to negotiate a different approach. And that goes double for independent producers. There are only about eight companies in the bargaining room when the AMPTP negotiates a union contract. Even a company as large as Lionsgate doesn't have a seat at the table, let alone a true, small independent producer.

● **Complexity:** The residual system is sclerotic – bound up in so many rules, caveats, carveouts and distinctions that it takes a full-color guidebook just to begin to understand them. (Ok, that's not necessarily how the argument is phrased, but you get the point.) That increases legal fees and payroll processing costs in an already challenging business.

● **Inflexibility:** That complexity makes the system inflexible when business models (i.e., typical reuse patterns) change. That's a stasis that the industry can't afford, particularly as it struggles to adapt to life in a world dominated by nimble technology companies. Silicon Valley is eating Hollywood's lunch, and residuals (and unions) are one reason why.

● **Administrability:** The system's complexity also makes residuals costly and error-prone to administer. Millions of paper residuals checks per year, a king's ransom spent on postage, processing clerks and the computer programmers who write and revise ten of thousands of lines of software that implement the system – it's simply an irrational way to spend money.

● **Strikes:** The residuals system has led to costly strikes for more than half a century and continues to do so. Neither management nor labor can afford to let this continue.

● **De-Residualization:** It may not be politically feasible to eliminate existing residuals; it may not be possible to reform entertainment residuals as the advertising industry and SAG-AFTRA are discussing for commercial residuals; but what is possible is de-residualization: resisting residuals in new types of media and reuse patterns, or ensuring that residuals in these new areas are a fraction of the size of residuals in traditional media.

## C. Solving the Fight over Union Residuals

By Schuyler Moore. 23(6) ENTERTAINMENT LAW & FINANCE (September 2007).
© 2007 ALM Properties, Inc. Reprinted by permission.

The Writers Guild of America has been negotiating with the Alliance of Motion Picture & Television Producers for a new collective bargaining agreement. The current agreement expires on Oct. 31, 2007. The current agreements of the Directors Guild of America and Screen Actors Guild of America end on June 30, 2008. This article summarizes some of the key conflicts that may trigger threatened guild strikes. Most of these issues relate to the income base and calculation of residuals. The article suggests a simple and fair alternative method for calculating residuals that eliminates all the contentious issues, not just in the pending negotiations of the guild agreements, but also in practice.

Residuals are contingent payments based on a percentage of a film's gross revenue. The majority of residuals are paid directly to the guild members, but some payments are also made to the guild's health and pension benefit plans. Residuals are calculated in the following manner:

- Residuals on theatrical films are only calculated based on video and television revenues, not theatrical revenues.

- Residuals [on theatrical films] are always calculated based on all or a portion of gross receipts. Thus, they are payable regardless of whether the film company makes a profit. From the film company's perspective, this is by far the worst aspect of residuals.

- For film companies that distribute their own videos (as opposed to sublicensing video rights), only 20% of video revenues are included in gross receipts as a deemed royalty.

Here are some of the issues being fought over:

### Video and DVD

The guilds agreed to include only 20% of video revenues in gross receipts as a deemed royalty back in the early 1980s, when manufacturing costs were much higher and video revenues were much lower. In its infancy, video was analogized to merchandising and it simply made sense to calculate gross revenue to the film company based on the sales margin of each unit.

The only problem is that margin has now vastly increased, while the 20% royalty has not. Video and DVD have now grown to be the largest income source for theatrical films and are of key importance to the guilds (in particular because residuals do not apply to theatrical revenues for theatrical films). The guilds are just not happy with the 20% royalty theory any more.

### Video-on-Demand

Video-on-demand over the Internet will create a huge new source of film revenue, which to a lesser or greater extent will cannibalize other revenue sources. The problem for the guilds is that the guild agreements divide the film world into theatrical, video, pay TV and free TV, and it is not clear just where Internet revenues (or any video-on-demand revenue for that matter) fall, if anywhere, under the current guild agreements.

In my book, THE BIZ, I suggested that the answer may be "nowhere," which triggered a quick invitation to lunch from the guilds, where they explained that they thought Internet revenues fell under every category that was subject to residuals (what a surprise!). In the pending negotiations, the guilds simply cannot risk missing the boat on Internet and video-on-demand revenue, particularly when that revenue will cannibalize other income streams that are currently subject to residuals.

Even if Internet revenues are included, the studios are arguing that only 20% of Internet revenues should be included in gross receipts, because such Internet revenue is likely to slowly cannibalize video and DVD revenues, which are currently on a 20% royalty basis. Because there are no manufacturing costs for distribution over the Internet, the guilds are not going to roll over lightly on this one.

### Allocations

It is bad enough when films are sold to third parties in packages (particularly television sales), resulting in skewed allocations to lower residual or non-guild films; but to add insult to injury, most of the studios are now vertically integrated with television networks or cable companies, so they are selling to themselves. This practice has lead to a number of lawsuits by talent claiming that their participations were short-changed by low-ball inter-company sales, and the guilds are lining up with the same grievance for residuals.

### Discounts and Buy-Outs

The guild agreements contain concessions intended to help once-struggling media, including discounts on residuals for programs made for basic and pay-cable television, and low buy-outs on foreign residuals for television shows. With the huge growth in all three of these markets, the guilds are no longer in the mood to subsidize them.

### Independent Film Companies

Even aside from these current issues on the negotiating table, the calculation of residuals is riddled with ambiguity, inconsistency and confusion. For example, the guild agreements are not designed to address independent film companies that use sales agents to pre-sell rights to various foreign countries. The guild agreements are negotiated between the studios and the guilds, and no one at the table is particularly thinking about how the agreements apply to independent film companies.

The current guild agreements thus fail to address many common business practices, leading to disputes between film companies and the guilds, such as:

● The guilds take the position that residuals should generally be calculated "at source," *i.e.*, based on the gross receipts of the lowest level subdistributor, including foreign subdistributors. This causes endless disputes about how the "at source" calculation is to be made, when it applies, and who is liable. For example, in the case of an "outright sale," residuals apply to the sale price, and are *not* calculated "at source." Unfortunately, the guild agreements do not define an "outright sale," so there are many disputes over this term.

● The guilds also take the position that when a distributor licenses video rights to a third party (as opposed to the distributor undertaking video distribution itself), 100% of the payments received are included in gross receipts, as opposed to only 20% being included, as in the case of self-distribution. Some distributors have taken the position that only 20% of video royalties received from third parties should be included in calculating residuals.

● When a film company receives a minimum guaranty from a distributor under a pre-sale agreement, the guilds take the position that the minimum guaranty should be allocated heavily to video and television, which are subject to residuals, while film companies like to allocate as much as possible to theatrical, which isn't.

● The guilds take the position that residuals must be calculated based on the greater of (a) the portion of a minimum guaranty allocated to video and television or (b) the gross receipts of the sub-distributor for the particular media (even if no overages are received by the film company). Film companies view this as an unfair one-way ratchet.

### A Solution to the Chaos

So, let me suggest one potential simple solution to all this chaos. Why not calculate residuals right up front as a percentage of a film's budget? The amount of residuals thus calculated could then be paid in installments (*e.g.*, one-fourth per year for four years) to more or less track the result under the current approach for the payment of residuals (where residuals are due as revenues are received).

Alternatively, the residuals could be paid all up front if the guilds would accept a reasonable discount for the time value of money and elimination of the risk of non-payment that is inherent in the installment approach.

There is tremendous logic for tying residuals to a film's budget. First, in the absence of knowing anything else, the best prediction of a film's gross receipts is based on its budget. In fact, almost all pre-sales and output agreements provide for payments based on a film's budget, so there is a direct correlation between the budget and receipts.

Second, residuals have been paid long enough that expected residuals can be calculated, on average, as a percentage of a film's budget. In fact, this is exactly what SAG does when SAG demands an advance bond to secure residuals. All I am suggesting is that this should be the end of the process, rather than the beginning.

Of course, historical averages will not match any particular film's exact revenue, but this brings me to the third and final logical argument: Why should residuals be tied to a film's revenues in the first place? The intent is just to provide extra compensation to the guild members, and it is just as logical to base this extra compensation on a film's budget as it is to base it on gross receipts.

### Setting the Percentage

So what percentage of the budget should residuals be? The starting point should simply be the historical average of residuals to film budgets, which will differ for each guild. From there, it is simply a matter of arm wrestling as to whether the percentage should be higher or lower when the guild agreements come up for renewal.

This will at least be an honest negotiation, as opposed to the artificial debate about what income streams should or should not be included, or whether a 20% video royalty is appropriate. In other words, money is money, and the bottom line is how much money will residuals cost, not whether any particular income stream is or is not included.

This suggested approach benefits everyone. The first and most obvious benefit is that it creates certainty as to how much residuals will be owed, and it eliminates all the current chaos, confusion and arguments over the calculation of residuals. It completely eliminates the time-consuming and expensive accounting and auditing process.

It might also benefit everyone if the film company could elect to pay residuals right up front as part of a film's budget. This has an obvious benefit to the guilds, in that it provides for certainty of payment and accelerated cash flow (albeit subject to a reasonable discount for the time value of money and elimination of risk).

### The Benefit for Film Companies

Counter-intuitively, up-front payments might also benefit many film companies for several reasons:

A film's budget would thus increase by the amount of residuals, and because presales and output agreements almost always calculate the amount owed as a function of the budget, an increase to the budget will increase the amount the film is sold for. I know this seems odd, but this is the way the film world works.

By including residuals in the budget, it becomes possible to finance residuals using standard film-financing techniques, such as bank financing, pre-sales, etc. It is typically far better to have this issue dealt with up front than to be caught owing residuals at a time when the film company does not have the cash to pay them; remember, residuals are calculated on gross — not net — receipts, so they apply even if a film is running at a loss.

As long as the up-front payment is discounted, the total amount of residuals owed is less than under the installment approach.

In all events, this suggested alternative is far better than the current lunacy. It would be a tragedy if the industry is shut down with strikes over issues as abstract as whether only 20% of Internet revenues should be included in gross receipts. This suggested alternative eliminates for all time the endless arguments that will otherwise occur as future media are developed.

But if this suggestion doesn't work, then my next suggestion is to include both video and Internet revenues at 100%, instead of the current 20% (so the guilds can declare victory), but make the residual rate 20% of the current rate (so the ultimate result doesn't change). Heck, if you can't fight the lunacy, you might as well join it!

## D. Dump Residuals

By Schuyler Moore. Excerpted with permission from *With biz at a crossroads, sharp turns from the current path are imperative,* THE HOLLYWOOD REPORTER, February 18, 2009.

Our industry is in economic trouble, and it isn't ending soon. The studios already know that bad times are a-comin', which is why they are letting so many people go. But firing staff doesn't solve the problem. So I offer here some tough medicine – economic triage – to get us through these tough times. And while some might not like this bitter pill, better to take it than have our industry bleed to death until bankruptcy. Because that is where it is going as we get destroyed by piracy, a free fall in ad revenue and a reduction in state tax credits. A previously mediocre business is now a loss leader.

*****

When residuals first snuck their nose under the tent, they were applied only to the then-tiny amount of TV revenue on theatrical films, since talent was paid their base compensation for the primary medium: theatrical. Remember that "residual" comes from the word "residue" and refers to the grime at the bottom of the pan.

Residuals then were applied in the 1970s to another ancillary medium called video, which through an unexpected fluke grew into the main event and now swamps theatrical revenue by a margin of 2-1. The guilds conveniently have forgotten history and now think that residuals on the primary media are a God-given entitlement.

And the worst part is that residuals are paid based on gross receipts, even if the studio is losing its shirt. It is time to dump residuals if this industry is going to survive. There is not a single other industry where union employees are entitled to a share of the employer's gross receipts. Please tell me why a Teamster driver should get a share of the "Batman" gross. And if SAG decides to commit suicide by going on strike, now is the time to fight this battle. *****

## E. Recoupment Based Residuals

By The Alliance of Motion Picture and Television Producers (AMPTP)
Excerpted from *Producers' Proposals to the WGA – Comprehensive Package* (July 16, 2007)
For readability, some formatting has been changed, paragraphs divided, and additional headings added in ( ).

### Introduction

We are committed to negotiating a deal that is fair to everyone, one that respects the needs and concerns of the WGA as well as all the AMPTP member companies, one that maintains industry stability, one that gives us the flexibility to adapt to the revolutionary changes in front of us, one that helps us manage our risks, grow our businesses and share our rewards.

The Companies and the Guilds must work together to re-position this industry to respond to the changing markets and the changing world. We must come together to avoid what has happened to industries that deny change or failed to adapt fast enough.

### Key Subject Areas

#### Recoupment

Today's residual formulas were based on the premise that producers recouped in the initial (primary) market. Revenues obtained in the initial market of release for the vast majority of product no longer cover costs of production, much less distribution and marketing expenses. These negotiations should explore new ways to ensure that we all share in successes while risks are appropriately balanced.

#### New Methods of Capturing and Re-Capturing Audience

Many provisions in our current contracts – some dating back 30 years – prohibit or inhibit us from promoting, re-purposing and exploiting our content to capture or recapture audiences or make additional revenue in traditional as well as New Media. With the revolutionary marketplace changes continuing unabated, these outmoded provisions deserve to be re-examined during these negotiations.

### Residual Payment Point

#### (A) Theatrical

Revise the MBA to provide that no residual payments (no payments of additional compensation) shall be made in connection with a theatrical motion picture, the literary material for which was written or acquired under the MBA and which is released theatrically for the first time on or after November 1, 2007, until the "residual payment point" has been reached.

#### (Definition of "Residual Payment Point")

The "residual payment point" is the date on which the revenues received by the Company from licensing the exhibition of the picture (hereinafter "exhibition revenues"), measured at the times and as hereafter provided, exceed the sum of the costs incurred by the Company:

(1) for the acquisition of any literary material or rights in connection therewith;

(2) for the development of the motion picture and any literary material connected therewith;

(3) for the production of the motion picture;

(4) for the advertising and marketing of the motion picture; and

(5) for distribution of the motion picture (including, but not limited to, the cost of prints).

The foregoing costs shall not include development costs other than those described in subparagraph (2) above, overhead or interest costs.

#### (Definition of "Exhibition Revenues")

"Exhibition revenues," for purposes of this provision, means those revenues received by the Company from exhibition of the theatrical motion picture in whole or in substantial part, and does not include revenues received from the exploitation of rights ancillary to or derivative of the theatrical motion picture, including, but not limited to, revenues received from merchandising, publication and music licensing.

(Determining When RPP Reached)

The Company shall determine whether the residual payment point has been reached on a quarterly basis following release of the theatrical motion picture, within sixty (60) days after the end of each calendar quarter.

(Payments After RPP Reached)

In the event that the Company determines that the residual payment point has been reached, then, beginning with the calendar quarter immediately following the quarter in which the residual payment point has been reached, the Company shall begin making payments of additional compensation in accordance with the terms of the MBA based upon revenues received in the quarter(s) following the quarter in which exhibition revenues exceeded the above-listed costs.

(Example)

For example, if the Company determines that the residual payment point for Theatrical Motion Picture A was reached on February 22, 2008, then the Company shall commence payment of residuals on Theatrical Motion Picture A as required by the MBA based on revenues received beginning in the second quarter of 2008.

(Audits)

The Companies and the Guild shall jointly appoint an independent third party auditor who shall have the right to examine those books and records of the Company which are relevant and necessary to determine whether the residual payment point has been reached and, if so, when such point was reached. It is understood that neither the Guild nor any of the individual writers from whom literary material was acquired or who were employed in writing the literary material for the picture shall have the right to examine such books and records. It is also agreed that the independent auditor shall maintain strict confidentiality of the information audited and shall not disclose to any person or entity (including the Guild) the amount of any cost incurred or exhibition revenue received, nor the aggregate of costs expended or of exhibition revenues received. The auditors shall execute appropriate confidentiality agreements.

In providing information to the Guild, the auditor shall be limited to a statement that the residual payment point has or has not been reached and the date on which the residual payment point was reached. The Guild shall not further disclose this information to any third party.

The cost of any audit conducted by the independent third party auditor to determine whether the residual payment point has been reached shall be paid one-half by the Guild and the remaining half by the Company. Other details with regard to the manner in which the audits will be conducted, including the timing, frequency and number of such audits, shall be discussed and agreed upon by the parties.

(B) Television

Revise the MBA to provide that no residual payments (no payments of additional compensation) shall be made in connection with a television motion picture, the literary material for which was written or acquired under the 2007 MBA, until such time as the "residual payment point" has been reached.

(Definition of "Residual Payment Point")

The "residual payment point" is the date on which the revenues received by the Company from licensing the exhibition of the picture (hereinafter "exhibition revenues"), measured at the times and as hereafter provided, exceed the sum of the costs incurred by the Company:

(1) for the acquisition of any literary material or rights in connection therewith;

(2) for the development of the television motion picture and any literary material connected therewith;

(3) for the production of the television motion picture;

(4) for the advertising and marketing of the television motion picture and

(5) for the distribution of the television motion picture.

The foregoing costs shall not include development costs other than those described in subparagraph (2) above, overhead or interest costs.

(Definition of "Exhibition Revenues")

"Exhibition revenues," for purposes of this provision, means those revenues received by the Company from exhibition of the television motion picture in whole or in substantial part, and does not include revenues received from the exploitation of rights ancillary to or derivative of the television motion picture, including, but not limited to, revenues received from merchandising, publication and music licensing.

(Applicability)

This provision shall be applicable to episodic series, serials and strip programs beginning with the first full season of the series, serial or strip program after the effective date of the 2007 Agreement.

(Determining When RPP Reached – Non-Series)

The Company shall determine whether the residual payment point has been reached with respect to each television motion picture (other than one that is part of an episodic series, serial, strip program or multi-part closed-end series) on a quarterly basis following initial exhibition of the television motion picture, within sixty (60) days after the end of each calendar quarter.

(Determining When RPP Reached – Closed-End Series)

With respect to multi-part closed-end series, the Company shall determine whether the residual payment point has been reached on a quarterly basis following exhibition of all parts of the multi-part closed-end series, within sixty (60) calendar days after the end of each calendar quarter, on the basis of the costs incurred and revenues generated on all parts of the multi-part closed-end series.

(Determining When RPP Reached – Open-Ended Series)

With respect to episodic series, serials and strip programs, the determination as to whether the residual payment point has been reached shall be made within ninety (90) days after the end of each season following exhibition of each episode or program produced for that season, on an aggregated season-by-season basis, on the basis of the costs incurred and revenues generated on all programs or episodes produced for the current and any previous seasons.

(Determining When RPP Reached – Discontinued Series)

In the event that production of an episodic series, serial or strip program is discontinued and such series, serial or strip program has not yet reached the residual payment point, the Company shall thereafter continue to examine, on a quarterly basis, within sixty (60) days after the end of each calendar quarter, whether the residual payment point has been reached.

(Payments After RPP Reached)

In the event that the Company determines that the residual payment point has been reached, then, beginning with the calendar quarter immediately following the quarter in which the residual payment point was reached, the Company shall begin making payments of additional compensation in accordance with the terms of the MBA.

Run-based residual payments shall be triggered by any run that takes place in the quarter(s) after the residual payment point is reached and shall be treated and paid for as the run next in order, counting the runs that occurred prior to the residual payment point.

Receipts-based residual payments shall be payable based on revenues received in the quarter(s) following the quarter in which the residual payment point was reached.

(Example – Season 1 of an Episodic Series)

As an example, suppose Company begins production of Season 1 of Episodic Series A in 2008. At the end of Season 1 (which may occur in 2009), Company will determine whether the exhibition revenues exceed the aggregate costs as outlined above.

If so, then the residual payment point has been reached and, beginning with the next calendar quarter following the quarter in which the residual payment point was reached, Company will: (1) begin making residual payments due under any run-based formula based on exhibitions of any episode of Episodic Series A occurring on or after the residual payment point; and/or (2) begin making residual payments due under any receipts-based formula based upon revenues received for any episode of Episodic Series A in the quarter after the residual payment point has been reached.

In this case, suppose the Company determined that revenues exceeded costs on Season 1 of Episodic Series A (which was produced for initial exhibition in network prime time) on June 28, 2009; suppose further that all episodes of Season 1 had been run twice in network prime time prior to June 30, 2009 and that each episode of Season 1 is run in syndication once in July of 2009.

In that case, the Company would make residual payments for the syndication run that took place in July as the third run under the syndication schedule.

Suppose further that Season 1 of Television [Series] A is licensed to basic cable in September of 2009 and that the first payments under that license are received by the Company at the end of that month. In that case, the Company shall make residual payments pursuant to the provisions of Article 58 based upon the revenues received during the third quarter of 2009 under that license.

On the other hand, if the exhibition revenues do not exceed the aggregate costs as outlined above, then the residual payment point has not been reached.

(Example – Season 2 of an Episodic Series)

Suppose, in the latter case, that Company resumes production of Episodic Series A, with Season 2, in 2009. At the end of Season 2, Company will determine whether the exhibition revenues for Seasons 1 and 2 exceed its aggregate costs as outlined above for both Season 1 and Season 2.

If so, then the residual payment point has been reached and Company will begin making residual payments due under a run-based formula for exhibitions of any episode of Episodic Series A occurring in the quarter(s) after the residual payment point was reached and/or residual payments due under a receipts-based formula based upon revenue received in the quarter(s) after the residual payment point has been reached for any episode of Episodic Series A.

If not, then the residual payment point has not been reached.

(Example – Season 3 of an Episodic Series)

In the latter case, suppose further that Company resumes production of Episodic Series A, with Season 3, in 2010. At the end of Season 3, Company will determine whether the aggregate costs as outlined above for Seasons 1, 2 and 3 exceed its exhibition revenues for those three seasons.

If so, then Company will begin making residual payments due under a run-based residual formula for exhibitions of any episode of Episodic Series A occurring in the quarter(s) after the residual payment point was reached and/or residual payments due under a receipts-based formula based upon revenue received in the quarter(s) after the residual payment point was reached for any episode of Episodic Series A.

If not, then the residual payment point has not been reached.

(Audits)

The Companies and the Guild shall jointly appoint an independent third party auditor who shall have the right to examine those books and records of the Company which are relevant and necessary to determine whether the residual payment point has been reached and, if so, when such point was reached. It is understood that neither the Guild nor any of the individual writers from whom literary material was acquired or who were employed in writing the literary material for the picture shall have the right to examine such books and records. It is also agreed that the auditors shall maintain strict confidentiality of the information audited and shall not disclose to any person or entity (including the Guild) the amount of any cost incurred or exhibition revenue received, nor the aggregate of costs expended or of exhibition revenues received. The auditors shall execute appropriate confidentiality agreements. In providing information to the Guild, the auditor shall be limited to a statement that the residual payment point has or has not been reached and the date on which the residual payment point was reached.

The Guild shall not further disclose this information to any third party.

The cost of any audit conducted by the independent third party auditor to determine whether the residual payment point has been reached shall be paid one-half by the Guild and the remaining half by the Company. Other details with regard to the manner in which the audits will be conducted, including the timing, frequency and number of such audits, shall be discussed and agreed upon by the parties.

## F. Reforming Residuals

This Section, which is reprinted from HOLLYWOOD ON STRIKE!, was first published in slightly different form in THE HOLLYWOOD REPORTER on July 24, 2009, under the title *There's a lot of residual pain ahead if current system isn't remedied.*

### Introduction

As my book HOLLYWOOD ON STRIKE! makes clear, much of the unrest of 2007-2009 can be traced to conflicting proposals regarding new media residuals, as well as the AMPTP's ill-advised proposal to reduce all residuals to a form of net profits, referred to as "recoupment based residuals."* Also a point of contention was the decades-old home video residuals formula.

Viewed through this lens, the two years of labor unrest can be understood largely as a dispute over residuals. Indeed, most above the line Hollywood strikes have centered on residuals, as the Prologue discusses. What can be done to fix the residual system in order to reduce the likelihood of strikes and stalemates in the future?

### The Need for Residuals

We should start by recognizing that the industry needs residuals because talent – especially actors, writers and TV directors – survive on them between gigs. In fact, residuals make up on average about one-third of the typical SAG actor's income. Without these payments, the industry's professional talent base would evaporate. Moreover, the expectation of residuals is built into the industry's collective psyche, and they're here to stay.

### The Problem with the Current System

The current system, however, is flawed.

First, it's expensive and time-consuming to monitor usage in diverse media then report, process and mail physical checks to a member's guild, which then processes the checks and remails them to the member – or to the agent, who may then take a commission where permitted and then mails a check again, this time to the guild member. The WGA alone received as many as 5,000 checks a day in 2002. SAG processes 2 million residuals checks a year and receives $2 million in residuals payments a day.† The volume coupled with the convoluted process result in a 48-day lag time in delivering residuals checks.‡

In addition, residuals checks are too often for absurdly small amounts. Some actors get checks for $2 – or even for a penny:

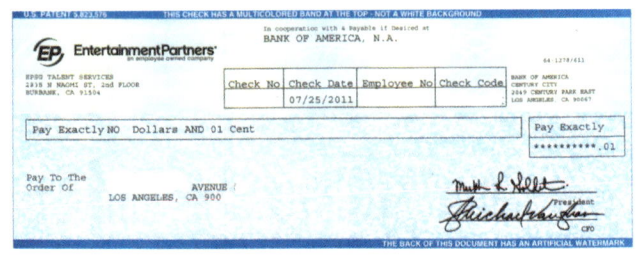

Some actors have even gotten checks for zero cents – the result of rounding down once taxes have been deducted.§ One actor told me she had received residuals statements for small negative amounts, when were then deducted from later payments.

In any case, SAG's average check amount is not publicly known, but the average for foreign levies (a specialized form of compensation some-

---

* See p. 170.
† http://www.variety.com/article/VR1118029219 (12/18/10).
‡ Id.
§ Some of these are on display at the bar called Residuals in Studio City, CA.

what analogous to residuals) is about $30 per check. That means that some of those are for larger amounts and many more are for smaller amounts. The takeaway: check processing costs often equal or exceed the amount of the check itself. It's a ridiculous system.

Second, there are too many different residuals formulas – dozens across the guilds, depending on the original medium and the reuse medium. That contributes to expense and confusion.

Third, since the formulas depend on the mediums, conflict and strikes result as distribution and revenue shift among platforms. This has been particularly true in home video, where the formula, unchanged since 1984, sweeps 80% of revenue off the table before the calculation even begins. The rise of made-for-cable programming during the 1990s brought new irritants.

Today, the Internet is the flashpoint, and the resolutions of the WGA strike and SAG stalemate are only a temporary pause. Many actors are understandably unhappy that network reruns are shifting to online platforms like Hulu and a host of others, where residuals are measured in tens of dollars a year rather than hundreds or thousands of dollars per rerun. As new media continues to evolve, so will platform conflicts.

What's the solution?

### Possible Approaches

Canada's ACTRA union offers producers a residuals buyout based on a percentage of the performer's upfront payment or session fee. U.S. guilds are unlikely to accept that because most U.S. residuals are a percentage of gross or a large fixed amount.

Another approach was offered by attorney Schuyler Moore, who proposed basing film residuals on percentage of budget; he didn't address TV.* In any case, the proposal falls short of the guilds' desire that members participate in the success of a project, which generally means via gross-based residuals. (Moore later came out in favor of eliminating residuals altogether.)†

---

\* See p. 166.
† See p. 169.

### Residuals "At the Wellhead"

A better approach would be to calculate residuals "at the wellhead" – in other words, aggregate all of a project's gross revenue from all platforms and then pay talent a percentage. That solution would be simpler and platform agnostic, benefiting everyone by reducing labor friction as distribution technologies evolve.

In this plan, "all" truly means "all": The residuals base would include all revenue from the "primary market" (the medium of first release, such as theatrical or broadcast) as well as 100% of revenue from all other markets. That 100% would include all home video rental, ending what the WGA has called "the hated DVD formula" that bases residuals on only 20% of home video revenue. Another sweetener for the guilds might be to end the rule that some older films and TV shows are not subject to residuals.

### Setting the Percentage

Since the proposal would pay talent a percentage of gross, the question naturally arises: What percentage of gross should be paid? The unions won't embrace a plan that reduces residuals, nor will the studios adopt one that increases them. Thus, to make both sides happy, the percentage should be set such that the initial year's residuals neither increase nor decrease in aggregate across all members of a particular guild.

Here's how this might work: SAG data show that actors working under the TV and theatrical agreements received about $471 million in residuals in 2008. Under this proposal, the 2008 percentage would have been set so that, when applied to 100% of gross, the resulting aggregate residual would be $471 million.

The question then becomes how successive years' percentages should be set – in other words, how much annually should residuals go up (or down, if the guilds are ever forced by the economy to accept actual rollbacks)? The percentage would be subject to tough negotiation, but the compound annual growth rate of residuals during a trailing period of previous years might provide a benchmark.

Also, if studios' gross revenues are increasing, then even if the percentage stayed constant, guild residuals would increase. In any case, negotiating a single percentage figure is far easier than endless debate over how to cram the square peg of new technologies into the round hole of existing business models.

## Increasing Efficiency

Let's also increase efficiency by defaulting to electronic data interchange between the studios and guilds, email communication regarding residuals due, direct deposit and an end to the small payments that are common with some guilds or unions, notably SAG. In the name of choice and privacy, let members opt out of these labor-saving changes if they wish; most probably won't because they'll get paid faster and because natural inertia means that most people won't bother to make a choice one way or another.

## Conclusion

Labor unrest and unnecessary costs make it harder for Hollywood to make money. Sticking with the current system guarantees that platform-related fights will worsen and that outdated processing techniques will continue to waste money. Change is essential, and it could start with a study, just as SAG, AFTRA and the ad industry are doing as they consider a revamp of their residuals. Perhaps that's a small step, but it's a start.

# APPENDIX: SOURCES AND CONTRACTS

This section lists the sources used in preparing this book, then provides guides to the union/guild agreements, their coverage, and the new media sideletters.

## Sources

Sources used in preparing the chart and this book include current and past union and guild agreements and MOAs/MOUs (Memorandums of Agreement / Understanding); the people noted in the Acknowledgments; web sites for the unions, guilds, pension & health plans, and the Film Musicians Secondary Markets Fund; Handel, HOLLYWOOD ON STRIKE!; Andy Selsor, ed., SHOWBIZ RESIDUALS GUIDE 2007-2008 (Los Angeles: Entertainment Publishers, Inc., 2007) (120 p.) (no longer updated and probably unavailable); WGA, *Residuals Survival Guide* (2013); a series of information sheets prepared by Entertainment Partners (2009); Eric B. Yeldell, THE MOTION PICTURE AND TELEVISION BUSINESS: CONTRACTS AND PRACTICES (2 v.) (Beverly Hills: Entertainment Business Publishing Co., 1985, revised 1987) (out of print); and numerous items listed in Handel, ENTERTAINMENT LABOR: AN INTERDISCIPLINARY BIBLIOGRAPHY (see "residuals" in index). In addition, miscellaneous sources are footnoted throughout the book.

## Overview of the Union and Guild Contracts

This book refers repeatedly to the various union and guild agreements, but it can be tough to actually find those agreements and know whether you're looking at the most up to date versions.

It helps to understand what's out there. Each guild/union has one or more main collective bargaining agreements, which are books generally ranging from 200-700 pages. Most of the TV/film agreements are an unusual size: 5-1/4" x 8-3/8", but some are 8-1/2" x 11", as are other agreements such as the commercials contracts.

There may be different agreements for television as opposed to theatrical work, and for independent producers and AMPTP members.

Legacy-SAG and Legacy-AFTRA also have separate agreements for basic cable production, whereas SAG-AFTRA, the DGA and WGA cover this field in their main agreements. The SAG and AFTRA ones are short 8-1/2" x 11" unbound documents.

Below are the agreements that cover key scripted entertainment programs – i.e., scripted non-low-budget product made for theatrical, primetime TV (but not daytime), pay TV, home video, basic cable or new media.

(For agreements relevant to daytime programs, see Chart 2 in the next section below.)

| Union | Agreements |
|---|---|
| DGA | Basic Agreement (BA) |
| WGA | Basic Agreement (MBA) (formerly called the Minimum Basic Agreement) |
| SAG-AFTRA | Codified Basic Agreement (CBA), Television Agreement (TVA) |
| L-SAG | Codified Basic Agreement (CBA), Television Agreement (TVA), Basic Cable Agt. |
| L-AFTRA | National Code of Fair Practice for Network Television Broadcasting (aka Network Code aka Netcode) Exs. A and E, 4 basic cable templates |
| IATSE | Basic Agreement (BA) |
| AFM | Basic Theatrical Motion Picture Agreement, Basic Television Film Agreement, Basic Cable Agreement, Ex. B to Basic Cable Agreement |

Many of the current agreements are available as PDFs on the various union websites, and from the AMPTP or the unions in hardcopy for a modest fee. Many are also available at https://entlabor.com/Guild_Contracts.html.
Many AFM agreements can be found at http://www.fmsmf.org/producerresources/afmagreements.html.

Also, some materials from the mid-2000's are available at http://digitalcommons.ilr.cornell.edu/blscontracts/. Other sources for agreements are listed at http://www.ilr.cornell.edu/library

/outreach/enz/upload/cbasources.2006a.pdf. However, even with these resources, it can be difficult to obtain a full set of the agreements, or even to determine what agreements exist.

Most of these agreements last for three years and are then re-negotiated. About a year after a new deal is reached, a new book often becomes available.

During the interim, people use the existing book plus an 8-1/2" x 11" printout of the newly negotiated modifications, generally known as a Memorandum of Agreement or Memorandum of Understanding or, occasionally, an Extension Agreement or a less-formal extension letter.

Sometimes books aren't issued for several years, in which case it may be necessary to use two or more MOAs, MOUs or extension documents.

Each union also publishes summaries of their minimum wage scales and some of the rules regarding working conditions. These generally have little relevance to residual calculations, however.

In addition to the above documents, many of the guilds and unions will offer individually-negotiated contracts, waivers, sideletters and the like. These are often available only to the affected producers and members.

## Made-for Media Cross-Reference by Union/Agreement

These charts show the subjects covered by the union agreements. Most of this book relates to Chart 1.

### Chart 1. Key Scripted Entertainment Program Types (see Chapters 1-14 and residuals chart)

| Made for | DGA | WGA | SAG | AFTRA | IATSE | AFM |
|---|---|---|---|---|---|---|
| Theatrical | Basic Agreement (BA) | Basic Agreement (formerly called the Minimum Basic Agreement) (MBA) | Codified Basic Agreement (CBA) | Not covered | Basic Agt (BA) or Area Standards Agt. (ASA), & ea. local's agt. | Basic Theatrical Motion Picture Agt. |
| Free TV | | | Television Agreement (TVA) plus CBA | Netcode Ex. A | | Basic Television Film Agt. |
| Pay TV | | | | Netcode Ex. E | [tbd] | Basic Cbl Agt. |
| Home video | | | | | [tbd] | Th. or TV Agt. |
| Basic cable | | | Basic Cbl Agt. | 4 templates | [tbd] | Basic Cbl Agt. |
| New media | Made for New Media SL to BA, MBA, CBA/TVA, Ex. A, IATSE BA or AFM Theatrical/TV Agt. | | | | | |
| Deriv NM from BC | Same as above row | | Not covered | | Same as above | Ex. B to BC Agt |
| High Budget SVOD | 2014 MOA to BA, MBA, CBA/TVA, Ex. A | | | | Not covered (as of 2014) | |

### Chart 2. Secondary Entertainment Program Types (see Chapter 15)

| Made for | DGA | WGA | SAG | AFTRA | IATSE | AFM |
|---|---|---|---|---|---|---|
| Non-primetime or non-network, but non-serial | Basic Agreement (BA) | MBA | Not covered | Netcode front of book (FOB) (i.e., not Exhibits A or E) | [tbd] | [tbd] |
| Non-primetime serials (soap operas) | Freelance Live and Tape Television Agt. (FLTTA) | MBA App. A | | | [tbd] | [tbd] |
| Unscripted | | | | | BA / ASA | [tbd] |
| NM based on non-primetime serials or unscripted | Same Sideletter as in Chart 1 | | | Made for New Media SL to Netcode front of book | [tbd] | [tbd] |
| Videogames | [tbd] | MBA Art. 64 | Expired Interactive Agt. | Interactive Agt. | [tbd] | [tbd] |

## Chart 2. Secondary Entertainment Program Types (see Chapter 15)

| Made for | DGA | WGA | SAG | AFTRA | IATSE | AFM |
|---|---|---|---|---|---|---|
| Low budget theatrical | Level 1a-4c LB [tbd] and BA | LB [tbd] and MBA | Ultra LB, Modified LB, LB, Student, Short, & CBA | Not covered | Ultra LB, Tiers I-III LB [tbd] | [tbd] |
| Animation - theatrical | Not covered | Not covered | TV Animation Agreement | | BA plus Animation Guild (Local 839) Agt. (except Fox PT animation writing is WGA) | [tbd] |
| Animation - free & pay TV | | | | [tbd] | | [tbd] |
| Animation - HV | | | [tbd] | [tbd] | | [tbd] |
| Anim. - BC | | | BC Anim. Agt | [tbd] | | [tbd] |
| Anim. - Fox PT | | Individ'l agts. | TV Anim. Agt. | [tbd] | | [tbd] |

## Chart 3. Commercials (see Chapter 16) and Industrials (see Section 15.F)

| Made for | DGA | WGA | SAG | AFTRA | IATSE | AFM |
|---|---|---|---|---|---|---|
| Commercials | Commercials Agt. | Not covered | Commercials Agt. | | [tbd] | Commercials Agt. |
| Industrials | [tbd] | [tbd] | [tbd] | [tbd] | [tbd] | [tbd] |

### Residuals and Reuse Cross Reference by Union/Agreement

This chart shows which union agreement provisions cover various aspects of residuals and other reuse. The headings show the primary contracts (BA, MBA, CBA/TVA, etc.); references are to these contracts unless otherwise indicated. "FOB" means the front of book portion of the AFTRA Netcode.

| Book Chptr | Reuse pattern, made-for medium, reuse market, etc. | DGA BA | WGA MBA | L-SAG or SAG-AFTRA* CBA/TVA | AFTRA Netcode Ex. A† | AFTRA Netcode FOB | IATSE BA | AFM Th/TV |
|---|---|---|---|---|---|---|---|---|
| 5.A | Theatrical to theatrical | No residuals | | | | | | |
| 5.B | Theatrical to free TV and foreign | Art. 19 | Art. 15.A | CBA 5.A | Not covered | | XIX(B) | Theat. 15(b) |
| 5.C | Theatrical to basic cable | Art. 18 | Art. 58 | | | | [tbd] | [tbd] |
| 6.A | Free TV to network primetime | Art. 11 | Art. 15.B; SL to Art. 13.B.7 re super-sized eps. | TVA 18, SL | | [tbd] | No residuals | |
| 6.B | Free TV to other than network primetime | Same as row 6.A, plus SLs: | | | Ex. A § 3 | [tbd] | | |
| | | SLs 10 & 12 | SLs 1 & 2 to Art. 15.B.1.b | SLs B, B-1, B-2 | | | | |
| 6.C | Free TV to foreign | Same as row 6.A | | | | [tbd] | No res. | [tbd] |
| 6.D | Free TV to basic cable | Art. 11 | Art. 58, SL (Amendment Agt.) | TVA 78 | | [tbd] | No residuals | |
| 7 | Theatrical to supp. markets | Art. 18 | Art. 51 & SL | CBA 5.2 | Not covered | | XXVIII | Theat 16 |
| | Free TV to supp. markets | | | TVA 20.1 | Ex. D | [tbd] | | TV 14 |
| 8 | Made for pay TV & home video | Art. 20 | Art 57, App B | TVA 78 | Ex. E | [tbd] | No res. | BC 17 [tbd] |

\* SAG CBA/TVA prior to July 1, 2014. SAG-AFTRA CBA/TVA from July 1, 2014 onward.
† Not applicable from July 1, 2014 except as to legacy product.

| Book Chptr | Reuse pattern, made-for medium, reuse market, etc. | DGA BA | WGA MBA | L-SAG or SAG-AFTRA* CBA/TVA | AFTRA Ex. A† | Netcode FOB | IATSE BA | AFM Th/TV |
|---|---|---|---|---|---|---|---|---|
| 9 | Made for BC | Art. 23 | App. C | BC Agt. | 4 diff templates | | No residuals | |
| 10 | Free TV, pay TV, HV to theatr. | Arts. 11, 20 | Art 15, App B | TVA 19,78 | Ex. A§3 | [tbd] | No res. | TV II.15 |
| 10 | Basic cable to theatrical | Art. 23 | App. C | BC § 1 | 4 diff templates | [tbd] | | [tbd] |
| 11 | Traditional media (theatrical free TV, pay TV, home video, basic cable) to new media | New Media Reuse Sideletter (to DGA BA, WGA MBA or SAG CBA/TVA) | | | NM Reuse SL to Ex. A | NM SLs to FOB | New Media Reuse Sideletter (to IATSE BA or AFM Th/TV) | |
| 12 | Original new media, derivative new media (other than next row) and High Budget SVOD* | Made for New Media Sideletter (to DGA BA, WGA MBA or SAG CBA/TVA) | | | Made for NM SL to Ex. A | | Made for New Media Side-letter | Made for New Media Sideletter |
| | Derivative new media based on basic cable | Same as derivative NM in preceding row | | Treated as *original* new media in preceding row | | | | BC Agt. Ex. B |
| 14 | Separated rights & similar | 10-103(d) | 16, others | Not applicable | | | | |
| 15.B | Clips (excerpts) (see also provisions in NM Reuse SLs) | 10-103(e), 11-201, 11-207, 11-209, 11-303, 20-909 | 15.A.3.j, 15.B.10 | CBA 22, TVA 35, 36 | [tbd] | [tbd] | [tbd] | Th. 8, 8A, 8B; TV 8, 8A, 8B |
| 15.I | Foreign levies | Country by country agts. | | | Handled by SAG | | Not applicable | |
| 15.A | Non-primetime or non-network, but non-serial | [tbd] | See row 6 above | | | FOB [tbd] | [tbd] | [tbd] |
| | Non-primetime serials (soap operas) | FLTTA [tbd] | Art. 36, App. A (Art. 15) | | | FOB [tbd] | [tbd] | [tbd] |
| 15.C | Unscripted (exact covered program types vary by union) | FLTTA [tbd] | | | | FOB [tbd] | No residuals | [tbd] |
| 15.A and 15.C | Non-PT or non-net, non-serial to NM | [tbd] | See row 11 above | Not covered | Not applicable | NM Reuse SL to FOB | [tbd] | [tbd] |
| | Non-primetime serials to NM | [tbd] | [tbd] | | | | [tbd] | [tbd] |
| | Unscripted to NM | [tbd] | [tbd] | | | | [tbd] | [tbd] |
| | New media based on or similar to non-PT or non-net, non-serial | [tbd] | See row 12 above | | | Made for NM SL to FOB | [tbd] | [tbd] |
| | New media based on or similar to non-primetime serials | [tbd] | [tbd] | | | | [tbd] | [tbd] |
| | New media based on or similar to unscripted | [tbd] | [tbd] | | | | [tbd] | [tbd] |
| 1.A | Videogames (interactive media) | [tbd] | Art. 64 | Expired | Interactive Agt. | NA | | [tbd] |
| 15.E | Animation – theatrical | Not covered | Not covered | | Not covered | No residuals | | [tbd] |
| | Animation – free & pay TV, HV | | | TV Anim. | [tbd] | | | [tbd] |
| | Animation – basic cable | | | BC Anim. | [tbd] | | | [tbd] |
| | Animation – Fox primetime | | Individ'l agts | TV Anim. | [tbd] | | | [tbd] |
| 15.F | Industrials | [tbd] | [tbd] | [tbd] | [tbd] | | | No residuals |

* High Budget SVOD is applicable to DGA, WGA and SAG-AFTRA, but not to AFTRA Ex. A nor (as of 2014) to Netcode, IATSE or AFM.

References – 181

| Book Chptr | Reuse pattern, made-for medium, reuse market, etc. | DGA BA | WGA MBA | L-SAG or SAG-AFTRA* CBA/TVA | AFTRA Netcode Ex. A† | IATSE FOB | AFM BA Th/TV |
|---|---|---|---|---|---|---|---|
| 15.G-H | Other types of music reuse | Not applicable |||||| See Sec. 15.G-H |
| 16 | Commercials | No residuals | Not covered | SAG-AFTRA Commercials Agt. || No residuals | Commercials Agt. |
| 18.K | Audits | [tbd] | Arts. 11H, 53 | [tbd] | [tbd] | [tbd] | [tbd] | [tbd] |
| 18 | Responsibility for payments | [tbd] | Art. 65 | [tbd] | [tbd] | [tbd] | [tbd] | [tbd] |
| 18 | Security deposits | [tbd] | Art. 46 | [tbd] | [tbd] | [tbd] | [tbd] | [tbd] |
| [tbd] | [tbd] | [tbd] | [tbd] | [tbd] | [tbd] | [tbd] | [tbd] | [tbd] |

## Current Theatrical and Television Live Action Contracts

The most current union contracts with the AMPTP, major studios or networks are listed below. Books are shown in SMALL CAPS. The other listed items are 8-1/2" x 11" printouts.

**DGA**
● 2011(-2014) DGA BASIC AGREEMENT
● 2011(-2014) DGA FREELANCE LIVE AND TAPE TELEVISION AGREEMENT (FLTTA)
● 2014(-2017) Memorandum of Agt to BA & FLTTA

**WGA**
● 2011(-2014) WGA BASIC AGREEMENT (MBA) (there may actually be two slightly different versions, one with the AMPTP and one with the networks – this has sometimes been the case in the past)
● 2014(-2017) Memorandum of Agt to MBA

**Legacy-SAG**
● 2005(-2008) SAG CODIFIED BASIC AGREEMENT
● 2005(-2008) SAG TELEVISION AGREEMENT
● (Note: in 2008-2009, SAG worked under the expired 2005 Agreements)
● 2009(-2011) Memorandum of Agreement for SAG CBA and SAG TV Agreement
● 2011(-2014) Memorandum of Agreement for SAG CBA and SAG TV Agreement
● 2011(-2014) SAG Basic Cable Agreement

**Legacy-AFTRA – Exhibit A**
● 2001(-2004) AFTRA NATIONAL CODE OF FAIR PRACTICE FOR NETWORK TELEVISION BROADCASTING (NETCODE)
● 2004(-2007) Memorandum of Agreement for Ex. A
● 2007(-2010) Memorandum of Agreement for Ex. A
● 2010(-2011) Extension Agreement for Ex. A
● [2011(-2014) Memorandum of Agreement for Netcode Ex. A]

**SAG-AFTRA**
● 2005-2014 SAG documents listed above
● 2014(-2017) SAG-AFTRA Memorandum of Agt.

**Legacy-AFTRA – Front of Book**
● 2011(-2014) AFTRA NATIONAL CODE OF FAIR PRACTICE FOR NETWORK TELEVISION BROADCASTING (NETCODE) (contains front of book only; omits Ex. A)
● 2014(-2017) Memorandum of Agt. for FOB

**IATSE**
● 2012(-2015) IATSE BASIC AGREEMENT (BA)

**AFM**
● 2010(-2013) BASIC THEATRICAL MOTION PICTURE AGREEMENT
● 2010(-2013) BASIC TELEVISION MOTION PICTURE AGREEMENT
● 2003(-2006) Basic Cable Television Agreement
● Unknown if there are 2006 and 2009/2010 basic cable MOUs
● Exhibit B to Basic Cable Agreement (addresses new media) (2010 draft or later; unsigned and still under negotiation; not publicly available)

## The New Media Sideletters

Finding the new media sideletters is almost as difficult as finding the agreements themselves.

With a couple of wrinkles noted below, each guild or union has a pair of new media sideletters, one on reuse of product on new media platforms (columns I-K) and one on product made for new media (rows 7-9).

In other words, one sideletter focuses on new media as a reuse market and the other as a made-for medium.

When new media is both the made-for and reuse market (I7-K9), the applicable provisions are usually found in the Made for New Media Sideletter, but in the Netcode Ex. A sideletters, this topic is addressed instead in the New Media Reuse sideletter.

The sideletters generally appear in the back of the 2008 or 2009 guild/union agreement, if any, or else in the 2008 or 2009 MOA/MOU.

➔ Several sideletters are unusual:

● The DGA has one pair of new media sideletters that apply to both the BA and FLTTA. They appear in both the BA and FLTTA.

● SAG-AFTRA and L-SAG have one pair of new media sideletters that apply to both the CBA and TV Agreement.

● AFTRA has *two pairs* of new media sideletters, one of which applies to the Netcode front of book and the other to Netcode Exhibit A.

● AFTRA also has two separate pairs of 2010 Extension Agreements and 2011 MOAs.

● AFTRA has a Sideletter (Netcode SL 42) in which it expresses its members' concern that "the Producers might use Experimental New Media Projects to circumvent the terms and conditions of the AFTRA TV Code" and in which the producers assure AFTRA that "they do not intend to use such projects as a subterfuge to allow the production of broadcast television programs outside the terms of the AFTRA TV Code."

● The AFM has *three* new media sideletters (one pair plus one unpaired). The main pair applies to (and appear in) the Theatrical and TV Agreements, while the third, unpaired sideletter applies to the Basic Cable agreement and relates only to derivative new media product that is based on basic cable shows. As various Sections in Chapter 12 discuss (and see also the note regarding AFM on p. 34), there are differences between this sideletter and the corresponding provisions in the primary AFM Made for New Media sideletter. This sideletter is still under negotiations, so changes are possible.

The sideletters have somewhat different names from union to union, but this book and the residuals chart use a uniform naming system: New Media Reuse Sideletter (NM Reuse SL) and Made for New Media Sideletter (Made for NM SL). Here are the precise names of the sideletters (with "Sideletter" abbreviated):

| Union | NM Reuse SL | Made for NM SL |
|---|---|---|
| DGA | SL 15: Exhibition of Motion Pictures Transmitted via New Media | SL 35: Programs Produced for New Media |
| WGA | SL on Exhibition of Motion Pictures Transmitted via New Media | SL on Literary Material Written for Programs Made for New Media |
| SAG or SAG-AFTRA | SL re NM Reuse: Exhibition of Motion Pictures Transmitted via New Media | SL re Programs Made for New Media |
| AFTRA Front of Book | SL on Exhibition of AFTRA National Code of Fair Practice for Network Television Broadcasting Programs Reused in New Media | SL on AFTRA National Code of Fair Practice for Network Television Broadcasting Programs Made for New Media |
| AFTRA Ex. A | Same names as SAG | |
| IATSE | Exhibition of Motion Pictures Transmitted Via New Media | Productions Made for New Media |
| AFM Th/TV | Same names as IATSE | |
| AFM Basic Cable | SL on Exhibition of Programs Produced Under the AFM Basic Cable Agreement in New Media | |

For reasons of space, the residuals chart sometimes says "same SL," meaning "the sideletter of the same name as the preceding one listed." For instance, in cell K8 on p. 3 of the chart, the phrase "BA Made for NM SL E.2.a. MBA same SL 3.b.(4)(a)" is a reference to Sec. E.2.a of the DGA Made for NM SL and to Sec. 3.b.(4)(a) of the WGA MBA Made for NM SL.

Also, in cell K2 on p. 3 of the chart, all of the references are to the NM Reuse SL, but for space reasons even the phrase "same SL" had to be omitted.

The sideletters were originally adopted in 2008-2010, depending on the union. There were few changes in the 2011-2014 MOAs, but the 2014 MOAs (negotiated in 2013 and 2014, primarily) made a variety of changes. See p. 160 for details.

In addition to the explicit changes, the annual increases in residual bases and applicable minimums also affect the new media residuals formulas for reuse of traditional product on ad-supported platforms (K3-K6), reuse of derivative new media product on ad-supported platforms (K7) and reuse of derivative or original new media on free TV (C7-D8)

The following chart shows the location of the new media sideletters, their numbering (if the union agreement numbers its sideletters) and the later MOAs that affect the sideletters.

| Subject | DGA BA/FLTTA | WGA MBA | SAG-AFTRA CBA/TVA | AFTRA Ex. A | Netcode FOB | IATSE BA | AFM Th/TV | BC |
|---|---|---|---|---|---|---|---|---|
| Physical location of the New Media Sideletters | 2011 BA & FLTTA | 2011 MBA | 2009 MOA | 2007 MOA | 2011 Netcode | 2012 BA | 2010 Th & TV agts. | BC Agt Ex. B |
| SL numbering | 15 & 35 BA 14 & 28 FLTTA | None | None | None | 29 & 30 | None | None | None |
| Later MOAs that modify SLs, residual bases or applicable minimums | 2014 MOA | 2014 MOA | 2011 MOA, 2014 MOA | 2010 Extn, [2011 MOA] | NA | NA | NA | NA. Ex. B is still in negot. |
| High Budget SVOD | 2014 MOA | 2014 MOA | 2014 MOA | | | | | NA |

## Tri-Guild Theatrical and Television Live Action Contracts Since 1960 & Some Earlier

*Source: The provisions of the DGA, WGA and SAG Agts. Relating to tri-guild audits list these agreements. No comparable lists are readily available for the other unions.*

**DGA**
1960 BA
1964 BA
1968 BA
1973 BA
1975 FLTTA
1978 BA
1978 FLTTA
1981 BA
1981 FLTTA
1984 BA
1984 FLTTA
1987 BA
1987 FLTTA
1990 BA
1990 FLTTA
1993 BA
1993 FLTTA
1996 BA
1996 FLTTA
1999 BA
1999 FLTTA
2002 BA
2002 FLTTA
2005 BA
2005 FLTTA
2008 BA
2008 FLTTA
2011 BA
2011 FLTTA
2014 MOA

**WGA**
1960 Network TV Film Agt.
1960 Network Live TV Agt.
1960 Network Documentary Agt.
1960 Theatrical Agt.
1960 Screen Agt. (Universal)
1960 TV Film Agt. (AMPP)
1960 TV Film Agt. (Independent)
1960 TV Film Agt. (Freelance)
1963 Live TV Agt. (Networks)
1963 Network Documentary Agt.
1963 Screen Agt.
1963 Screen Agt. (Universal)
1965 Live TV Agt. (Networks)
1965 Network Documentary Agt.
1965 Screen Agt. (Universal)
1966 Theatrical Agt. (Independent)
1966 TV Film Agt. (Freelance)
1967 Ext. (to 1966 TV Film Agt. (Freelance))
1968 Live TV Agt. (Networks)
1968 Network Documentary Agt.
1970 Network Film MBA
1970 Theatrical & TV Agt. (AMPTP)
1971 Ext. to 1968 Live TV Agt. (Networks)
1971 Network Documentary Agt.
1973 Networks Basic Agt.
1973 Network Documentary Agt.
1973 Theatr. & TV Agt. (AMPTP)
1977 Networks Basic Agt.
1977 Network Documentary Agt.
1977 Theatr. & TV Agt. (AMPTP)
1977 Theatr. & TV Agt. (8 Cos.)
1981 Theatr. & TV Agt. (AMPTP)
1985 Theatr. & TV Agt. (AMPTP)
1988 Theatr. & TV Agt. (Indep.)
1988 Theatr. & TV Agt. (Indep. Revised)
1988 Theatr. & TV Agt. (AMPTP)
1992 Ext. to 1988 Theatr. & TV Agt.
1995 Theatr. & TV Agt. (AMPTP)
1995 Theatr. & TV Agt. (Networks)
1998 Theatr. & TV Agt. (AMPTP)
1998 Theatr. & TV Agt. (Networks)
2001 Theatr. & TV Agt. (AMPTP)
2001 Theatr. & TV Agt. (Networks)
2004 Theatr. & TV Agt. (AMPTP)
2004 Theatr. & TV Agt. (Networks)
2008 Theatr. & TV Agt. (AMPTP)
2008 Theatr. & TV Agt. (Networks)
2011 Theatr. & TV Agt. (AMPTP)
2011 Theatr. & TV Agt. (Networks)
2014 MOA (unk. if two versions)

**SAG**
1952 CBA
1956 Supp. (to 1952 CBA)
1960 MOA (to 1956 Supp.)
1960 TV Agt.
1963 MOA (to 1960 MOA)
1964 TV Agt.
1965 MOA (to 1963 MOA)
1967 CBA
1967 TV Agt.
1971 Supp. (to 1967 CBA)
1971 TV Agt.
1974 MOA (to 1971 Supp. & 1971 TV Agt.)
1974 TV Agt.
1977 CBA
1977 TV Agt.
1980 Supp. (to 1977 CBA & 1977 TV Agt.)
1983 MOA (AMPTP) (to 1980 Supp.)
1986 CBA
1986 TV Agt.
1986 MOA (Indep. Producers) (to 1983 MOA (AMPTP))
1989 CBA
1989 TV Agt.
1989 CBA (Indep. Producers)
1992 CBA
1992 TV Agt.
1992 MOA (Indep. Producers) (to 1989 CBA (Indep. Producers) & 1989 TV Agt. (Indep. Producers))
1995 CBA
1995 TV Agt.
1995 CBA (Indep. Producers)
1995 TV Agt. (Indep. Producers)
1998 CBA
1998 TV Agt.

1998 CBA (Indep. Producers)
1998 TV Agt. (Indep. Producers)
2001 CBA
2001 TV Agt.
2001 CBA (Indep. Producers)
2001 TV Agt. (Indep. Producers)
2004 Ext. Agt(s). (to all four 2001 agts.)
2005 CBA
2005 TV Agt.
2005 CBA (Indep. Producers)
2005 TV Agt. (Indep. Producers)
2009 CBA
2009 TV Agt.
2009 CBA (Indep. Producers)
2009 TV Agt. (Indep. Producers)

Note – the four 2009 agts. are listed in a Sideletter but what actually exists is a 2009 MOA (perhaps in two versions); no codified 2009 CBA or TV Agt. Was ever released

2011 MOA to CBA & TV Agt. (perhaps two versions)

## SAG-AFTRA

2014 MOA to CBA & TV Agt.

# INDEX

## $

$2 billion per year, 2
$2.2 billion, 2
$700 million, 2

## 1

1930s, 162
1940s, 162
1950s, 162
1952, 162
1959, 162
1960, 162
1960s, 162
1970s, 162
1980s, 162
1984, 175
1988 writers strike, 162
1990s, 162, 163, 175

## 2

20% home video royalty, 175
2000, 163
2000s, 163
2001, 163
2002, 155, 174
2003, 10
2004, 163
2005, 163
2005 SAG contract, 163
2006, 163
2007, 163
2007-2008 Writers Guild strike, 4

## A

a basic cable, 2
above the line, 5
above the line strikes, 174
actors, 147
ACTRA, 175
AFM, 4
AFTRA, 4
agents, 12
Alice in Wonderland, 2
Alliance of Motion Picture and Television Producers, 9, 177
Amazon Video on Demand, 2
AMC, 8, 30
American Federation of Musicians, 4, 177
American Federation of Radio Artists, 15
American Federation of Radio Artists: The Formation of the Los Angeles Local, 15
American Federation of Television and Radio Artists, 4, 15, 164, 176, 177, 181
AMPTP, 9
Arbitration Decisions, 11
Arkoff, Samuel, 11
assumption agreement, 8
at the wellhead, 175
Ayling, Phillip, vi

## B

Barrett, Christopher, vi
basic cable, 2, 3, 163
Becker, William Franklin, 15
Besbris, David, vi
blacklists, 162
Blu-ray, 2, 3, 22, 29
bolded green, 7
broadcast TV, 2, 3

## C

cable TV, 162
Calley, John, 11
Canada, 175
Candygrams, 11
Carroll, Lewis, 2
cell phones, 2
color television, 162
commercials, 2, 163
commercials strike, 163
Company, 8
contract expiration, 163
contract negotiating cycle, 5
Cope, James, vi
credited writers, 7
CW, 10
CW network, 163
cycle, 5

## D

dark purple, 7
definition of residuals, 3
DeHaan, Christopher, vi
Depression, 162
Dexter, 2, 3
DGA, 4
digital media, 163
direct deposit, 176
directors, 147
Directors, 7
Directors Guild of America, 4, 147, 164, 181
direct-to-video, 2, 29
download-to-own, 2
Dr. Horrible's Sing-Along Blog, 2
Dreith, Dennis, vi
dues paying non-members, 8
DVD, 2, 3, 22, 29
DVDs, 163

## E

effective dates, 10
elections, 2005 SAG, 163
elections, 2005 WGA, 163
electronic data interchange, 176
Employer, 8
eparation of Rights for Screen and Television Writers, 141
expired contracts, 10
extension of contract, 163

## F

film, 10
financial core members, 8
Financial Interest and Syndication rules, 163
Fin-Syn rules, 163
first assistant director, 7
fixed residuals, 4, 175
foreign levies, 147, 174
foreign television, 2
foreign television sales, 162
foreign TV, 3
Fox, 10
Fox network, 162
free TV, 3
freeze, 18, 60, 119, 160
Freeze, 72
FX, 2, 3

## G

GCC, 10
green, 7
gross deals, 4
gross revenues, 175
gross-based residuals, 175
Guaranteed Completion Contracts, 10

## H

H&R, 13
Hair, Ray, vi
Halloween, 10
Harvey, Rita Morley, 15
hated DVD formula, 175
HBO, 2, 162
health and retirement, 13
Heller, George, 15
Hobbit affair in New Zealand, 192
holiday specials, 10
Holloway, Daniel, i, vi
HOLLYWOOD REPORTER, 174
home video, 3, 162, 163
Home Video, 21
home video residuals formula, 162, 163, 174, 175
Hot in Cleveland, 3
Hulu, 2, 175

## I

IATSE, 4
in pattern, 5
interim agreements, 10
International Alliance of Theatrical Stage Employees, 4, 181
Internet, 2, 3, 163, 175
Internet streaming, 2
italics, 7
iTunes, 2

## K

key second assistant director, 7
King of Hearts, 2

## L

labor peace, 162
Ladd, Jr., Alan, 11
lawyers, 175
letters of adherence, 9
Lionsgate, 8
literary material, 47

## M

Mad Men, 8
made-for medium, 3
made-for-cable programming, 175
Markley, Tom, vi
Melnick, Daniel, 11
Miller, Ron, 11
Mirisch, Marvin, 11
Moore, Schuyler, vi, 175
Motion Picture and Television Business: Contracts and Practices, 177
movie, 2

## N

net profits, 4, 174
Netflix, 2
network primetime, 2, 3
new media, 2
new media residuals, 174
new media template, 164
New Zealand, 192
New Zealand Hobbit Crisis, 192
no pattern, 5
Non-union members, 8
novel, 7

## O

one production only, 9
OPO, 9
out of pattern, 5

## P

P&H, 13
paid download, 2
Paramount, 163
Participating musicians, 7
pattern, 5
pattern bargaining, 5, 11
patterns, 5
pay TV, 2, 3, 163
Pay TV, 21
pension and health, 12, 13
pension, health and welfare, 13
percentage residuals, 4
perpetuity, 8
PH&W, 13
primary market, 3, 175
Producer, 8
promulgated agreements, 9
purple, 7

## R

ratification, 10
recoupment based residuals, 174
red arrow, 7
Red scares, 162
red-boxed text, 7
Reforming Residuals, 174
Reiner, Grace, 141
residual system, 174
residuals, 162
residuals checks, 155, 174
residuals follow credits, 7
residuals formulas, 175
residuals, older films and TV shows, 175
retroactive, 10
reuse market, 3
reuse pattern, 3
rollbacks, 175

## S

SAG, 4
Saturday Evening Post, 11
Screen Actors Guild, 4, 147, 155, 163, 164, 174, 175, 176, 177, 181
Selsor, Andy, 177
separated rights, 144
session fees, 175
Showbiz Residuals Guide 2007-2008, 177
Showtime, 2
sideletters, 9
source material, 7
SpikeTV, 3
stockpiling, 163
story, 48
streaming via paid subscription, 2
streaming-to-own, 2
strike fatigue, 162
strikes, 174
Supplemental Markets, 21
syndication, 2, 3, 163

## T

tape, 10
tax, 147
telegram, 11
telegraph, 11
television directors, 174
television film, 10
The Shield, 3
theatrical exhibition, 3
theatrical film, 10
theatrical motion picture, 3
*There's a lot of residual pain ahead if current system isn't remedied*, 174
Those Wonderful, Terrible Years: George Heller and the American Federation of Television and Radio Artists, 15
treatment, 48
TV Land, 3

## U

UCLA, 15
Understanding Separated Rights, 141
unit production managers, 7
UPN, 163

## V

video, 10
videocassettes, 162
videogames, 163

## W

waivers, 9
Walker, Cardon, 11
Warner Bros., 163
Watching Paint Dry, 38
WB, 163
Weise, Joan Halpern, vi
wellhead, 175
WGA, 4
WGA strike of 2007-2008, 2
Whedon, Joss, 2
writers, 144, 147
Writers Guild of America, 4, 141, 155, 163, 164, 174, 175

## Y

Yeldell, Eric B., 177

| A1 Reused in: 1/25/15 Residuals chart v. 2015-2.doc Made for: | B Theatrical | C Free TV - Network Primetime | D Free TV - Syndication or Non-Primetime | E Foreign (Free TV; BC; & Ad-Supported Streaming of TV/HV) | F/G Supplemental Mkts. & some in-flight, F4 & F5 may=F3 — Pay TV / Home Video | H Domestic Basic Cable | I/J New Media - Consumer Paid — eRental / EST | K New Media – Ad-Supported (incl. AVOD; excl. foreign streaming of TV/HV) |
|---|---|---|---|---|---|---|---|---|
| 2 **Theatrical** Only for "Post-'60" (DGA 5/1/60; SAG 6/13/60; IA, AFM 1/31/60). WGA + post-1948 Universal. | No residuals (even for re-releases, foreign theatrical releases, or extended runs). | See notes & definitions in col. & row headings, p. 4. *nearby cells*, and **C3-D3**. RB/AM & ceiling for **C4-C8** may not be the same as **C3** (fit's unclear). **C3-H3, I3-J3?, K3** are subject to **H3** note re exhausted free TV product. | | | 1.2% of gross (SAG-AFTRA 3x, IATSE 4.5x). AFM post-7/1/71 theatrical & | 1.5% to 1.8% of Producer's GR (=20% of worldwide wholesale GR if affili-ated video co.; else, | 1.2% of gross (SAG-AFTRA 3x, IATSE 4.5x). AFM: 1% of gross. | 1.2% of gross (SAG-AFTRA 3x, IATSE 4.5x, AFM 1%) | 1.8% to 3.25% of 20% of GR (SAG 3x, IATSE 4.5x, AFM 1% to 1.8%). Break =50K units. Notes: 13-16 | 1.2% of gross (SAG 3x, IATSE 4.5x, AFM 1%) for post-7/1/71 product. No residuals for older product. See also AVOD note below. |
| | | 1.2% of gross (1.8% if "outright sale"; rarely used provision) (SAG-AFTRA 3x, IATSE 4.5x). AFM: 1% of gross (1.5% if outright sale). | | | | | | | |
| 3 **Free TV (all)** DGA C3, D3 & E3 RB's differ. WGA uses non network-PT AM (high or low budget) for all AM residuals. | DGA: U.S./ Canada, 150% theatrical AM; non-U.S./ Canada, 100% of same; both, 150% of same. WGA - made for free TV or basic cable: U.S., greater of theatrical AM or 150% of the non network-PT TV AM; non-U.S., same formula but 100% instead of 150%; both, use U.S. formula. SAG-AFTRA: U.S./Canada, 150% TAM; non-U.S./Canada, same (alt: 50% TAM per ea. non-U.S./Canada zone); both, 200% TAM. AFTRA: BC unclear. AFM: 50% TV scale. IATSE, AFM BC: $0 | One free run, then per-run; 100% of: **RB** Residual Base, DGA); **RB** (WGA); or **TAC** 50% (network) or subject to ceiling 40% (off-net) to 5% of RB/AM **TAM** (Total Applicable Min... SAG-AFTRA). IATSE, AFM: no residuals. | One free run on C3 or D3 & then (subj-ect to important SLs): run by run declining from two GR breaks; then 1.2% of gross (SAG-AFTRA 3x) after GR break. AFM: 1% of 20%). See F2-F3 notes. | 15%, 10%, 10% (one-time 35% for some 1 hrs.) of RB/AM/TAM trigg-ered by telecast or two GR breaks; then 1.2% of gross (SAG-AFTRA 3x) after GR break. AFM: 1% of 20%. AGICOA. IATSE: $0. | TV only (date) 100% of fee applies for all AFM **F2-G3**): 1% of gross. Re non-AFM, see H3 note re exhausted free TV product. | 100% of fee received by producer (1.8% at $1M Prod. GR) (SAG-AFTRA 3x, IATSE 4.5x, AFM 1% (of 20%)). See F2-F3 notes. | 2% of gross (SAG-AFTRA 3x). No **C3-H3, I3-J3?, K3** resids on exhausted TV product (i.e., if netwrk rerun resids not still payable (generally, pre-7/1/71 product). IA, AFM: no residuals. | 1.2% of gross (SAG-AFTRA 3x, IATSE 4.5x, AFM non BC 1%, AFM BC 3x). Residuals only for post-x/x product (unless n.d.). x/x/x = DGA n.d.(?); WGA n.d. (?); SAG th.n.d. (?); SAG TV 7/20/52; AFTRA n.d. (?); IATSE 2/1/73; AFM 7/1/71; AFM BC n.d. No residuals for older product. Date cut-offs apply even to theat & non-exhausted free TV. | 1.8%-3.5% of 20% of gross (SAG-AFTRA, AFM BC 3x, IATSE 4.5x, AFM non BC 1%—1.9% (vs. J2)). Break = 100K units. WGA - per arbitration: No residuals for pre-2/13/08 TV product. AFM: ratifi-cation date. AFM BC date tbd. Other un-ions: unclear if no resids before dates in 12-16, or if eff. date of 2008/09 agt. is cut-off, or none. | Current product: Free win. of 7 days or 24 days (1st 7 eps. of a new series and any one-time programs) or 17 days (kids shows) (but always 7 days for K3), then two 26 wk. windows ea. @ 4% (rising in contract year 2 to 4.5% then 5% in contract year 3) of RB/AM/TAM, then (1 year after end of free win) 2% GR (SAG-AFTRA, AFM BC 3x). RB/AM is non net-work-PT. AFM BC: RB = scale wages earned. Note: former WGA imputed gross formula was deleted in 2014. WGA, SAG-AFTRA: No residuals for AVOD use of pre-2014 product. DGA – implicit? Product prior to 2008/09 Agt. (but see H3 note): 2% of gross (SAG-AFTRA, AFM BC 3x). Foreign streaming: use E3-E6. IATSE, AFM non-BC: no residuals. |
| 4 **Pay TV** (for SVOD, see row 10) WGA: For made for pay TV product of a type not gener-ally produced for network PT TV: F5-G5 not F4-G4 for pay TV & HV uses. IATSE F4-G5? | | C4-E5 are same as made for free TV (C3-E3). DGA - high budget pay television picture (product >=80 min and >= $5M budget): 1.2% of gross. DGA - other product: 20% discount on residuals until gross break. IATSE: no residuals. AFM: made for pay TV (C4-E4) treated as made for theatrical (C2-E2). AFM: made for HV (A5-K5) treated as made for theatrical (A2-K2) or free TV (A3-K3) depending on whether created under Theatrical MP Agt. or TV Agt.: except HV to theatrical (B5) always as free TV (B3) and HV to foreign (E5) always as free TV (E3). AGICOA? | | | DGA (max = AM/yr.): Dom cbl: sub fees % yr (+ possible 2%, GR>brk): PPV 2% GR > brk. WGA dom fixed $/yr. for >10 exhib days or 1 yr. SAG-AFTRA dom after same: 6% GR; & 2nd svc. pay TV, GR break can foreign svc 2% GR trigger. AFM: $0 in F4-G4. | 2% of GR (SAG-AFTRA 3x) after 100K units (WGA, SAG: 75K for 30/60 min. pay TV). DGA: if initial release is on 4 performers; 1.5% of GR times no. of performers. Applies to all 6% or "3x" figures in F4-H5 (but not to H3). | 2% of gross (2.5% for pre-7/1/84 product) (SAG-AFTRA 3x). IATSE, AFM: no residuals. SAG-AFTRA: <= 4 performers; 1.5% of GR times no. of performers. | | |
| 5 **Home Video** IATSE: F4-G5? AFM: see C5-E5 note | | | | | DGA & SAG-AFTRA: see F4-G4. SAG: G5 break = 100K. WGA: 2% of aggregate (pay + HV) GR > aggregate GR brk. | Same as made for free TV (F3-G3). IATSE: no residuals. | | | |
| 6 **Basic Cable** DGA, WGA: high budget only (ea. have diff. cutoffs); low is negotiable. L-AFTRA: BC templates vary. | | DGA, SAG: C3, WGA: if {>= 10 runs or 1 yr on BC: or <= 66 episodes in series}, or {Hitchcock}, use H3, else C3. IA, AFM: $0. | WGA: H3 or D3 as per C6. DGA. SAG: if {>= 10 runs or 1 yr on BC: DGA (declining D3 SAG 25% to 5% of TAM, w/ large discount based on GR), else D3. D3 starts at 40%. IA, AFM: $0. | Same as made for free TV (E3). IATSE, AFM: no residuals. AGICOA? | | "Sanchez" = run by run declining 17%–1.5% of RB/AM/TAM) WGA alt: "Hitchcock" = 120% AM difference pmt; H3 when > 1 AFTRA alt: Exhib days yr by yr declin. % of scale, IA, AFM:$0. 2nd lic: 2% GR (SAG-AFTRA 3X). | | | |

| [A1] Reused in: 1/25/15 Residuals chart v. 2015-2.doc  Made for: | [B] Theatrical | [C] Free TV - Network Primetime | [D] Free TV - Syndication or Non-Primetime | [E] Foreign (Free TV; BC; & Ad-Supported Streaming of TV/HV) | [F/G] Supplemental Mkts. Pay TV (&some in-flight) / Home Video | [H] Domestic Basic Cable | [I/J] New Media - Consumer Paid  eRental / EST | [K] New Media – Ad-Supported (incl. AVOD; excl. foreign streaming of TV/HV) |
|---|---|---|---|---|---|---|---|---|
| [7] **Derivative NM** Def'n of **Deriv. NM**: DGA, WGA, IA: NM based on for TV. SAG: & th. & HV, delete BC. AFTRA=SAG but no th. *AFM*: free TV, BC. | Not explicitly specified for ATL. Also, bargaining history varies among ATL unions. IATSE, AFM Orig. NM, AFM Free TV Deriv: no residuals. | C7-D8 is like C3-D3 (except AFM BC-Deriv). *DGA* RB: D3 RB. *WGA* AM: D3 bargain rate (high budget for Deriv. NM, low for Orig. NM), prorated for NM<=15 min. WGA. C7-D8. & **K7** residuals are aggregate, not per writer. *SAG-AFTRA* RB: for Deriv NM: C3 resid ceiling for source program, prorated; for Orig NM: C3 resid ceiling (if NM < half hr use prorated half hr ceiling; else closest <= NM length). E7-E8 = B7-B8. AFM BC-Deriv: 100% (for C7) or 75%-5% (for C8) of AFTRA program fee. DGA, WGA, AFM BC-Deriv: PT runs of NM<=15 mins treated as non-PT. IATSE, AFM Original NM, AFM Free TV Deriv: no residuals. | See D7-D8. | See E7-E8. | Same as if made for free TV (F3-G3); except *AFM BC-Derivative NM*: pay TV 3.6% of gross; HV 3.6% (of 20%) of gross. | Same as if made for free TV (H3); except *AFM BC-Derivative NM*: 3.6% of gross. IATSE, AFM Original NM, AFM Free TV Deriv: $0. | 26 wk. free win. then 1.2% of GR (SAG-AFTRA, *AFM BC-Deriv.* 3x; IATSE 4.5x, other AFM 1%). No resids if {for C8)}, {AFM BC-Deriv: Orig. NM. budget <= $25K/min.}; or {for Orig. NM or Deriv. NM except AFM BC-Deriv} if {IA: 2 IA crew} or {IA, other AFM: 1st release is consumer paid}. | 13 wk free win; then two 26-wk wins. @ {{3.5% (was 3%) of {DGA, WGA, RB/AM (C7-BC8)}, {AFM BC-Deriv: 1st TV replay fee}}; {SAG-AFTRA: $20-$25/actor} ea win; & (1 yr after free win ends) 2% GR (SAG-AFTRA, AFM BC-Deriv 3x). IATSE, AFM Free TV Deriv: no residuals. No residuals. |
| [8] **Original NM** | | | | | | | | |
| [9] **Experim. NM** | Optional coverage. Definition of **Experimental New Media**: (a) budget ≤ $15K/min. & ≤ $300K/episode & ≤ $500K/order and (b) no DGA prior e/ee; or no professional writer; or no covered performer; or < 4 experienced crew; or < 2 active AFM musicians. | | | | | | | |
| [10] **High Budget SVOD** Def'n: Original & derivative dramatic NM made for initial exhibition on a subscription consumer pay platform (e.g., Netflix) ≥ 20 mins. & > various per-episode budget thresholds. | See B7-B8. | See C7-C8. | See D7-D8. | See E7-E8. | See F7-G8. | See H7-H8. | On the original subscription platform (or related or affiliated foreign platforms): 1 free year and, thereafter, a year by year declining 30%-1.5% of network PT RB/RB/TAC); or 65% of foregoing if < 15m subs in U.S. & Canada. Other pay platforms (incl. other subscrptn platforms): 1.2% GR (SAG-AFTRA 3x). | 7 day free window (for one-time program or first 3 episodes of a new series) then 2% GR (SAG-AFTRA 3x). |

- TV product to secondary digital channels (D3, D4, D6): 2% of GR (SAG-AFTRA 3x) if out of production and out of fixed residual-able reuse for specified periods.
- Live simultaneous linear streaming of TV product: no residuals (treated as part of the broadcast/cablecast, not as separate K3, K4, K6).
- For the above two points, see DGA 2014 MOA ¶¶ 8, 12; WGA 2014 MOA ¶¶ 10, 12.b; SAG-AFTRA 2014 MOA ¶¶ 18, 19.

| A1 **Reused in:** Residuals chart v. 2015-2.doc **Made for:** | B **Theatrical** | C **Free TV - Network Primetime** | D **Free TV - Syndication or Non-Primetime** | E **Foreign (Free TV; BC; & Ad-Supported Streaming of TV/HV Product)** | F/G **Supplemental Mkts.** (& some in-flight) Pay TV | F/G Home Video | H **Domestic Basic Cable** | I/J **New Media - Consumer Paid** eRental | I/J EST | K **New Media – Ad-Supported** (incl. AVOD; excl. foreign streaming of TV/HV) |
|---|---|---|---|---|---|---|---|---|---|---|
| 2 **Theatrical** | No residuals. | BA 19-101 to 104. MBA 15.A.2, 3 (preamble), 3.a, b. CBA 5.A. IATSE BA XIX(b)(1)-(3). AFM Theatrical 15(b)(i)(1) & (2). | | | BA 18-101, 102, 103. MBA 51.C.1.a. CBA 5.2.A (1), E(1), (2). TVA 20.1. Netcode Ex. D § 3.A, 4.A, B. IATSE BA XXVIII(b)(1). AFM Theatr. 16(b)(i) & TV 14(b)(i). | BA 18-101, 102, 104. MBA 51.C.1.b. SL to Art. 51. CBA 5.2.A (2), E(1), (3). TVA 20.1. Netcode Ex. D § 3.A, 4.A, B. IATSE BA XXVIII(b)(2). AFM Theatr. 16(b)(i) & TV 14(b)(i). | BA 18-102 (2nd to last para). MBA 58. CBA 5.A (implicit). IATSE ? AFM ? | BA NM Reuse SL 1, 5. MBA same SL 1.a, 3.a, 5. CBA/TVA same SL 1.A, 4.A. Netcode Ex. A | BA NM Reuse SL 2, 5. MBA same SL 1.b, 3.a, 5 (& arb decn) CBA/TVA same SL 1.B, 4.A. | NM Reuse SL: BA SL 3.B, 5. MBA SL 2.a, 3.a. CBA/TVA SL 2.D, 4.A. IA SL 2, 3.a. AFM SL 2, 3(a). |
| 3 **Free TV (all)** | BA 11-201. MBA 15.B.13.a-c. TVA 19(a)-(c). Netcode Ex. A § 3. AFM TV II. 15(b)(17)(i). | BA 11-101(b) (1)(i). MBA 15.B.1.a, b(1), (2)(a), (d), (3). DGA & WGA 2011 MOUs. TVA 18(a), (b) (1), (3), (4). Netcode Ex. A § 3. Ex. A § 3. | BA 11-101(b)(2)-(5), 24-301, SLs 10 & 12. MBA 15.B.1.a. b.(1), (2)(o), (d), (3). SLs 1 & 2 to Art. 15.B.1.b. (2)(c). TVA 18(a), (b)(2), (3), (4). SLs B, Ex. B-1 & B-2. Netcode Ex. A § 3. | BA 11-102. MBA 15.B.2. TVA 18(c)(1)-(4). Netcode Ex. A § 3. AFM:? | BA 20-100, 400, 600, 804, SL 7. MBA App. B § D.2, 3.a, G.4. TVA 78(c)(1a)-c), 78(d)(5). Netcode Ex. E § 2.B, 3.A(1), 4.E. AFM BC 17.E.2 | BA 20-100, 400, 700, SL 7. MBA App. B § D.2, 3.b. TVA 78(c)(2a)-e). Netcode Ex. E § 2.B.3.B(1).AF M BC 17.C.3.b | BA 11-108. MBA 58. TVA 18.1(a). Netcode Ex. A § 3. | BA NM Reuse SL 3. 1.a, 3.a, 5. CBA/TVA same SL 1.A, 4.A. Netcode Ex. A | same SL 1.b, 3.a. Netcode Ex. A same SL 1.B, 5.A. IATSE same SL 1.a, 3.a. AFM same SL 4(1)(a), AFM BC 4(3)(a). | BA NM Reuse SL 3. A, 5. MBA same SL 2.b, 3.a. CBA/TVA same SL 2.A, B, 4.A. Netcode Ex. A same SL 2.A, B, 5.A. AFM same SL 4(2). AFM BC Ex. B NM Reuse SL 2.A. |
| 4 **Pay TV** | BA 20-803. MBA App. B § G.2. TVA 78(d) (3). Netcode Ex. E § 4.C. AFM TV II. 15(b)(17)(i). | BA 20-801. MBA App. B § G.1. TVA 78(d)(1). Netcode Ex. E § 4.A. (Applicability of TVA and Netcode provisions to reuse in foreign (i.e., E4-E5) is implicit.) AFM made for pay TV: AFM Basic Cable 17.D.2 (& AFM Theatrical 15). AFM made for home video: AFM Theatrical 16(b)(i)(17)-(19) and AFM TV 14(b)(i)(18). | | | | | BA 20-802. MBA App. B § G.3. TVA 78(d)(4). Netcode Ex. E § 4.D. | same SL 4(1)(a), AFM BC Ex. B same SL § 1A. | Netcode Ex. A same SL 1.B, 5.A. IATSE same SL § 1B. AFM BC Ex. B same SL § 1B. | *Finding the NM SLs: DGA, WGA: 2011 Agt. AFTRA Netcode (front of book). 2007 Netcode. AFM NM SLs to BC Agt. (aka AFM BC Ex. B) draft in process. Other unions: see 2008 or 2009 MOUs/MOAs. All: see also subsequent MOUs/MOAs.* |
| 5 **Home Video** | | | | | See F4-G4 for DGA, SAG, AFTRA. MBA App. B § C.2, 3, G.4. | | | | | |
| 6 **Basic Cable** L-AFTRA: four template agts (not shown). | BA 23-104(f). MBA App. C § 2(b)(1), (2). SAG Basic Cable 1. AFM (re BC to theat): ? | BA 23-104(f). MBA App. C § 2 (b)(1), (2). (e). MBA App. C § 2 (b)(1), (2). Netcode Ex. A NM Reuse SL 4.A(5)(a)(i). AFM BC Ex. B § A(5)(a), (also Netcode 2(A)(2)(a)(i), 73). | BA 23-104(b)-(e). MBA App. C § 2 (b)(1), (2). SAG BC 5-8. | BA 23-104(f). MBA App. C § 2(b)(1), (2). SAG BC 1. | BA 23-104(f). MBA App. C § 2(b)(1), (2). SAG BC 1. AFM ? | BA 23-104(f). MBA App. C § 2(b)(1), (2). SAG BC 1. | BA 23-104(a). MBA App. C § 2(b)(1)-(3). SAG BC 3. | | | |
| 7 **Derivative New Media** | Not explicitly specified. See provisions listed in C7-D8. | BA Made for NM SL E.1.e.(1). MBA same SL 2. b.(4)(e)(I). CBA/TVA same SL B.3(c)(i). Netcode Ex. A NM Reuse SL 4.A(5)(a)(i). AFM BC Ex. B § A(5)(a) (also Netcode 2(A)(2)(a)(i), 73). | | Not explicitly specified. See provisions listed in C7-D8. | BA Made for NM SL E.1.e.(2). MBA same SL 2.b.(4)(e)(ii). CBA/TVA same SL B.3(e)(ii). IATSE BA Made for NM SL F(2). AFM BC Ex. B § A(5)(b) (& Netcode Ex. D § 3(A)(1)). IATSE and AFM (except AFM BC-Deriv) apply only to pay TV and HV (F7-G7), not BC (H7). | BA Made for NM SL E.1.e.(2). MBA same SL B.3(e)(ii). Netcode Ex. A NM Reuse SL 4.A(5)(a)(ii). IATSE BA Made for NM SL F(2). AFM BC Ex. B § A(5)(b) (& Netcode Ex. D § 3(A)(1)). IATSE and AFM (except AFM BC-Deriv) apply only to pay TV and HV (F7-G7), not BC (H7). | BA Made for NM SL E.1.e.(2). MBA same SL B.3(e)(ii) & Netcode 4.D. | BA Made for NM SL E.1. a-c (& NM Reuse SL 5). MBA same SL 2 b.(4)(a)-(c). CBA/TVA same SL B. 3(a), (d) (& NM Reuse SL 4.A). Netcode Ex. A NM Reuse SL 4.A(4), 5. IA BA Made for NM SL F(1)(c), (d). AFM same SL F(1)(b)-(d). AFM BC Ex. B same SL A(1), (4). | BA Made for NM SL E. 1. a-c (& NM Reuse SL 5). MBA same SL B 3(a)+(c) (& NM Reuse SL 4.A). Netcode Ex. A NM Reuse SL 4.A(1)-(3), 5.A. IATSE BA Made for NM SL F(1)(a), (b)(i). AFM same SL F(1)(a), (b)(ii). AFM BC Ex. B same SL A(1)+3). |
| 8 **Original New Media** | | BA Made for NM SL E.2.c(1). MBA same SL 3.b.(4)(c)(i). CBA/TVA same SL D.3(c)(i). Netcode Ex. A NM Reuse SL 4.B(3)(a). | BA Made for NM SL E.2.c(1). MBA same SL 3.b.(4)(c)(i). CBA/TVA same SL D.3(c)(i). Netcode Ex. A NM Reuse SL 4.B(3)(a). | | BA Made for NM SL E.2.c(2). MBA Made for NM SL 3.b.(4)(c)(i). CBA/TVA same SL D.3(c)(ii). Netcode Ex. A NM Reuse SL 4.B(3)(b). IATSE BA Made for NM SL F(2). AFM same SL F(2). IATSE and AFM apply only to pay TV and HV (F8-G8), not BC (H8). | BA Made for NM SL E.2.c(2). MBA Made for NM SL 3.b.(4)(c)(i). CBA/TVA same SL D.3(c)(ii). Netcode Ex. A NM Reuse SL 4.B(3)(b). IATSE same SL F(2). AFM same SL F(2). IATSE and AFM apply only to pay TV and HV (F8-G8), not BC (H8). | BA 23-104(a). MBA E.2.c(2). MBA same SL 3.b.(4)(c)(i). CBA/TVA same SL D.3(c)(ii). Netcode Ex. A NM Reuse SL 4.B(3)(b). IATSE same SL F(2). AFM same SL F(2). | BA Made for NM SL E.2.a, b (& NM Reuse SL 5). MBA same SL 3.b.(4)(a), (b). CBA/TVA same SL D.3(a), (b) (& NM Reuse SL 4.A). Netcode Ex. A NM Reuse SL 4.B(2). IA BA Made for NM SL F(1)(a), (b)(ii), (c), (d). AFM same SL F(1). | BA Made for NM SL E.2.a.b. MBA same SL 3.b.(4)(a). CBA/TVA same SL D.3(a). Netcode Ex. A NM Reuse SL 4.B(1). IATSE BA Made for NM SL F(1)(a), (b)(i). AFM same SL F(1). |
| 9 **Experim. NM** | | | | | | | | | | |
| 10 **HB SVOD** | | | | | | | | | | |

§ or ¶ of Made for NM SL, as follows: BA SL § B. MBA SL § 1. CBA/TVA SL § C. Netcode Ex. A SL § C. IATSE BA SL ¶ B. AFM SL ¶ 6(B). DGA 2014 MOA ¶ 11.a.D. WGA 2014 MOA ¶ 11.a.4.e. SAG-AFTRA 2014 MOA ¶ 10. IATSE & AFM: not yet negotiated.

Read the book and see residuals as a system

Download an excerpt at jhandel.com/residuals

Sign up for updates at jhandel.com/contact

# Entertainment Residuals: A Full Color Guide

## Part I – Overview
- Ch. 1 Introduction
- Ch. 2 The Residuals Chart
- Ch. 3 Media, Markets, Unions & More
- Ch. 4 Residuals Formulas

## Part II – Cell by Cell Analysis
- Ch. 5 Made for Theatrical
- Ch. 6 Made for Free TV
- Ch. 7 Reuse in Supplemental Markets
- Ch. 8 Made for Pay TV & Home Video
- Ch. 9 Made for Basic Cable
- Ch. 10 Theatrical Use of TV and Home Video Product
- Ch. 11 New Media Reuse of Traditional Product
- Ch. 12 Made for New Media

## Part III – Additional Topics
- Ch. 13 Payment Calculation
- Ch. 14 Separated Rights and Similar Reuse Provisions
- Ch. 15 Other Entertainment Residuals and Reuse Payments
- Ch. 16 Commercials
- Ch. 17 Economics
- Ch. 18 Payment Mechanics
- Ch. 19 International and Linguistic Issues
- Ch. 20 Recent History
- Ch. 21 Policy Issues

## Part IV – Reference
- App. Sources and Contracts
- Index
- Residuals Chart

| Abbrev. | Meaning |
|---|---|
| "NM Reuse" is aka "NM Exhibition." | |
| **Examples** | |
| BA 19-101 | DGA BA Sec. 19-101 |
| MBA 15.A.2 | WGA MBA Art. 15.A.2 |
| Netcode Ex. A NM Reuse SL § 4.B(1) | Sec. 4.B(1) of the NM Reuse SL to Ex. A of AFTRA National Code of Fair Practice for Network TV Broadcasting |

**Omissions from chart (see book for discussion):** daytime (DGA FLTTA, WGA App A, AFTRA FOB, AFM TV Video Agt.), AFM SRLA, **videogames** (WGA Art 64, AFTRA Interactive Media Agt.), SAG-AFTRA & AFM **Commercials** Agts., **animation**, **other:** AFTRA basic cable templates, SLs (esp. important in C3-D3), waivers, one production only agts. & special deals, pilots & promotional launch periods, CW, MyNetworkTV, holiday program exhibition days, initial release in other than the made-for market, supersized episodes, serials, production for initial release in foreign media, foreign language production, remakes, WGA separated rights, script publication fee, etc., DGA series bonus pmts., low budget productions, bargaining history, arbitration decisions, custom & practice, proration, allocation, P&H, AICF, IACF, member dues, agent commissions, payment due dates, clips / excerpts, some music reuse, foreign levies, or Copyright Royalty Tribunal monies.

1/25/15 Residuals chart v. 2015-2.doc

This chart is excerpted from a forthcoming book, *Entertainment Residuals: A Full Color Guide*, which explains the entire residuals system. Visit jhandel.com/residuals or scan the QR code for more info.

| Abbrev. | Meaning |
|---|---|
| win. | Window |
| *Italics* = out-of-pattern or no pattern. | |
| RB/AM/TAC/TAM are usually per person; GR % are aggregate. | |
| **Unions** | |
| ATL | Above the line (DGA, WGA, SAG, AFTRA, SAG-AFTRA) |
| L-AFTRA, L-SAG | Legacy AFTRA or SAG Agts. (pre 7/1/14) |
| **Documents** | |
| AFM BC | AFM Basic Cable TV Agt. |
| AFM BC | Ex. B (new media) to AFM BC |
| Ex. B | |
| AFM Theatrical | AFM Basic Theatrical Motion Picture Agt. |
| AFM TV | AFM Basic TV Film Agt. |
| Agt. | Agreement |
| App. | Appendix |
| Art. | Article |
| BA | DGA Basic Agreement |
| CBA | SAG-AFTRA Codified Basic Agreement |
| Ex. | Exhibit |
| Ex. A | Usually means Netcode Ex. A |
| FLTTA | DGA Freelance Live & Tape TV Agt. |
| FOB | AFTRA Netcode front of book |
| IATSE BA | IATSE Basic Agreement |
| MBA | WGA Basic Agreement |
| Netcode | AFTRA Network Code |
| Para., ¶ | Paragraph |
| Same SL | The same SL as earlier in the sentence |
| Sch. | Schedule |
| Sec., § | Section |
| SL/SLs | Sideletter(s) |
| Supp. | Supplement |
| TVA | SAG / SAG-AFTRA TV Agt. |
| "Art.," "Sec.," "Para." usu. omitted. § or ¶ usually mean w/in Ex., App., Sch. or SL. | |

| Abbrev. | Meaning |
|---|---|
| **Media and Markets** | |
| AVOD | Ad-supported VOD |
| BC | Basic cable |
| BC Deriv | Derivative NM based on a basic cable series |
| cbl | Cable |
| Deriv NM | Derivative new media |
| dom | Domestic |
| EST | Electronic Sell Through |
| HV | Home video |
| NM | New media |
| Orig NM | Original new media |
| PPV | Pay per view |
| PT | Primetime |
| SVOD | Subscription VOD |
| Th, Theat(r) | Theatrical |
| VOD | Video On Demand |
| **Formulas** | |
| $0 | Same as "no residuals" |
| 1.2%, 1.5%, 1.8%, 2%, etc. | Indicates the DGA and WGA gross % (other unions shown in parens) |
| alt. | Alternate, alternatively |
| AM | Applicable minimum |
| brk | Gross break |
| comp | Compensation |
| ep(s) | Episode(s) |
| exhib day | Exhibition day |
| GR | Gross |
| Hitchcock | An alt. BC to BC (H6) formula |
| n.d.; na | No date; not applicable |
| RB | Residual base |
| Sanchez | Run by run declining % fixed resids. for BC (H6) |
| sub fee | Per-subscriber fee |
| TAC | Total actual compensation |
| TAM | Total applicable minimum (note – legacy AFTRA TAM is higher than SAG-AFTRA or legacy SAG) |
| Unk | Unknown |

# ALSO OF INTEREST

## ENTERTAINMENT UNIONS AND GUILDS: AN INTERDISCIPLINARY BIBLIOGRAPHY

A must-have for attorneys, union officials and academics working in entertainment labor, ENTERTAINMENT LABOR: AN INTERDISCIPLINARY BIBLIOGRAPHY is a 345 page annotated bibliography of over 1,500 books, articles, dissertations, legal cases, websites and other resources through early 2013 dealing with entertainment unions and guilds and various other aspects of entertainment labor. It includes both U.S. and foreign materials – and provides URLs for materials available online. The product of literally dozens of database searches and hours of research, there's no other resource like it. Available at https://www.createspace.com/3368648 or http://amzn.to/Z4cyt5.

## THE NEW ZEALAND HOBBIT CRISIS

After the third *Lord of the Rings* movie premiered in 2003, fans of the series eagerly anticipated production and release of its prequel, *The Hobbit.* It turned out they had a while to wait, as a series of troubles delayed production for years.

Then, in September 2010, when almost everything seemed resolved, U.S. and international actors unions suddenly issued an alert advising their members "not to accept work on this non-union production."

Events quickly spiraled out of control and New Zealand plunged into crisis. Saving the *Hobbit* was do or die for the local film industry, and the government scrambled to avoid disaster. Protests and rallies erupted as word spread that the studio might rip the troubled production from the country. The island nation's currency fell on the possibility of losing the half-billion dollar project. What happened next was almost unbelievable – and proved, if nothing else, that not all Hollywood drama is on the screen. Available at https://www.createspace.com/3352289 (paper) or http://amzn.to/SiHUX2 (paper, Kindle or audio).

## HOLLYWOOD ON STRIKE!

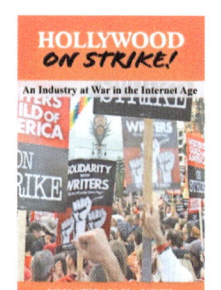

The Writers Guild went on strike in 2007. The big issue: fees for programs released on new media such as the Internet.

The strike was settled one hundred turbulent days later – but then the Screen Actors Guild spiraled out of control, unwilling to accept the same terms but unable to muster a second strike. As the national economy collapsed, idled writers and actors sacrificed millions of dollars in film and TV wages in order to pursue pennies in new media. All told, the turmoil lasted about two years.

HOLLYWOOD ON STRIKE! analyzes events as they unfolded and lays bare the contracts, economics and politics swirling behind the paradox of Hollywood labor relations. It includes 80 pages of reference materials: abbreviations/glossary, a graphic timeline, index, and more. Available at https://www.createspace.com/3344392 or http://amzn.to/1wj7VoW.

Made in the USA
Charleston, SC
23 December 2015